HOCKEY NIGHT IN DIXIE

MINOR PRO HOCKEY IN THE AMERICAN SOUTH

Jon C. Stott

Victoria • Calgary • Vancouver

Heritage House Publishing Company Ltd.
#108–17665 66A Avenue
Surrey, BC, Canada V3S 2A7
www.heritagehouse.ca

Heritage House Publishing Company Ltd.
PO Box 468
Custer, WA, USA
98240–0468

LIBRARY AND ARCHIVES CANADA CATALOGUING IN PUBLICATION
Stott, Jon C.
Hockey night in Dixie: minor pro hockey in the American south / Jon C. Stott.
ISBN-13: 978-1-894974-21-9   ISBN-10: 1-894974-21-2

1. Hockey teams–Southern States–History. 2. Hockey–Southern States–History.
I. Title.
GV848.4.U6S76 2006   796.962'64090750949   C2006-903847-3

LIBRARY OF CONGRESS CONTROL NUMBER: 2006932617

Edited by Audrey McClellan
Cover design by Jacqui Thomas
Interior design by Duncan Turner
Front-cover photo by Jon C. Stott
All interior photos provided by Jon C. Stott, except where noted

Printed in Canada

Heritage House acknowledges the financial support for its publishing program from the Government of Canada through the Book Publishing Industry Development Program (BPIDP), Canada Council for the Arts, and the province of British Columbia through the British Columbia Arts Council and the Book Publishing Tax Credit.

The Canada Council | Le Conseil des Arts
for the Arts | du Canada

BRITISH COLUMBIA
ARTS COUNCIL
Supported by the Province of British Columbia

This book has been produced on 100% post-consumer paper, processed chlorine free and printed with vegetable-based inks.

CONTENTS

For Andrew (#14)
&
Craig (#23)

my favorite hockey players

PREFACE

Between the fall of 1988 and the spring of 2005, 233 teams played in a total of 160 cities in 13 minor professional hockey leagues. The total number of clubs and cities is not so surprising, considering that minor-league franchises in all sports frequently move from city to city and even from league to league. Expansion franchises are granted; teams become defunct; old leagues disband or combine with other leagues; and new leagues are formed. What is surprising is where the 233 teams played. Only 21 Canadian cities hosted minor-league hockey teams; in contrast, 123 teams played in southern American cities.

Minor-league hockey had been played in the South before 1988. From the 1960s to the 1980s, cities such as Charlotte, North Carolina; Roanoke, Virginia; Knoxville, Tennessee; Macon, Georgia; and St. Petersburg, Florida, had iced teams in the Eastern, Southern, and Atlantic Coast hockey leagues. After the Second World War, the southwestern cities of Tulsa, Oklahoma; Wichita, Kansas; and Fort Worth and Houston, Texas, were members of the United States and, later, Central Professional hockey leagues.

However, in the years following 1988, hockey was also played in places like South Carolina, Louisiana and the hinterlands of west Texas, where few people had ever seen games before, let alone knew the rules. Teams such as the Augusta (Georgia) Lynx, South Carolina (Charleston) Stingrays, Monroe (Louisiana) Moccasins, Arkansas (Little Rock) River Blades, Lubbock (Texas) Cotton Kings and Tallahassee (Florida) Tiger Sharks provided southern sports fans with a totally foreign form of winter entertainment, and athletes from northern Europe, the northern United States and Canada discovered unusual new environments in which to skate, pass, shoot and (not infrequently and to the delight of the spectators) fight—and get paid for it.

The growth of minor-league hockey in the southern United States began slowly. In 1988, four southern teams competed in two leagues. By the 1998–99 season, however, 56 of the 110 teams that made up the seven operating leagues were based in the South. Since that time the number has decreased slightly; during the 2004–05 season, 41 of the 95 teams in five leagues were based in southern states.

Hockey Night in Dixie examines the phenomenon of minor-league professional hockey as it has been played in the American South since 1988. Part One, "The Ice Men of Dixie," profiles one southern team from each of the four lower-level minor leagues: the ECHL (formerly the East Coast Hockey League), the Central Hockey League, the United Hockey League and the Southern Professional Hockey League. It does not include a team from the top-level American Hockey League because most of the AHL teams are based in the Northeast and Midwest, and several of them are owned by National Hockey League clubs, which means that nearly all of the players are under contract to NHL teams. It is a high-level developmental league, and a large percentage of its players will graduate to the major league, something that is rarely the case in the other minor leagues.

Part Two, "An Ice Age in Dixie," presents a historical overview, surveying the fortunes of all minor leagues that operated during the period, with a focus on those leagues in which most, if not all, of the teams were based in southern cities.

☉   ☉   ☉

In writing this book, I have been helped greatly by the officials, players, coaches, trainers, fans and media people involved with the Roanoke Valley Vipers, the Odessa Jackalopes, the South Carolina Stingrays and the Fayetteville FireAntz. I spent a week with each of these teams during the 2005–06 season. Dozens of people kindly and patiently answered questions, posed for photographs and submitted to lengthy interviews. Six people—Amy Webb, Jack Carnefix, Don McKee, Brett Friedlander, Jason Fitzsimmons and Steve Cherwonak—went far beyond the call of duty to assist me in this project.

During the research and writing of this book, several printed and online services were extremely valuable. I constantly referred to *Total Hockey*, second edition (edited by Dan Diamond and published by Total

Sports), and the annual media guides of the various professional leagues. Ralph Slate's www.hockeydb.com, an incredible statistical record that includes league, team and individual statistics, was indispensable. I regularly consulted www.factiva.com to retrieve old newspaper articles and www.oursportscentral.com to keep up on current news about minor-league teams.

I want to thank Don LePan, who put me in contact with Fraser Seely of Heritage House, and to thank Fraser for having faith in the project. Audrey McClellan provided excellent editorial guidance, for which I am very grateful. As always, my children, Clare and Andrew, have provided great love and support. Researching, visiting the four teams, and writing have all been enlightening, rewarding and incredibly enjoyable. To everyone involved—thank you! I've had a wonderful time.

Professional Hockey Leagues Mentioned in This Book

ACHL	Atlantic Coast Hockey League
AHL	American Hockey League
CHL	Central Hockey League
ECHL	East Coast Hockey League
IHL	International Hockey League
NHL	National Hockey League
SEHL	South East Hockey League
SPHL	Southern Professional Hockey League
UHL	United Hockey League *(formerly the Colonial Hockey League)*
WHA2	World Hockey Association 2
WCHL	West Coast Hockey League
WPHL	Western Professional Hockey League

INTRODUCTION

Return to the Minors

"**Y**ou know," I said to my daughter as I glanced at the sports listings in the *TV Weekly*, "I'm really beginning to miss hockey." It was December 2004 and Day 97 of the National Hockey League lockout. I'd arrived in Albuquerque, New Mexico, for an extended Christmas vacation, and if I wanted sports, it seemed I'd have to watch football bowl games, the NFL playoffs or college basketball.

"Why don't you see if the Scorpions are in town?" she replied. "Maybe you could go to one of their games. The rink's only a 10-minute drive away." The Scorpions were the local minor-league hockey team, and they were, indeed, playing in town a couple of days later, so I decided that I'd go to Tingley Coliseum to get my hockey fix.

It would be the first minor-league hockey game I'd attended in over four decades. As a boy and later a university student in the 1950s and early 1960s, Friday night had been hockey night for me—watching the Victoria Cougars and the Vancouver Canucks of the Western Hockey League. Until the late 1950s, when the CBC television network arrived on Canada's west coast, the National Hockey League existed in sound only—Saturday's *Hockey Night in Canada* radio broadcasts of Toronto Maple Leafs games called by Foster Hewitt and, occasionally, Thursday night Montreal Canadiens games called by a relative newcomer named Danny Gallivan. The minor leaguers I watched regularly, few of whom ever became major leaguers, were larger-than-life heroes, gods of the ice.

After I graduated from the University of British Columbia, I left the minors behind, watching *Hockey Night in Canada* on television; university games in Kalamazoo, Michigan, and Edmonton, Alberta; and, most important, my young son's contests played on the outdoor rinks near our home in Edmonton.

But, on a Sunday afternoon in 2004, I arrived at Tingley Coliseum over an hour before the opening faceoff. The sun, although low in the early winter sky, shone warmly and brightly on a dozen or so people who stood chatting as they waited for the doors to open. A good two-thirds of them wore Scorpions hockey sweaters that bore the names of their favorite players on the back (including, I later learned, the names of players who had departed a few seasons earlier), and they discussed the previous night's game, a 5–4 overtime win at San Angelo, Texas, which several of them had followed on the radio. These diehard fans, wearing their loyalties on their backs, were knowledgeable about the team; they stood up fiercely for their favorites; and, as their frequent glances at the still-locked door indicated, being at the arena watching the Scorpions was one of their favorite activities.

I purchased a $25 ticket in the platinum zone, joined the line, which had doubled in size, and at five o'clock followed the loyalists inside. To my right, a souvenir counter displayed the usual parapher-nalia—baseball caps, foam fingers, regulation jerseys (both home and away) priced at nearly $100 each (numbers and lettering extra)—along with a seasonal special. Prominently placed was a sample of the special Christmas jerseys that the players would be wearing during their four pre-Christmas games. These would be auctioned off. Winning bids, the attendant told me, ranged from $250 to $1,000 depending on the pop-ularity of the player. Profits after expenses went into the merchandise revenue fund, with a portion of that donated to charity. I passed by the souvenir stand, purchased a program, entered the nearly empty arena and searched for my platinum seat—a thinly padded theater-style seat behind the goal.

The teams had not yet taken the ice for pre-game practice, and it was likely that, when they did, their warm-ups would be short. Both teams were probably very tired. The visiting Tulsa Oilers had played two nights earlier in Loveland, Colorado, 506 miles to the north, while the Scorpions had climbed on the bus after the previous night's game against San Angelo and made the 514-mile trip home from west Texas. Tonight's game would be their third in as many days. The Oilers and Scorpions were members of the 17-team Central Hockey League (CHL), which extended from Memphis in the east to Albuquerque in the west, and from Loveland, north of Denver, to Hidalgo, a city on the Texas–Mexico border near the mouth of the Rio Grande.

Located on the New Mexico State Fairgrounds in Albuquerque, Tingley Coliseum, home of the New Mexico Scorpions until the spring of 2005, was originally built as a rodeo and horse-show auditorium.

I had plenty of time to look around the quiet, nearly empty arena. The building seemed old. The arched roof was supported by girders, and an angular-looking press box leaned over the top of the $16 center-ice seats. At each end of the rink loomed large video screens that had already begun to beam messages and commercials. Two elements of the arena caught my attention. No clock-scoreboard hung over center ice. Instead, wall-mounted devices were positioned at each end of the rink. Not only might the more conventional type of scoreboard have been too heavy for the roof supports, but the building had not been built for hockey.

This became obvious when I looked from my third-row seat toward the ice. All around the rink there was a 25-foot space between the boards and the 8-foot wall in front of the first row of fixed seats. This wall marked the boundary of the arena floor, the large area on which the ice surface had been placed. Behind the glass there were temporary risers holding two rows of folding chairs; skirting in red, yellow and black— the Scorpions' colors—adorned the edges of each section of the risers. These were the premium box seats, sold only on a season's basis, and they were located on the floor of the horse-show and rodeo arena that Tingley Coliseum had originally been and still was. The ice rink was far away from most of the fans, and, as I noticed during the first period, the separation seemed to take them out of the game.

Just as the teams arrived on the ice, the message boards flashed the statement "It's about hockey, eh!"—a local tribute to the sport's Canadian origins. The players glided about slowly, stretching, skating lazily over the blue lines, flicking gentle shots at the goalies. A small crowd filtered into the stands. On the last Sunday of shopping before Christmas, perhaps a thousand people responded loudly as the lights were dimmed; Stanley the Scorpion, the club's bright-green mascot, skated onto the ice; and the announcer's voice boomed out over the PA: "Are you ready for some hockey?"

The first period was a sluggish affair, with neither team scoring. The most exciting moment occurred 5 minutes and 31 seconds into the game when Doug Pirnak of the Oilers and Konrad McKay of the Scorpions glared at each other from 20 feet apart and began circling each other. The crowd, which by this time had reached about 1,500 and seemed much smaller, scattered, as it was, around the 11,571-seat Coliseum, began to yell. "Poke him in the eye," one fan exhorted. Both players threw their arms above their heads, sending their gloves sailing in small arcs behind them, and then moved toward the other. As if on cue, the other players on the ice skated to the boards, one team on each side of the rink. At this moment, the fans turned their attention away from the ice to gaze at the giant video screens. There, larger than life, McKay and Pirnak traded a few punches before embracing and wrestling each other to the ice. The other players tapped their sticks politely on the ice, just as they had before the opening faceoff, when the player of the month had been announced. After each combatant received a five-minute penalty for what was officially called "fisticuffs," the fans settled back happily into their seats, and the game resumed its sluggish pace.

During the first intermission, a group of mite players skated, often on their ankles, in a 10-minute game; Stanley the Scorpion, having removed his skates, drove a very loud quad—which displayed the dealer's name prominently—in circles between the blue lines; and the Zamboni—the mechanics of which were illustrated and explained in a full-page article in the program—performed its ice-cleaning functions. I wandered into the lobby, where I introduced myself to Geoff Kent, a hockey-sweater-wearing member of the Scorpions' front-office staff, whose name and face I recognized from the program. Kent was the club's senior vice-president and general manager, a native of Halifax, Nova Scotia, who had moved to the southern United States to work for hockey teams in Little Rock, Arkansas, and Fort Worth, Texas, before coming to Albuquerque.

When I asked if he felt that the National Hockey League lockout had refocused local attention on the Scorpions and helped to increase attendance at Tingley Coliseum, he replied no, noting that the club was slightly behind the previous year's attendance figures, when they had averaged 4,481 a game. "If anything, the lockout may have hurt us. People are used to seeing the Colorado Avalanche and Phoenix Coyotes' games on the sports channels; that gets them thinking about hockey and our games. This isn't happening this year, so we have to work harder to get people into the games." He explained that the club was not in competition for fans with the hugely popular University of New Mexico men's and women's basketball teams. "Our demographics are different; we're after the people who go to the movies or casinos. We try to give away something nearly every night, and we make sure there are lots of things going on between periods and during stoppages of play. We've got a midweek game coming up after Christmas, and we're offering six-dollar tickets to anyone under 18. We hope that will bring more families to the game, that they'll have a good time and that they'll come back later in the season."

As the Zamboni chugged off the ice and Stanley performed a few final donuts at center ice, I climbed to the back row of the grandstand and positioned myself where the support pillars didn't block my view. The Scorpions returned to the ice after their 15 minutes of rest, but the time off didn't help them. The Oilers outshot them 18 to 9 and also scored three unanswered goals. Watching the game from a higher vantage point, I saw just how slowly the New Mexico players were moving. Three games in as many nights were certainly taking their toll. Team owners faced a dilemma: in order to attract the largest crowds possible, they had to schedule most of their games on Fridays, Saturdays and Sundays. But that meant the members of the relatively small 17- to 19-man rosters, some of them playing with aches, pains and minor injuries, were game- and, frequently, travel-weary by Sunday night's game. When the Oilers arrived back in their Oklahoma home early Monday morning, the two teams would have traveled a combined total of nearly 3,000 miles over the weekend.

If there was a bright spot in the second period, it occurred during a play stoppage when two pigeons flew across the rink before roosting on one of the roof beams, a place that presumably gave them a bird's-eye view of the so-called action. Their flight produced a few lame witticisms. One fan remarked loudly, "This game really is for the birds." Another hoped that the birds would not physically display their judgment of the quality of the game below them.

During the second intermission, Stanley cavorted on his quad again, two fans tried unsuccessfully to fire a puck from center ice through a four-inch opening on the bottom of a large plywood sheet (painted with advertisements) that covered the net, and a small remote-controlled blimp, also with advertising on it, cruised over the stands, dropping leaflets.

I decided to look at the biographies in the program to get an idea of who these Scorpions were. They ranged in age from 19 to 33, with half of them between 22 and 25. Most came from Canada, and there were two each from the United States and Europe. Just two players—33-year-old assistant coach Peter Ambroziak, the only player on either team to have played in the NHL (12 games), and Dennis Tetrault—had been selected in the NHL entry draft. The Scorpions seemed to be made up of good but not great players, working for an average of about $500 a week at the game they loved.

Just before the beginning of the third period, two middle-aged men climbed the stairs to the last row and sat a couple of seats down from me. As we chatted briefly about the progress of the game, the pigeons made another flypast. "Well," one of the men remarked, "we won't have to worry about them when the team moves to the new arena." He explained that Tingley Coliseum would be the Scorpions' home for just another year. After that, they'd be moving to a new arena in the town of Rio Rancho, a rapidly expanding bedroom community, 12 miles to the north. "It would be nice to watch a game in a new arena," he continued. "The sightlines would be a lot better than they are here, and the lights would be brighter. But it would be quite a drive for fans who live in Albuquerque. I don't think I'd go to as many games."

During the third period, both clubs seemed to be doing no more than going through the motions. The off-ice activities became more interesting than the game. Each time the puck was about to be dropped, female ushers stood up and held large signs reading "Puck in Play" over their heads. During several stoppages in play, a young man wearing a lab coat and carrying a cordless mike asked fans simple questions about hockey rules. Usually they couldn't answer, and when that was the case, Doctor Hockey, as he called himself, provided the answers. The announced crowd of 2,854—it seemed much smaller—had little else to amuse itself. Neither team scored and no fights broke out. When the final buzzer sounded and the Scorpions wound up with their fifth loss in six games, the fans did not appear too unhappy.

However, a few dozen of them lingered along the boards, lacing up skates. It was "Skate with the Scorpions" night. As soon as the road-weary ice warriors had showered and changed, they'd be joining their admirers on the ice. On the way out, I stopped at the souvenir table to pick up a copy of *The Hockey News* and a book I'd heard about a couple of years earlier, *Zamboni Rodeo: Chasing Hockey Dreams from Austin to Albuquerque*, by Jason Cohen, a Texas journalist. The dust-jacket copy described it as a "rollicking ride through a season in the life of a minor pro hockey team in Texas." The team, the Austin Ice Bats played in the same league as the Scorpions. Maybe the book would help me find out more about minor-league hockey in the early 21st century.

⊙　　⊙　　⊙

After Christmas, I began to read my purchases. On the statistics page of *The Hockey News*, I learned that the CHL was one of five minor leagues. The American Hockey League, which had been around when I was a kid, was considered the premier league for developing future NHLers. The ECHL (which had formerly been called the East Coast Hockey League) was seen as the best league for developing less-experienced and less-polished young pros. The United Hockey League, along with the CHL, was a step lower, and the Southern Professional Hockey League was, as someone later explained it to me, the destination of players with "no-where else to go."

The five leagues iced teams in 95 cities extending from St. John's, Newfoundland, to Anchorage, Alaska, and from Estero (a suburb of Fort Myers), Florida, to San Diego, California. What was surprising was that only 5 of the clubs were based in Canada, while 41 of them played in 14 southern states. Texas cities alone hosted 12 teams (in three different leagues). There were four teams in each of North Carolina, South

Carolina and Georgia. Many of the teams played in places that most Canadians, and no doubt a lot of Americans from northern states, had never heard of: Hidalgo, Texas; Lafayette, Louisiana: Biloxi, Mississippi; Duluth, Georgia; and Florence, South Carolina.

I turned from the news to *Zamboni Rodeo*. An account of the 1997–98 season of the Austin Ice Bats, it was more sad than rollicking, describing 12-hour road trips on unreliable buses to play four games over four nights in converted horse-show arenas in front of vociferous but relatively unknowledgeable fans—all for a few hundred dollars a week and no job security. Some of the players were enjoying a couple of years being paid to play the game they loved before they entered the real world. Some were convinced that they had been unjustly overlooked or ignored by scouts for NHL teams, that they should have been drafted, and that their performance with the Ice Bats might provide them with the break they needed to move, even slightly, up the professional hockey ladder. The rest were hockey lifers, older men who had at one time shown promise, had plateaued early and were now playing out the string at a much lower level than what had been predicted for them.

Like so many books written about a specific athletic team, *Zamboni Rodeo* ended with a section entitled "Where Are They Now?" that was written by Cohen three years after the season covered in the book. A few Ice Bats had moved to higher minor leagues; some were still playing in the lower minors; a couple had entered the coaching ranks; several had retired. Of the 11 teams that Austin had played that year, 5 no longer existed.

After reading Cohen's book, I returned to the biographical sketches in the Scorpions' program. The information in them had acquired new meaning. For example, I now saw Peter Ambroziak as a player who had never fulfilled the potential scouts had long ago seen in him. In the 1994–95 season, he had played 12 games for the Buffalo Sabres, earning one assist. However, in six years in the higher minors, he'd never got more than 29 points in one season. In 1999 he joined New Mexico, tallied 87 and 78 points in his first two years and then averaged just over 40 points in the next three. With the Scorpions, he appeared to have found his niche, one that had extended his life as a professional hockey player.

For the Scorpions' two rookies, Jordan Bianchin, the 23-year-old son of former NHLer Wayne, and 19-year-old Slovakian Ivan Svarny, playing with the Scorpions was an opportunity to continue playing competitive hockey after their United States college and Junior A years. Bianchin had been a low-scoring center at the University of Denver and Northern Michigan University; Svarny had not been drafted when he'd turned 19 and had chosen the uncertain life of a professional in the lower minors over continuing in the junior leagues. Up until Christmas he'd appeared in all of the team's games, scoring a goal and amassing only 10 minutes in penalties, a small total for a defenseman and far behind Sean Legault's team-leading 108 minutes. It would not be surprising if either man's hockey career ended when the season was over. But even if it did, Bianchin and Svarny were currently enjoying an experience denied most of their college and junior teammates.

When I returned to Edmonton, I began to look at the hockey sections of Our Sports Central (www.oursportscentral.com), a website that provided links to newspaper articles about teams in various minor-league sports. In addition to game stories and feature articles, I read about a female defenseman who played for the Tulsa Oilers; about the lifetime suspension that the United Hockey League (UHL) imposed on the head coach of the Motor City Mechanics because he had offered a $200 bounty to anyone on the team who "got" a specific member of one of the opposing clubs; and about the increasing number of locked-out NHLers signing contracts, which were often worth less than 5 percent of their major-league pay, to play in the lower minors—to the considerable displeasure of the journeymen they were displacing.

But most interesting were newspaper reports of franchise moves that were predicted to take place in the off-season. The Worcester IceCats, claiming their market had too small a corporate base to provide adequate sponsorships and luxury box sales, planned to move to Peoria, Illinois, presently the host city of the ECHL. The Cleveland Barons had apparently received inquiries about relocating to Tulsa, Oklahoma, or Quad Cities, Iowa/Illinois. The ECHL had assumed operations of the financially troubled Louisiana IceGators. Once one of the most successful teams in all of minor-league hockey, the IceGators were not expected to survive to the next season. In the CHL, an expansion franchise would begin play in the fall in Youngstown, Ohio, a city over 800 miles from Memphis, its nearest opponent. The UHL's Port Huron (Michigan) Beacons announced they would be discontinuing operations after the season, stating that they had lost close to half a million dollars over each of the previous three seasons. Change seemed to be a major characteristic of minor-league hockey.

In late February, after I had completed a long-term non-sports-related project, I found myself thinking more and more about minor-league hockey, particularly in the southern states, and wondering what the answers might be to a number of questions that had arisen since my visit to Tingley Coliseum just two months earlier. The first and biggest question was easy to ask: Why did minor-league professional hockey experience such tremendous growth during the past decade and a half, especially in the American South? However, thinking about possible answers raised many more questions: Why did sports entrepreneurs want to invest in minor-league hockey teams? How were the various leagues formed and cities chosen? Why did cities where football and basketball dominated the fall and winter sports scenes court professional hockey leagues? Why did athletes want to go to places most of them had only just heard of to play hockey for a few hundred dollars a week? Why did people in places like Charleston, South Carolina; Tallahassee, Florida; Baton Rouge, Louisiana; Lubbock, Texas; and Reno, Nevada, become avid—some might say rabid—hockey fans? What caused the unbelievably rapid increase in the number of minor-league franchises in the mid-1990s, and, a few years later, what caused the shifting of franchises to different cities and the folding of teams, sometimes in midseason? And finally, how long could the interest in minor-league hockey be sustained in the southern states? Would the incredible ice explosion be followed by a catastrophic meltdown?

During the next 14 months, I searched for answers to these and other questions, reading about minor-league hockey in the American South, talking to league and team officials and, most important, attending hockey games in four southern cities, one in each of the ECHL, CHL, UHL and SPHL; visiting with coaches, players, referees and fans; and watching more minor-league games than I had done since I'd finished university and left Vancouver almost 45 years earlier.

PART ONE

THE ICE MEN OF DIXIE

Visits and Conversations

APPALACHIAN AUTUMN

The Roanoke Valley Vipers of the United Hockey League

The Roanoke Valley, nestled in the mountains of western Virginia, is one of the most traditional of minor-league hockey's nontraditional markets. Professional hockey has been played in Salem, Roanoke and the nearby town of Vinton since 1967. Clubs have been members of the Eastern Hockey League, Southern Hockey League, Atlantic Coast Hockey League and All-American Hockey League. The Virginia Lancers, playing first in Vinton and later in Roanoke, were a charter member of the East Coast Hockey League in 1988, and as the Lancers, Rebels, Rampage and Express they remained ECHL members until July 20, 2004, when the league revoked the franchise. In the spring of 2005, the United Hockey League awarded an expansion franchise to Roanoke.

MONDAY NOVEMBER 7, 2005

During the first week of November 2005, the Roanoke Valley didn't seem like hockey country. The Appalachian Mountains to the east were dappled with green and russet colors, indicative of the fall season just beginning. The Monday morning sports section of the *Roanoke Times* featured front-page stories about college and professional football and NASCAR racing. On page three, a small, 150-word story and accompanying summary recounted the Sunday night victory of the Roanoke Valley Vipers, who had traveled to Connecticut to defeat the Danbury Trashers. On the statistics page, the UHL and NHL results and standings followed auto racing, football and golf statistics. The Vipers, with three wins and three losses, occupied third place in the five-team Eastern Division.

The Roanoke Civic Center, which first opened in 1971, was the home of both the Vipers and the Dazzle, a minor-league basketball team. Both clubs folded after the 2005-06 season, leaving Center officials with 60 open dates to fill for the upcoming fall and winter.

In the breakfast room of the Comfort Inn, half-a-dozen tall, lanky young men wearing basketball warm-up pants and T-shirts with such slogans as "Charleston Basketball Classic 2000" sat awkwardly on too-small chairs around too-small tables, eating cereal and muffins. They were attending the training camp of the Roanoke Dazzle, a team in the National Basketball Developmental League, the Vipers' chief rival for minor-league sports fans and, with the Vipers and the Roanoke Symphony, co-tenants of the Roanoke Civic Center. Three weeks earlier, hockey players had stayed at the same hotel, but somehow the young basketball hopefuls seemed more natural in the setting.

In Valley View Mall, a 10-minute walk from the hotel, six stores sold athletic apparel—hats, T-shirts and jackets—bearing the names of various local and national teams. One store carried nothing but Washington Redskins merchandise, the Redskins being the area's National Football League team of choice. Another offered only clothing bearing the logo of college football power Virginia Tech, which is located in nearby Blacksburg. The other stores featured college apparel along with NFL, National Basketball Association and Major League Baseball hats and uniforms. There was no NHL merchandise and none from the Roanoke Valley Vipers.

By the early afternoon, the temperature in Roanoke had risen to the low 70s. Downtown, at the Civic Center, sweaters or jackets were unnecessary, even for people standing next to the boards. That was because there was no ice. The ice-making machinery had broken down late Thursday night, and the Vipers' Friday and Saturday night hockey games had been canceled. No practice had been scheduled for Monday, and Civic Center workers were correcting the mechanical problems and preparing to lay a new ice surface so that the team could practice on Tuesday. Monday would be the Vipers' only day off for the week.

The front-office staff—at five people, one of the smallest in the league—didn't have time to lament the weekend's lost games and revenue; they had to prepare for four home games in five days. They held the usual front-office hockey jobs: business and game-day operations, media and community relations, broadcasting, corporate sales and group sales. There was no general manager; co-owner Kristen Dixon coordinated business activities from her home in Canton, Ohio. However, with a busy home schedule ahead, she would be arriving in Roanoke any day.

What was surprising about the group was that the two most experienced members were women: Amy Webb, a Roanoke resident, who had worked for the Vipers' ECHL predecessor, the Express; and Kris House, who arrived in Roanoke during the summer of 2005 after several seasons working for pro hockey teams in Binghamton, New York. Different in background, age and temperament, the two had in common a love of hockey and an enthusiasm for, and real competence in, their jobs.

When Amy Webb was in her final year of high school, she took an internship with the Roanoke Express as part of her program of studies in sports management. "I was a gofer in the press box during game day, getting information for the announcers and phoning in scores. I really enjoyed the experience and wanted to stay on after the season had ended. It took a long time to make contact with the owners, but finally they offered me a job at $230 a week. I spent the summer calling people, trying to get them to buy season tickets, and in the fall, when the players were back, I took them to schools and other places. There was one old lady who was in a nursing home; one of the players and I visited her regularly—she loved it."

Although Webb was working long hours as director of media and community relations, and loving every minute of it, the Express's fortunes were in decline. The hands-off ownership group had disillusioned both corporate sponsors and fans, the team's main sources of revenue.

"When the season ended, we had to go on as if everything was fine, and so we began to work on season-ticket renewals. Then came 2:30 pm, Tuesday, July 20, 2004. The league called to say that the franchise had been revoked." Webb gathered her stuff, along with a few game-worn jerseys. They had been marked for sale, but with no organization to sell them, she sent them to the players. "I think it gave me a kind of closure." The next eight months were difficult for Webb. "I wanted hockey; I wanted the Express back."

Amy Webb, the Vipers' community and media relations director, has yet to play goal for the team. But there's no doubt she would try if she felt it would help the club and bring more fans into the Roanoke Civic Center.

Then, in March 2005, she learned that the UHL was going to place a franchise in the Civic Center for the 2005–06 season. "A friend who'd worked with the Express had contacted [UHL commissioner] Richard Brosal and, in the conversation, had mentioned my work in hockey. I said to myself, 'It was a sign!'"

Within a couple of weeks, the new owners, Ken and Kristen Dixon, had offered her a job. As the franchise's only employee, she set up a long banquet table and a folding chair, picked up the telephone and began calling people on a list of prospective season-ticket holders.

Webb admitted that she faced many challenges during the long summer hours that followed. "We didn't hire a sales person until the end of May, and it was only then that we were able to go after corporate sponsors." At the same time, she coordinated the team's efforts to create a visible identity, announcing the team name, displaying the new logo—a coiled snake behind the word "Viper," which is underlined with a hockey stick—introducing the mascot and conducting a name-the-mascot contest. One of the most effective strategies for bringing the new team to the public's attention involved six billboards placed around the town. On them, a family—two parents and two children—smiled happily. Three were missing teeth. Beneath the picture ran the slogan "It's a family affair—Roanoke Valley Vipers." It certainly drew a more favorable response than a Christmas billboard created by the Express two years earlier: the picture of a hockey player with a raised fist and the slogan "Season's Beatings."

Not only did the Vipers have to make Roanoke Valley sports fans aware that there was a new hockey team in town, they also had to overcome the skepticism about hockey that the locals had developed during the last few seasons of the Express. "Some of the people we talked to felt that the new league might not be as good as the ECHL," Webb explained. Would it be a *Slap Shot* league, with aging goons dragging out their careers? The job, she said, was to win people over one at a time. "We promised them affordable family entertainment, and we planned an environment for both adults and kids." In October, when the public criticized ticket prices, which ranged from $8.50 to $22.00 and were higher than Express tickets had been, the Vipers' management mounted two marketing campaigns: "Under 6 for 6"— a low price for small children—and "8 for 8," the price for a ticket in the back eight rows of the end zone. "We wanted the people to know we were listening to them," Webb remarked.

Amy Webb clearly enjoyed her work in hockey. While discussing the new team, she had to pause frequently to take questions from other staff members, quickly and effectively supplying answers. But she did have regrets about the job. She'd had to cut back considerably on her university studies, and she wasn't able to spend time on Opportunity for Baseball, a charitable organization she started after graduating from high school that gathered baseball equipment for underprivileged children in the United States and the Dominican Republic.

As director of community and media relations, Webb's main job was to let the people of the Roanoke Valley know about the new hockey team and to encourage them to come to the Civic Center. The task for Kris House, director of business and game-day operations, was to make sure they had a good time when they got there, even if the Vipers didn't win. Webb had noted, "We've got a good core of real hockey fans, but not enough to support the team. We want families to know that they can have a good time when they show up. If they do, they'll come back, and that's what we need."

It was after two in the afternoon, and House was just beginning to eat her lunch. The next home game was 53 hours in the future, but she'd been busy since 8:30 that morning preparing for it. Now in her seventh year working in minor-league hockey, the 31-year-old Indianapolis, Indiana, native was perhaps the only university student in the United States to change schools because she wanted to be able to watch intercollegiate hockey. "I was in the Athletic Training program at Indiana State University at Terre Haute in southwestern Indiana, and after my second year I realized how much I missed hockey. I used to go to a lot of the Indianapolis Ice games." A year later she headed 600 miles north to the shore of Lake Superior, where she completed her studies and watched Northern Michigan University's hockey Wildcats. After graduation, House worked in the front office of the Ice and then moved to Binghamton. "After several years in there, I found myself plateaued. I made a conscious decision to move. My goal was to reach the NHL, and I knew I needed new and more management experience." She arrived in western Virginia in the early summer.

She described the challenge of reintroducing professional hockey to Roanoke. "Because we're selling family-oriented entertainment, we set out to educate and entertain. We're preparing hockey brochures about hockey rules so that fans who don't know the game very well can enjoy it more. But it's more than just hockey. So we're working at creating an energetic, fun game-day experience for fans. We prepare the music to enhance the game, and we've created a 'Kids' Zone' with coloring and other activities. If the kids are busy, they won't be running around the stands, and their parents can relax and enjoy the game. We also have intermission events, including mini-games with local kids' teams, and giveaways. The idea is for everyone in the family to have such a good night's entertainment that they'll want to come to another game."

Like Amy Webb, House exuded enthusiasm for her work, although in a quieter, more intense manner. "Hockey is my life. I can't imagine another career. The game is fast and there's lots of action. Sure, it's rough, but it's also highly skilled. I live for game-day operations, bringing the fans and the game together. That's why I don't like summer— there are no hockey games. If you want to sum me up, just say, 'I'm a hockey person.'"

. Although there hadn't been any ice at the Civic Center for three days, there was still hockey in western Virginia on the first Monday in November. Webb had observed that it was necessary to woo the community, so

Roanoke Valley Vipers' radio broadcaster Matt Rosen (left) and rookie forward Mike Krelove discuss hockey with youngsters in the southwestern Virginia town of Bedford. Player appearances are an important element of all minor-league teams' efforts to become better known in their communities.

for the past few Mondays, play-by-play man Matt Rosen and one of the Viper players had driven 20 miles east to Bedford, a village nestled in the Appalachians. Their destination was the local YMCA, where two New York transplants, brothers David and Richard Sperrazza, both still devoted Ranger fans, had convinced the recreation director to reserve half of the gym each Monday evening for children's ball hockey. Rosen and, on this night, Mike Krelove, a very blond and very young-looking player from Thunder Bay, Ontario, demonstrated basic passing and shooting techniques and joined the children in a rough-and-ready scrimmage. The session ended with a shootout that continued until each of the dozen or so 8-to-12-year-olds had put the orange street-hockey ball behind a very lackluster goalie—Krelove, a left-winger—and won a ticket to Friday night's Vipers game.

The session over, the parents thanked the Vipers, and the Sperrazzas, on learning that Rosen was from New York, talked with him about the Rangers' winning teams of the 1990s. They also asked how to purchase group tickets so they could bring a children's organization to a hockey game. "I want the local kids to see that there's nothing like hockey," David Sperrazza remarked. The excursion had been a success: the kids had a good time, and the Vipers had become better known.

TUESDAY NOVEMBER 8, 2005

By Tuesday morning, the ice surface at the Civic Center had been sufficiently restored for the Vipers to practice for the first time in five days. Shortly before ten o'clock, players clomped from the dressing room in ones and twos and began to skate tentatively, testing the new playing surface. A few minutes later, Daniel Berthiaume, the flamboyant assistant coach and former NHL goaltender, burst onto the ice, his stick held high, and announced, "La première étoile ... numéro soixante-six, Mario Lemieux." For each of the following mornings the ritual was the same, except for the name of the first star (always a French Canadian), and it signaled that practice was about to begin.

One thing was quickly apparent about the Roanoke Valley Vipers. It was—by minor-league standards—a young team. A check of the 19-man roster revealed that 7 players were 23 or under and only 1 was over 30. The average age was just over 22. David Shillington, who turned 20 late in the spring, was the second-youngest player in the league. Travis Smith was the oldest Viper at 32. Eight players were rookies, and the average number of pro seasons played was just over two. David Beauregard, the only Viper to have been selected in the NHL draft, had 10 seasons of experience.

The instructional circle is a familiar sight at hockey rinks everywhere. Here, coach Jim Wiley talks with members of the Roanoke Valley Vipers.

Because only four of the players had been together in the 2004–05 season, and because coach Jim Wiley had been appointed only a month before training camp, much of the practice was spent getting players to work together smoothly and to develop his system—which involved a lot of movement and a series of quick, short passes. Wiley spoke quietly and never used a whistle. His instructions were simple and clear, as were his explanations of the purposes of the drills. He'd begun his coaching career in 1984 in the United States Hockey League, where the players are teenagers preparing for athletic scholarships at American colleges, and he'd had to do a great deal of teaching. A rink-side observer listening to him and watching the players' reactions could tell that he was good at it and that he loved it. He closed the practice with a short, simple statement, "We've got to be willing to battle for the puck every shift," and then remained behind with veteran Mark Scott and rookie Mike Krelove, helping the older player fine-tune his game and the younger learn strategies and techniques that would enable him to adapt to hockey at the professional level.

During the practice, three or four people wandered into the arena and stopped for a few minutes to watch the activities. One of them, Robyn Schon, assistant facilities manager of the Civic Center, had a double interest. She was an avid hockey fan, having caught the fever after she'd moved to Detroit from Greensboro, North Carolina, to become the marketing director for the Detroit Red Wings. "I'm such a Red Wings fan," she remarked, "that my license plate reads WNGNUT—and I really am a nut for the game." But more important, she was checking on the state of the ice. She wanted the best possible conditions for the Vipers.

Having a hockey team was crucial to the Center. "Last year, after the Express disbanded, we lost a great deal of budgeted revenue. But having a year with no hockey did give us the time we needed to find a suitable tenant. In July 2004, as soon as we learned that the Express would not be returning, we put the word out that we'd be interested in attracting a new team." Three leagues—the UHL, the Southern Hockey League (as the short-lived World Hockey Association 2 had been renamed) and the South East Hockey League (which merged with the SHL in summer 2005 to form the Southern Professional Hockey League)—quickly showed interest. The Civic Center also began accepting deposits on season tickets for whatever new team arrived. "We went for the UHL," Robyn explained, "because it had longevity and stability. As a municipality, we couldn't afford a team from a shaky, embryonic league. If it failed, fans and business would lose faith and hockey would be gone from the Roanoke Valley. I'm really glad hockey is back. As a business person, I know how important it is for the area. And I'm a fan. It will be great to watch hockey again."

After practice, David Shillington sat down to talk about his career. He looked like a hockey player—there was a missing tooth and also a fleck of red in his left eye that he'd acquired during an opening-night fight—but his conversation wasn't limited to hockey. It included comments about American novelist John Steinbeck, federalist politics in Canada and plans for a political career after hockey.

Southern hockey fans display their love of hockey on their cars. Roanoke Civic Center official Robyn Schon's license plate proclaims her allegiance to the Detroit Red Wings, a team she followed while working in Michigan.

He grew up in Calgary, playing his way through the ranks and admiring Mike Bossy, whom he'd only seen on videos that his father had purchased, and current Calgary Flames star Jarome Iginla. But it wasn't until he took his Grade 12 year at Saskatchewan's famous Athol Murray College of Notre Dame that the passion for hockey gripped him. "It was the best experience I'd ever had—scholastics, hockey and religion. At Notre Dame, Terry O'Malley and all the faculty stressed that if I wanted to be a success, I had to be passionate, intense. I left Notre Dame a changed person and hockey player."

After a year in the Alberta Junior Hockey League, Shillington headed east to study political science and to play hockey for the University of Ottawa Gee-Gees. He arrived on campus early and, seeking some ice time, asked legendary junior coach Brian Kilrea of the Ottawa 67s if he could practice with the Ontario Hockey League team. A few days later, he limped off the ice with what everyone thought was a charley horse. "By that night my thigh was twice its normal size and the doctors operated right away." Shillington had suffered compartment syndrome, a limb- and sometimes life-threatening condition in which a muscle swells so much that it becomes constricted within the other muscles and bone that surround it. "I stayed in the hospital for a month," Shillington remembered. When he returned to the ice, he scored a goal on his first shift for the Gee-Gees. It was the only game he played that season.

In the fall of 2005, Shillington returned to Ottawa and began to practice with the university team. But he was let go before the season began. "I think that they made a mistake, but that was how things go. I decided I'd leave Ottawa. There was no hockey for me there and, being a good westerner, I really didn't like the East. So I quit the university, packed up my truck and headed to the [American Hockey League] Cleveland Barons' tryout camp." He was realistic in his expectations, knowing that he had little chance to make it with the AHL team. "I went for the experience. It was a great camp and I got to play in an exhibition game." What did he learn? The game was much faster and he had to think quickly and know what was going on all over the rink.

At the end of September, Shillington again packed his truck and started driving—this time to a place he'd only just heard of: Roanoke. He had told Cleveland's coach, Roy Sommer, about his desire to find a place where he could get enough ice time to develop his playing skills. Sommer recommended his friend Jim Wiley, who had just been named coach of the Vipers. "I've ended up in a perfect setting," Shillington said. "I don't have to play in every game, but I need direction, which Coach Wiley gives. I'm learning a very good system—one with short passes and lots of movement."

It had not only been a learning experience for the young rookie, it had also been fun. "Opening night was a great experience, hearing your name, then skating through the tunnel, through the fog and into the spotlights. In the first game I discovered how fast and tough the league is. And it was a surprise just how knowledgeable the fans are. But some of them would rather see a fight than a goal. I think it's sad when people come expecting a World Wrestling Federation kind of show. But there's [sic] not as many of these people as I thought there would be."

Like all pro hockey players, Shillington would like to reach as high a level as he can. "I'd like to make it to the AHL," he explained. But already he'd begun preparing for a life after hockey, putting the long hours spent on the bus to good use. "On road trips, I'm reading American novels for a course I'm taking online from [Alberta's] Athabasca University. I've just finished Steinbeck's *The Grapes of Wrath*, and next I'll read *Of Mice and Men*. I'm not much of a sleeper, and I don't take pre-game naps—I like to read."

His reading also included studies of federalism in Canada and global-ization movements. When the name of former Canadian prime minister Pierre Elliott Trudeau was mentioned, he snorted and expressed a fairly typical western Canadian attitude toward the eastern leader's view of a united Canada. It wasn't surprising to learn that his father had owned an oil company in Calgary and that Shillington was keenly aware of national energy policies. "The oil industry has been very good to me and my family," said the young left-winger, who has spent considerable time working for Canada's right-wing political organizations, first the Reform Party and then the Conservative Party. "When I finish hockey and my education, I'd like to work maybe as a lobbyist, helping the oil industry in its relationships with the federal government." But he readily admitted that that was in the future. Steinbeck and slap shots were his immediate concerns.

As the Zamboni made its final circle of the ice, Shillington and his new friends left the Civic Center and headed downtown to the Cornerstone Restaurant. There they'd enjoy a post-practice meal for only five dollars, one of the benefits of being a hockey player in Roanoke. The annual sal-ary cap in the UHL was $275,000 for a 19-man roster, an average of just under $14,500 a player for the six-month season. Although that worked out to around $600 a week, many rookies received only the weekly mini-mum of $250. However, players were given free housing, and the perks like five-dollar meals at the Cornerstone, discounts at pizza and Subway restaurants, free movies at one of the local theaters and reduced rates at golf courses helped to stretch what were usually very tight budgets.

Unfortunately, these discounts weren't portable. On the road, players received a $25 meal allowance, based on $5 for breakfast, $8 for lunch and $12 for dinner. It wasn't surprising to find the fridge on the team bus crammed with snacks, although they weren't always the most whole-some or nourishing food.

WEDNESDAY, NOVEMBER 9, 2005

As busy as the Vipers' week was going to be with four home games, the visiting Elmira Jackals' week would be even more hectic. They had ar-rived in town late Tuesday evening and checked in at the visiting team hotel. Immediately after Wednesday's game, they would reboard their bus—which was outfitted with bunks—to make the 10-hour, 472-mile return trip to upstate New York. Then, after Friday and Saturday night games in their own rink, the Jackals would again board the bus to return to Roanoke for a late Sunday afternoon game. In just over five days, the club would have traveled 1,888 miles, the distance from Vancouver to Dryden, Ontario, or from Dallas to Hartford, Connecticut, and played four games. Although the league tried to arrange schedules so that visiting teams played consecutive games in the same city, schedule makers also had to work with open dates in the various arenas. "It's just something you get used to," remarked one Elmira player as he sat in the bus after practice, reading *The Hockey News*.

As Jackals coach Perry Florio put his team through its practice, Branislav Kvetan, one of the Vipers' defensemen, sat in the stands watching the players he'd be facing in a few hours. The 28-year-old native of Trencin, Slovakia, was playing in his first UHL season, but had four years' experience in the North American minor leagues. Kvetan was one of four Europeans on the Vipers' roster, along with Jan Jas, an eight-year pro from Slovakia, and rookies Petr Jelinek from the Czech Republic and Alex Jerofejevs from Latvia. Jerofejevs, Jas and Jelinek had originally come to North America to play junior hockey and then stayed to play professionally. Kvetan had come directly from Europe to play professional hockey. "The higher you get in my country," he explained, "the less opportunity there is to play. Many of us come to North America so that we can continue our careers."

Kvetan came from an athletic family. "My father was a national coach for the Slovakian cycling team, and I think I'd have gone into road racing if I hadn't begun hockey." Like his North American counterparts, he'd started young, at six years old, and had to show up for practice at six in the morning. "There was only one rink in

For Vipers defenseman Branislav Kvetan, a native of Slovakia, playing minor-league hockey in North America is, in part, a way to fulfill his love of traveling to new places.

our town of 70,000, so you had to get up early." He played through
high school, enjoying the camaraderie and the chance to visit different
places in Europe, and then spent a year in the army. "When I came out,
it was difficult to find a place on a good team. I had friends in the NHL
and they put me in touch with an agent. That's how I got to play in Birmingham in the ECHL."

Coming to the Alabama metropolis for his first professional season
was a major learning experience, both on and off the ice. "Compared to
my hometown, it was a really huge city to me. I had very little English,
just two years in school. Of course, we all learned the bad words, but
now we had to learn how to get along. On the ice, I found that there was
a lot more hitting than I was used to back home. The players were more
aggressive, and there was a lot more fighting. Also, I had to adapt to the
smaller ice surfaces." And the bus trips! At home, five hours was the
longest time he'd had to spend on the bus. During the 2000–01 season
he spent with the Birmingham Bulls, the ECHL stretched from Toledo,
Ohio, and Trenton, New Jersey, in the north, to Fort Myers, Florida,
and Lafayette, Louisiana, in the south. He quickly became acquainted
with a basic fact of life in the North American minor leagues: the bus is
a second home.

After his year with the Bulls, Kvetan spent three more seasons in the
South, two with the Louisiana IceGators of the ECHL and one with the
Tulsa Oilers of the Central Hockey League. "After I'd been here for four
seasons, I decided it was time to go back to Europe. I signed a contract
with Znojemsti Excalibur Orli of the Czech Republic. I played in 15
games, but because of the NHL work stoppage, more and more players
were coming home to play. The hockey was fast and there were big
crowds. It was a very good experience, but because of all the NHLers I
had limited ice time, and eventually I got dropped to Division Two." His
contract was only for one year, and Kvetan found himself missing the
United States. "So I contacted my agent and he contacted Jim Wiley. I
wanted to play here, to see new places, meet new people and learn more
English. I don't make a lot of money, but it's enough to live on. I enjoy
being with the players, making new friends."

Kvetan didn't know how long his present stint in the United States
would last. But he thought that when he finally hung up his skates, he'd
return to Slovakia and stay involved in sports. "It's in the family. Who
knows? Coaching maybe." But for now he was having fun and getting

ready for the evening's game. His friends Jan Jas, Petr Jelinek and Alex Jerofejevs joined him, and the four headed back to their apartment for lunch and a pre-game nap.

Although the players' preparations for the game had ended, those of the front-office staff had just begun to move into high gear. Kris House unloaded boxes from a cluttered cupboard on the arena's concourse and began to set up the "Kids' Zone." At one end of the rink, Tim Callahan and Jae McCadden, the Vipers' two-person sales staff, checked the scaffolding, on top of which were placed two oversized recliners. Named "The Best Seats in the House" and sponsored by a local furniture store, they rose above the boards behind the glass, providing a close-up view of action in the corner. Early in the first period, the announcer would call the names of two fans who would be escorted to the recliners. Unlike most Canadian fans, who favor a location high above the ice where they can see plays developing, a large number of southern fans prefer seats next to the glass. Although they lose sight of play along the boards away from them, they enjoy the noise and sheer physicality of events right in front of them and the opportunity to pound on the Plexiglas and shriek at the athletes.

Upstairs in the Vipers' offices, play-by-play announcer Matt Rosen was nearing the end of several hours of preparation for the night's broadcast of the game against the Jackals, a team he'd seen only once so far in the season. He'd been reinforcing his knowledge of names and numbers, repeating them aloud time and time again so that he could recall them without hesitation as he called the game. But his groundwork went far beyond that. He carefully studied the game notes that Amy Webb had put together for the press, noting career highlights and background facts about each player. Then he watched a tape of a game between the Jackals and the Adirondack Frostbite, who would be in town on Friday and Saturday. As he watched, he noted distinctive characteristics and playing styles and practiced his recall of the names linked to the numbers on the sweaters. "I may only use 25 percent of the information I've gathered," he commented, "but without that other 75 percent, the broadcast would be weaker."

Rosen was in his first year of calling professional hockey, his second season broadcasting games overall. However, he'd been around hockey play-by-play all his life. His father, Sam, has been the TV voice of the New York Rangers for over two decades. "I don't remember a time when I didn't hear him calling hockey, and I've always wanted to be like him." After he'd finished his studies at the University of Arizona in Tucson, Rosen enrolled in a broadcasting school and learned technical elements of the trade and methods of becoming comfortable in front of a microphone. "But everything else, I'd been learning from my father for years," he said. "He emphasized the importance of preparation—I saw the hours of work he put in before each game, and I listened to him. I heard how his voice inflections caught the rhythms of the game and the pace of the play."

Matt Rosen was definitely goal-oriented. "I want to broadcast in the NHL. In fact, I want to succeed my father when he decides to retire. I have no doubt I'll get there; I'm driven to get there. I won't accept less. A few years ago, I was working at a financially rewarding job. But I said to myself, 'Where do I want to be in five years; do I still want to be at this job?' The answer was no; I could only be happy in sports broadcasting. I'm making a lot less money now, but I'm very happy. I'm learning every day. It's a wonderful experience."

Just before seven o'clock, the Zamboni left the ice and Kris House finished assembling the inflatable tunnel through which the players would emerge. Matt Rosen welcomed his radio audience and set the scene. Tonight's was the second of what would be 14 games between the two clubs. The Jackals won the first game, in Elmira, 7–5. This season, in an attempt to keep travel costs down, the Vipers would play 56 of their 76 games against the other four teams in their own division—the Jackals, Adirondack Frostbite of Glens Falls (New York), Danbury (Connecticut) Trashers and Richmond (Virginia) RiverDogs.

Just after seven o'clock, the Vipers skated out of the tunnel and began to circle lazily at their own end of the ice. They rocked nervously from side to side as they stood along the blue line during the singing of the national anthem. The crowd cheered loudly as the two teams lined up for the opening faceoff, but a minute later it fell silent. That was because, during the first shift, the system that Jim Wiley had been teaching was little in evidence. The puck was stolen from a Viper forward, and rookie Jarrett Konkle, the Jackals' leading scorer, broke toward the Roanoke goal, only to be dragged down by David Beauregard. Konkle scored on the ensuing penalty shot.

The Vipers' disorganized play continued for five more minutes before the system kicked in. Then Mark Scott and Petr Jelinek scored, and for nearly 20 minutes, from the middle of the first period to the middle of the second, the Jackals had no shots on goal. The Vipers added two more goals in the second and one in the third, earning their fourth victory. As the visitors fell behind, their frustration became apparent: they were assessed five slashing penalties, three majors for fighting and two misconducts.

During the second period, one of the members of the press box ran a sweepstakes in which people paid 25 cents to guess the evening's attendance. "Can you wait a couple of minutes?" one wag remarked. "I think I can probably count them." This would not have been a difficult task, as in some sections of the stands there were only five or six people. When the official attendance of 826 was announced in the third period, a veteran press box observer hypothesized, "That's the number of tickets out, not the number in the building. It's the worst attendance since the blizzard." This was a reference to the great snowstorm of March 1991, when 67 people braved the elements to attend an ECHL contest in Vinton. Midway through the game, players and fans were evacuated as the roof began to buckle under the weight of the heavy, wet snow that had fallen throughout the day.

The Vipers are the most recent in a long line of minor-league hockey teams that have played in the Roanoke area. Here, fans wearing jerseys of earlier teams cheer a Roanoke goal. (Photo by Amy Webb)

The attendance for the game was well under the 3,600 that owners Ken and Kristen Dixon had said they'd need each game if they were to break even. Three members of the press box offered possible explanations for the low turnout: fans were still skeptical about the quality of play in the new league; there hadn't been a sufficiently aggressive marketing campaign; and the area's many churches scheduled major activities on Wednesday evenings. Kristen Dixon was not there to see the small crowd; she was now expected to arrive from Canton in time for Friday's game.

Moments before the end of the third period, *Roanoke Times* hockey writer Katrina Waugh headed to the hallway outside the Vipers' dressing room to gather quotes for her game story. As she waited for Vipers coach Jim Wiley to emerge from his office to talk with her, Waugh discussed the constant struggle to get space in the sports pages for stories about hockey. "I began covering professional hockey and baseball here nine years ago, and it's become increasingly difficult to provide the hockey coverage I'd like. I have to fight for a non-game story, to provide my boss with a compelling reason for printing a feature story. I don't schedule any interviews before I get clearance for a story." With high school and Virginia Tech sports, along with major-league football and NASCAR, hockey was a minor priority in the paper. "Of course, I've never had to fight for a breaking news story, such as the decision of the ECHL to shut down the Express or the arrival of the UHL in town."

Some fans and Vipers employees had objected to what they considered a negative tone in her writing about the new hockey team. For example, her story on the announcement that the UHL's Port Huron franchise would be transferred to Roanoke began with this lead: "It's a match made in minor-league hockey's financial purgatory. Ken and Kristen Dixon were losing money on their United Hockey League franchise in Port Huron, Mich., and were looking for a new home. Roanoke lost its debt-ridden franchise and was looking for a new team." Asked about her supposedly cynical attitude, Waugh remarked, "As we get older, we learn more and become more skeptical. I want to be honest as a writer, not a cheerleader. I think that's my responsibility to my readers."

Just then, Jim Wiley emerged from his office to discuss the contest against Elmira. About the penalty shot, he commended Beauregard's action on the breakaway, even if it had resulted in a goal. "It wasn't his mistake. You can't be angry at a player for trying to stop a goal." He attributed the high number of penalties to the referee's adjusting to the newly introduced NHL rules regarding interference. "Gradually consistency will emerge. But it is every coach's dream to have nothing but full-strength hockey. That gives a flow, a rhythm to the game. The number of penalties broke up the rhythm; it was hard for us to get back in sync." Generally, he concluded, he was pleased with the team's performance. "We're moving in the right direction."

THURSDAY NOVEMBER 10, 2005

Thursday's practice was a short one; it gave the players a chance to keep loose, to iron out a few wrinkles in the system and, toward the end of the hour, to enjoy a few high jinks on the ice. After the Vipers were finished, the Adirondack Frostbite, Friday and Saturday nights' opponents, made an unexpected appearance. Their Wednesday night contest in Richmond against the RiverDogs had been canceled because of bad ice, so they'd arrived in Roanoke early. The previous weekend the Richmond Coliseum had been the site of a monster-truck rally, and on Tuesday a sellout crowd attended an Elton John concert. Although crews had worked all Tuesday night and during the day on Wednesday, they couldn't get the ice into a condition that would be safe for playing hockey.

In his office, Jim Wiley, who'd left the Vipers' practice a few minutes early, allowing the players time on their own, discussed his life as a coach. Since the end of his seven-year playing career, which had included 62 NHL games with the Pittsburgh Penguins and Vancouver Canucks, he'd coached at every level from junior to the majors (57 games as a replacement coach for the San Jose Sharks during the 1995–96 season). He had also worked as a director of hockey operations and a scout for the Sharks organization, and during the 2004–05 season he'd served as vice-president and general manager of the Louisiana IceGators during their final year in the ECHL.

Wiley agreed with the remark that he appeared to love the teaching aspects of his job, and he went on to praise those who'd taught him. "When I played, I learned mainly by instinct, as most of us did during the 1960s. But things have certainly changed. Talent is not enough anymore. You need to be scientific, as a coach and a player, and I've had a lot of people help me. I remember in the 1970s, people like Orland Kurtenbach and Kevin Constantine introducing me to modern thought. I've had great assistant coaches who've really helped me. I've really been taught well."

His work as a teacher began in 1984 with Des Moines of the United States Hockey League, a junior circuit in the American Midwest. "At that time, a lot of young men were playing until they were too old for junior. But while I was there, we began to work with people in high school. It was a job that involved a great deal more than teaching hockey. I went to parent-teacher conferences, and I arranged for host families for out-of-town players. You had to deal with homesickness, girlfriend problems and all the difficulties of adolescence. And on top of all that, I was learning to coach, to do something I'd wanted to do all my life."

Wiley was proud of what the USHL had become, and started to become, during his coaching tenure in Des Moines: a place where young men could become good enough—athletically and scholastically—to earn college scholarships. "One season," Wiley remembered, "the USHL had more players earning scholarships to play university hockey than all of the Tier II Junior A leagues in western Canada. It was a banner year for the USHL."

Whether it was in the junior- or major-league ranks, the elements of coaching remained fairly constant. "The talent levels differ," Wiley explained, "and at the lower levels there's more grassroots instruction. But even in the major leagues, you often have to go back to basics, to the fundamentals, and expand from there. And at each level it's essential that the players love hockey. Somebody once asked me how I motivate players in leagues like the ECHL and the UHL, where many of the players realize that they're never going to make it to the NHL. I told them what Lou Holtz, the Notre Dame football coach once said: 'I don't motivate players; I get rid of those who aren't motivated.' The ones without desire get weeded out fairly quickly."

Wiley was appointed head coach of the Vipers just five weeks before the season's opening game. The original coach, Rick Adduono, who'd come from Port Huron, resigned just after Labor Day in order to pursue other career opportunities—which in his case happened to be a higher-paying job as a coach in the ECHL. It was, Wiley admitted, a challenge. "I had to ascertain the makeup of the team that was in place when I arrived. You start with where you are and figure out how to get everyone on the same page. This has been a good team to work with. They have a strong work ethic; they're intense and disciplined, and they're willing to be coached. They want to win. It's my job to challenge them to be the best they can. I'm like a teacher in school: I make the lesson plans, set out the objectives and decide the methods for achieving them. Then I motivate them to want to learn."

Out in the stands, Travis Smith watched the Adirondack team practice. The 32-year-old defenseman was not only the oldest Roanoke player, but was also the team's "hometown" hero. He'd played all but 9 of his 235 professional games in the western Virginia city and lived and worked there during the off-season. Born in Creelman, Saskatchewan, a town of a hundred people southeast of Regina, he'd never really thought about a career in hockey until late high school, when his skills attracted the attention of recruiters from the University of Denver, which had consistently iced some of the best college hockey teams in the United States.

"I had a wonderful four years at university; it was a real education on and off the ice. In juniors I'd been the fastest player, but in Denver everyone was fast, and they were bigger and stronger. I'd been a scorer in juniors, but I now had to learn to be more defensive."

Veteran Vipers defenseman Travis Smith sits in the stands to watch the visiting team practice. A year-round resident in Roanoke, Smith is now pondering his future after hockey.

Smith hadn't been picked up in the NHL draft while he was in junior hockey, so, as his university hockey career wound down, he prepared to take his degree in business management and enter the workforce. "But near the end of my senior year, Frank Anzalone called me from Roanoke, Virginia. He was a friend of my college coach, Frank Serratore, and he wanted to know if I'd like to play for the Express after I graduated. I'd never heard of Roanoke; I had to look it up on the map." He found it, went there and stayed. The boy from the flatlands of southern Saskatchewan established a home in the Blue Ridge Mountains of Virginia.

"At first it seemed strange to me that there was hockey so far south, and I didn't know what to expect. But I soon found out that there had been a team in Roanoke for a long time. In some places in the South, they just come out for the fights. They like fights in Roanoke, too, but a lot of the people who come to the games really understand hockey. Some of the places we played in, the rinks weren't built for hockey. I'd say that Tallahassee was definitely not hockey friendly."

Not everyone in Roanoke was a hockey fan, as Smith found out one night after a game, when he and his teammates dropped into a tavern for a couple of beer. "I started talking to this person. She was an elementary schoolteacher, and the only time she'd ever been to a game was when some of the classes came to the arena on a field trip. She didn't know I was a player, but we hit it off." The two married after the 1998–99 season, and Smith became Roanoke's hometown hockey player.

After the 2001–02 season with the Express, Smith decided to retire from hockey. He was working in the city, and he and his wife were planning a family. "The next year the Greensboro team called me up to fill in for a game, but I knew they weren't going to re-sign me. I figured I'd had enough." And he had—for nearly a year. Then in January 2004, as the Express began what would be their last four months in the ECHL, Smith received a call for help from coach Tony MacAulay. Several players were hurt and he needed replacements. Smith answered the call and appeared in 16 games before suffering a season-ending concussion.

In 2004–05, with the Express gone and no NHL games to watch, Smith discovered how much he missed hockey. He realized that he'd have come back had the Express remained in the league, and he kept in shape by playing with a senior amateur club in town. "I didn't want to go somewhere else to play, but I discovered that this was what I still wanted to do. I'm still not sure what I'd like to do after hockey, and I'm taking the winter to sort things out. I've made a lot of contacts in my years here, and I'll probably send out resumes after Christmas. But I don't want to do just anything. After I leave hockey, it will have to be challenging and satisfying."

FRIDAY NOVEMBER 11, 2005

One of the most significant days in the life of a teenage hockey player occurs on a late Saturday in June. That is when the NHL conducts its annual entry draft, selecting some 300 amateurs from North American university and junior teams, U.S. high school clubs and European squads. A few of the chosen, such as Sidney Crosby, the first pick in 2005, go directly to the NHL; more are returned to their junior clubs or sent to the AHL or ECHL for further seasoning; a few elect to take scholarships and play collegiate hockey.

An even smaller number of drafted players make it to the rosters of UHL clubs. In fact, only 7 of the 57 players on the three teams who appeared at the Roanoke Civic Center this week in November had been selected by NHL teams: three each for the Vipers and Frostbite, and one for the Jackals. Two—Adirondack's Sylvain Cloutier and Roanoke's Jamie Hodson—had been selected in the third rounds of their draft years. Only one of the drafted players had made it to the NHL: Cloutier appeared in seven games for Chicago during the 1998–99 season.

On June 28, 1994, the San Jose Sharks selected David Beauregard in the 11th round. "I thought I had a chance of being picked because I had always been a scorer. When I was seven years old, I scored 230 goals in 43 games. I knew when the draft came along that San Jose was interested, but I knew that I was too small to be selected early. I was 5 feet 10 inches and only weighed 165 pounds. So that day a friend and I went to Olympic Stadium to watch the Expos play the Atlanta Braves. My dad called me and said that I'd been picked by the Sharks. At first I thought that he was kidding."

Because of his size and weight, the Sharks sent Beauregard back to junior hockey, and he went on a scoring binge, with 15 goals in his first 12 games for the St. Hyacinthe Lasers of the Quebec Major Junior Hockey League. At this point it appeared that Beauregard's dream of playing in the NHL would be realized within two or three seasons. But on October 16, 1994, tragedy struck. "I was on a breakaway and got hit in the eye by the stick of the guy chasing me. I was taken to the hospital and the doctors told me I was blind in the left eye." Because the NHL prohibits anyone blind in one eye from signing a contract, the dream was over.

Beauregard returned to his junior club late in the season, appearing in 22 games and scoring in 12 of them. "But I was one of the worst players on the ice. I'd lost my depth perception and it took me two months to get some sense of where the puck was." The Sharks dropped him from their protected list, and even though he had a five-game tryout with Kentucky of the AHL during the 1996–97 season, he saw limited ice time. The young players with NHL contracts got the attention and playing time.

In 1997, his junior career over, he signed a contract with the Wichita Thunder of the Central Hockey League, an assignment that saw him shuttling back and forth between the Thunder and the Kansas City

Blades of the higher-level International Hockey League. His 42 goals for Wichita earned him the CHL Rookie of the Year award. But what he remembers most about that season is one of his single-game call-ups to the IHL. "I flew to Chicago to join the Blades and sat on the bench for most of the game. I didn't get a shift until there were only 52 seconds left in the third period. I scored to tie the game. There was a shootout and I got the winning goal. Then, after the game, I showered, headed to the airport and flew back to Wichita."

Beauregard's stint with the Blades marked the end of his playing time in the higher minor leagues. Over the next seven seasons he skated for Muskegon, Flint, Port Huron and Fort Wayne of the UHL; Greensboro and Charlotte of the ECHL; and St. Jean and Sorel-Tracy of the Quebec Senior Hockey League. He hadn't lost his scoring touch, having three 50-goal seasons and one of 49. "I remember the last game of the 2001–02 season. I was with Port Huron and we were playing one of the best defensive teams in the league. I had 46 goals, but I got four more to reach 50. I still have the tape, and when I'm in a slump, I watch it to make me feel better."

Beauregard was realistic about his hockey future. Not only was the NHL out of the question, but also, with each passing season, it became increasingly unlikely that he'd get even a brief call-up to the AHL, focused as that league was on developing young talent for NHL teams. But that did not worry him. "I still play because I still love to play," he remarked. "I get up in the morning and I can't wait to go to practice. The pay is pretty good, and it's a fine game. I'll play as long as I can."

Although only two of the players on the three teams—Cloutier and Derek Gustafson of Adirondack—had made very brief trips to the NHL, all were well traveled, having, among the 57 of them, skated for 106 different teams in 10 different minor leagues. Forty-year-old Scott Drevitch of the Frostbite held the record: 16 teams in a 17-year career. If the total number of teams hints at the nomadic lives of minor-league journeymen (an appropriate professional term), the fact that 54 of these teams no longer exist indicates the unstable nature of the minor-league hockey business.

The playing career of Bob Rapoza, Adirondack's 31-year-old defenseman, illustrated both the nomadism and instability. In his first eight professional seasons, he skated for eight teams in five different leagues. Seven of the teams and one of the leagues no longer existed. After his final year of junior hockey, Rapoza had tryouts with Detroit of the Colonial Hockey League and the ECHL's South Carolina Stingrays. "Things didn't work out with these teams, and so I headed to Daytona Beach of the Sunshine Hockey League." Reminded that during the 1995–96 season, when he played, the league was called the Southern Hockey League, he replied, "Yes, but we still called it 'The Sunshine.' It was a league for playing and having fun. We stayed at hotels with kitchens; we were close to the beach. And we got paid $250 a week."

The sun set on the league after the 1995–96 season. Huntsville joined the CHL, and the other teams, playing before fewer than 1,500 people a game—"mostly sunbirds and locals who liked to watch fights" was how Rapoza described them—gave up the ghost. He headed north and joined the Dayton (Ohio) Ice Bandits of the Colonial League. The team played across town from the more established and financially secure Bombers of the ECHL. After finishing with the worst record in both standings and attendance, the Ice Bandits folded, and Rapoza made another long trip in search of a team to play for, this time to another snowbird destination, southern Arizona.

Once again he found himself in cities with two hockey teams, playing for the one in a shaky financial situation. The Tucson Gila Monsters of the West Coast Hockey League played in a building they shared with the University of Arizona club team, which attracted huge crowds from both the student body and the local population. The pro team folded midway through its second season; by that time, Rapoza had moved a couple of hundred miles west on Interstate 10 to Phoenix, where he played with the Mustangs of the WCHL. "There were more fans in Phoenix, but with the NHL's Coyotes also there, we couldn't survive. Playing in the WCHL was a good experience. There were lots of veterans in the league, and you had to use your head to survive."

After one season in Phoenix, Rapoza took to the road again, this time ending up in Georgia. Playing for the Macon Whoopee of the CHL was also a good experience, with a high level of play. However, the fan base was small and "they seemed to like drinking beer and watching fights." The Whoopee lasted only three years in the CHL, drawing progressively smaller crowds, and when the CHL merged with the Western Professional Hockey League after the 2000–01 season, it and the other eastern teams were jettisoned.

Rapoza had already moved on, and he spent the 2000–01 and

2001–02 seasons with the Asheville Smoke in the UHL. Yet again, he found himself with a team in a weakened financial condition. Located in a nontraditional market in western North Carolina, the Smoke was owned by a pair of brothers who also controlled the Knoxville Speed in the same league. When the Tennessee team experienced financial problems, it dragged its sister team down as well. "It was another example," Rapoza commented, "of successful businessmen having difficulties because they didn't understand the hockey business."

When the Smoke dissipated, Rapoza again headed west, joining the CHL's Wichita Thunder, a long-established and stable franchise. Two months into the season he was traded to the El Paso Buzzards of the WPHL and began a three-month experience unlike anything he'd been through with his earlier unstable teams. "Players had talked about El Paso having poor ownership, a bad rink and inferior living conditions. I refused to report when I was first traded. But it was go or be suspended and not play anywhere." What he'd heard about the team was true—and worse. "By January, there was no one in the front office. We had no sticks, no equipment. We had to play with mismatched socks."

One day the players arrived at the arena to discover 14 pairs of skates missing. "Mine were gone. The league got us some for our next game. By this time, the cops were looking for the owner, but apparently he'd skipped town. Some of the guys quit, so we finished the season with 13 players. I was ready to pack it up, but I'd promised the coach and the league president that I'd stick it out."

Because the Buzzards finished out of the playoffs, Rapoza was eligible to sign with another team and prepared to join the Adirondack IceHawks of the UHL. "El Paso's final game was in Amarillo, so my girlfriend and I drove our truck there. The game was on a Saturday night, and as soon as it was over we drove over 700 miles to Memphis. I caught a morning flight to Detroit and then drove to Flint, where Adirondack was playing."

Rapoza's odyssey wasn't over. The next two seasons he played with the UHL's Missouri River Otters in suburban St. Louis. During the first season it seemed like déjà vu—financially struggling owners and small crowds. However, with league help, the franchise established a strong financial base. Although Rapoza headed back to Adirondack after his second season, he had at last left a club that wasn't about to disappear.

Rapoza admitted that, despite the public statements players often make about ignoring front-office difficulties, off-ice problems do hurt a team. This had been the case in Dayton and especially in El Paso. "There's no doubt about it—when you travel to a place that you've heard bad things about, it's unsettling. It really takes the wind out of your sails. Everyone's nervous because you'll be playing tonight without knowing whether there's going to be a team tomorrow. It's tough to swallow. But if you want to play, you suck it up. This year is so much better." He can worry about getting ready for tonight's game and know that there'll be another one tomorrow—both of them against the Vipers.

Considered one of the strongest teams in the UHL, the Adirondack Frostbite demonstrated its experience and expertise during Friday night's game. It outmaneuvered the Vipers and capitalized on the home team's mistakes to score the game's opening goal just 70 seconds into the first period. The contest was tied 2–2 after two periods, but Mark Hurtubise scored midway through the third on another Viper mistake, and Lyon Porter put the puck in the empty net in the final minute to give the Frostbite a 4–2 win. The announced attendance was 1,376. Kristen Dixon was not among the crowd; she was in Canton, where she was reported to be fighting a cold.

During the Adirondack practice on Friday afternoon, Frostbite equipment manager David Baglio had approached his Viper opposite, Mike Brown, with a request for the loan of a pair of hockey pants. "We just got a new player, and his equipment hasn't arrived yet," Baglio explained. The new player was 21-year-old rookie Mark Hurtubise, who had been cut by the ECHL's Columbia Inferno during training camp. On Friday night, his game-winning goal and two assists earned him the game's first star. In response to Katrina Waugh's questions about how it felt to be named first star in his first professional game, he began modestly and with a standard response: "I was just happy I could help the team win." Then he revealed how important his on-ice performance was to him. "I was glad I showed them I can play. I needed to prove myself after my release from Columbia." Asked how it felt to be the youngest member of the team, he thought for several seconds, smiled and said, "One of the guys [Scott Drevitch] is as old as my dad."

SATURDAY NOVEMBER 12, 2005

Late Saturday afternoon, Tim Callahan remarked that he expected a good crowd for the evening game, the best since opening night. By six o'clock, some of the regulars had arrived. Two of them, Steven Watkins and Richard Hankins, worked part-time on hockey game nights, the former as a ticket-taker and usher, the latter as team photographer. Both spoke of their love of hockey, their delight in seeing a professional team back in town, their concern about the small size of the crowds, and their memories of more than three decades of watching hockey in the Roanoke Valley. A third early arrival, Bob Bandy, also recalled the old days of attending games regularly with his family. His daughter Kendra was such a fan that for a high school research project she created a data CD entitled *A Tribute to Hockey in the Roanoke Valley 1967 Thru 2003*, which contained player records and team standings over the years.

These three were typical of the group of hard-core hockey followers that forms the fan base for any professional sports team. Knowledgeable, enthusiastic and loyal, they can be counted on to support a team through winning and losing seasons and to attend games whether the weather is fair or foul.

On this night, the Vipers expected a good representation of the other group of fans, who are also essential for financial success: the casual attendees—couples, families and groups—who, having had an enjoyable time at the arena, will return three or four times a season and will tell their friends about their good experience. This evening a group of Boy Scouts, their leaders and several parents had arrived early at the Civic Center to listen to coach Jim Wiley explain a game that few of them knew anything about. Ever the teacher, he gave simple explanations of the basic rules, pointed out things to look for in that night's game and invited questions from the audience. Both the scouts and their parents responded, and their questions indicated the impression of hockey held by most people in the area. "Are there lots of fights?" one small boy asked. Another wanted to know when the last fight had occurred, while a third got personal: "Have you ever been in a fight?" A father, thinking in football terms, wanted to know how many plays the team had and how the coach sent them into the game. A mother, more familiar with basketball, asked which parts of the ice were out-of-bounds. Wiley provided clear, simple answers. "And now," he concluded, "I must go and get ready for the game. Like yours, my motto is 'Be Prepared.'"

As the Boy Scouts headed toward the concession stands, they passed Ken Gallagher, Jeff Nygaard and Jeremi DelCampo, the referee and two linesmen for the game, who were standing near the glass, looking out at

Ever the teacher, Roanoke coach Jim Wiley explains the rules and strategies of hockey to a group of Boy Scouts.

the ice. Nygaard and DelCampo left to scout out a pre-game meal, while Gallagher remained behind. A native of Wayne Gretzky's hometown of Brantford, Ontario, the 32-year-old official laughed when asked if an irate fan had ever yelled at him not to quit his day job. In point of fact, he had a day job and a very good one: he worked for the Canadian Imperial Bank of Commerce as a national project leader, traveling across Canada to meet with employees and clients. Officiating in the UHL was a weekend labor of love. Officials did get paid—referees received $450 a game, while linesmen got $150—but they had to cover their travel, lodging and meal expenses from this amount.

As a teenager, Gallagher both played and refereed. Like the young players whose games he began officiating, he showed up before sunrise at small arenas around Brantford. At age 17, after he had undergone a knee operation that ended his playing career, he entered the Hockey Canada officiating system. "I love hockey and I didn't want to leave the game. I love to skate, and officiating allowed me to continue that." As he reached higher levels of certification, he began to officiate in the Ontario Hockey Association's junior leagues. "It was tough at that level because the players had so much to lose, and that increased the intensity and pressure. I learned alongside the players. Refereeing in those small rinks with big, noisy crowds was very exciting."

This was his third season in the pro ranks. It was an exciting and grueling job as he covered the entire league from Iowa to Connecticut to Virginia. "I flew here, but most of the places I can drive to in five hours or less. This season I'll probably put 75,000 kilometers on my vehicle." He would be doing two games in Roanoke that weekend before flying to Detroit and driving home. The next week he'd drive to Port Huron and then to Muskegon in Michigan, and the weekend after that to Glens Falls, New York; Danbury, Connecticut; and Elmira, New York.

UHL referee Ken Gallagher laces up his skates before a game. During the week he travels across Canada for his employer, the Canadian Imperial Bank of Commerce. On weekends he can be found in an arena in one of the UHL's 14 cities.

Shortly before the players were introduced, Stryker, the Vipers' purple and white snake-like mascot, skated onto the ice with a bucket of used tennis balls clutched in one fist. One by one, he passed the balls to an assistant who threw them, usually successfully, over the glass into the stands, where young fans scrambled after them. Their excitement, often rising to the level of frenzy, became understandable when the announcer explained that each of the 16 balls had a Viper's number on it, and should that player score within the first five minutes of the game, the possessor of the tennis ball would win $100. Near the end of the second period, the fans would again scramble over seats and up the steep aisles, this time in a race for one of several cheap T-shirts, each one stamped with a sponsor's logo, that Stryker launched over the glass with an air cannon. While the holder of the lucky tennis ball went home richer, the retriever of a T-shirt, which might have been torn in the struggle for possession, had little to show for his or her efforts.

The Frostbite scored just after the game was a minute old when Blue Bennefield tucked the puck behind Jamie Hodson. But the Vipers tied the game less than two minutes later as Josh Tataryn scored on a power play and made the holder of one tennis ball a very happy fan. The teams played evenly the rest of the period, neither scoring. Referee Ken Gallagher handed out seven minor penalties, including two each for hooking and interference and one for holding—an indication of the close, tight-checking nature of the period. The much-improved Vipers were holding their own against the visitors.

At the end of the first period, after the players had left the ice, more hockey—of sorts—was played. Kris House walked onto the ice with an armful of hockey pads and two sticks and made two separate piles of the equipment along the blue line. To these she led two fans and announced the rules: each was to don a pair of hockey pants, shoulder pads and a set of gloves; grab a stick; walk, slide or slip to the opposite blue line steering a puck; and then shoot it. The winner, the person who got the puck into or closest to the net, took home a prize.

No goals were scored, and neither of the pucks came close to the net. It was a challenge for the contestants to slip-slide to the first blue line, a struggle to don the unfamiliar equipment and a nearly impossible task to control the puck well enough to get it to the other blue line. But the fans who had stayed in their seats cheered enthusiastically, finding the slapstick antics of these novices as interesting as the slap shots of the professional Vipers.

During the second period, Adirondack outshot the Vipers 12–9, but at 16:51, with two Frostbite players in the penalty box, rookie Louis-Philippe Martin put Roanoke ahead 2–1. However, as the period was drawing to a close, the Vipers made two costly mistakes. Martin went to the penalty box when the Vipers had too many men on the ice, and, with six seconds left in the period, Jan Jas took a slashing penalty.

The players headed to the dressing rooms, and a large pickup truck, the passenger window wide open, edged onto the ice and began circling the playing surface. As it did, fans stood along the concourse, throwing small foam footballs—which they'd purchased for a dollar apiece—toward the open windows. Each person who succeeded in throwing a ball into the truck won a prize.

In the first row of section nine, above center ice, an individual described as the Roanoke Valley's most dedicated hockey fan paid little attention to the activities on the ice, but discussed the serious situation the Vipers had placed themselves in. She didn't wear a replica sweater or other paraphernalia like the club's more vocal supporters, and she didn't yell loudly or gesture wildly as play resumed in the third period. But when Mark Hurtubise, the rookie Frostbite who'd won the first star the previous evening, scored a game-tying power-play goal early in the third period, she gave a short sigh of disappointment and commented on the consequences of foolish, unnecessary penalties.

For three decades, Maggie Drewry had been bleeding Roanoke green, navy blue, purple or whatever was the dominant color of the current team. She attended her first hockey game in 1973 and, she says, "fell in love with the game instantly—the speed, the goals, the crowd's excitement. I like aggressive hockey, but not the fights," she added, expressing an attitude unusual among southern hockey fans. "The early leagues were pretty rough," she remembered. "But when the ECHL was formed, the talent level rose. The players were younger and faster, and they wanted to play well so that they would move up."

Drewry looked back, as had several other fans, to the golden days of the mid-1990s, when, for four straight seasons, an average of over 5,500 fans came to each game at the Civic Center. But attendance had declined after that as the team changed ownership. Like Amy Webb, Maggie Drewry remembered July 20, 2004, the day the ECHL announced that the league had revoked the Roanoke franchise. "I saw it on the five o'clock news. I wasn't surprised, but I was devastated. It seemed like the owners hadn't cared about hockey—there wasn't much promotion of the team, and I heard that they were slow in paying bills. Last year was awful without hockey. I kept busy with booster club meetings, and we went to the Civic Center to plead for a new hockey team."

She hadn't been excited when she heard that the UHL was bringing a team into Roanoke. "I thought it was a league of goons and has-beens. But when I came to the practices, I was surprised at the youth of the players. Jim Wiley and Matt Rosen came to the booster club the day they arrived in town—something they didn't really have to do. The hockey is slower than in the ECHL—but I'm happy again."

When the third period was over, Drewry was not so happy, nor were the other members of a crowd announced as 2,053. The Vipers' attack floundered as they managed only 6 shots to the Frostbite's 12. Moreover, they took two slashing penalties and one for high-sticking, and only the goaltending heroics of Jamie Hodson—who was named the game's first star—kept Adirondack off the score sheet for the rest of the third period.

During the shootout after regulation time, the Vipers' second of the season, Mark Hurtubise again proved that he deserved a spot on the Adirondack roster. With the shootout tied at one goal each, he moved in on Hodson and let go a 15-footer that hit the goalie's left pad and trickled in just as the shooter bumped into Hodson. The goalie angrily argued—to no avail—that the collision with Hurtubise had knocked the puck in, that he had made the save and thus the puck should have been whistled dead. After the game, Katrina Waugh waited a good 15 minutes, in vain, for quotes from coach Jim Wiley.

Still struggling with what now appeared to be the flu, Kristen Dixon did not come to Roanoke, nor was she expected for Sunday's game.

POSTSEASON POSTSCRIPT

For the Vipers, the remaining 22 weeks of the season were times of losing and leaving. The team endured losing streaks of 7, 5, 10 and 8 games, and over a 48-game stretch it won two consecutive games only once. It finished the year with 40 points, bottom of the 15-team league. As a result of the team's poor performance during the first half of the season, coach Jim Wiley lost his job. On February 6, the Dixons announced from Canton, Ohio, that he would be replaced by Daniel Berthiaume, who had been a member of their club in Port Huron. In early December, the owners fired Kris House, director of business operations, and named Tim Callahan general manager. Later in the month the team announced a three-dollar reduction in the price of the majority of the arena's tickets. However, attendance continued to drop; at the end of the 37-game home schedule, an average of only 1,521 fans had attended each game at the Civic Center. The figure was the lowest in the league and the second lowest in all the minor leagues. David Shillington left the team in January to return to Canada; Branislav Kvetan missed 20 games with injuries; and in March, leading scorer David Beauregard was traded to the Danbury Trashers. Late in the season, fan Maggie Drewry remarked: "In all the years I've been watching games, this has been the worst season—on and off the ice. Some nights I don't even feel like coming to the arena, it's so depressing." On May 15, the Vipers issued a press release announcing that the team had ceased operations. When the Adirondack Frostbite suspended operations shortly after the season ended, Bob Rapoza once again had to look for a new team to play for.

2

FRIDAY NIGHT ICE

The Odessa Jackalopes of the Central Hockey League

The "Jack-Shack," Ector County Coliseum, was built in 1954 and is the oldest arena in the Central Hockey League. Each January it becomes home for a month to a major rodeo, and animals are kept in a large hall at one end of the arena—an area where, before hockey games, group picnics are served to as many as 500 people.

In the fall of 1996, Bob Hards, radio announcer for the Midland (Texas) Angels minor-league baseball team, wrote a friend in Washington state to tell him that Odessa, a west Texas city of 100,000 people, would have a professional hockey team the following year and that it would be called the Jackalopes. "You're kidding," his friend replied in disbelief—about both the idea of a team in Odessa and, if there was one, its unusual nickname. His incredulity was shared by people in Odessa. In fact, just before the Western Professional Hockey League announced its expansion to that city, a local TV sportscaster stated that the hockey rumors circulating in the area should be ignored—it was silly even to consider the notion.

The reaction of both Hards's friend and the TV announcer were understandable. At the time, the Permian Basin, where the neighboring cities of Odessa and Midland are located, was famous for its thriving oil industry and for being the home, during the later 1940s, of former president George Bush and his son George W. Bush, who was Texas governor in 1996. Odessa was also the site of the made-for-TV movie *Everybody's Baby*, the story of the rescue of a tiny child trapped in a well, and of *Friday Night Lights*, a 1990 book about the city and its passionate relationship with the Permian Panthers, a high school football team that regularly attracted 20,000 fans to its games. But hockey? There wasn't an artificial ice surface within a hundred miles, and the demographics were definitely against establishing Canada's great winter game as a spectator sport: nearly 45 percent of Ector County was Hispanic.

But ever since 1995, when Rick Kozuback, Brad Treliving and Ralph Backstrom were considering cities in which to place franchises in their planned Western Professional Hockey League, Odessa had been a potential location. The population of Ector and Midland counties combined was just over a quarter of a million people, the right size to support a team in their league, and Odessa possessed Ector County Coliseum, a 45-year-old building that held 5,000 people and could be adapted to house a regulation-sized hockey rink.

In October 1997, Odessa joined the WPHL and, in the first season, drew an average of 4,000 fans a game. That number dropped by 200 in the second season and later leveled off at just over 3,200 spectators a game. The Jackalope—an oversized, antler-sporting jackrabbit—quickly became one of the most popular mascots in hockey's minor leagues. Team merchandise, which pictured a frowning, snarling, antlered rabbit with a hockey stick slung over its shoulder, sold well not only in west Texas, but also across the country and in Canada.

The city of Odessa, located on plains where the sparse vegetation is relieved by silhouettes of oil rigs, and where the southern horizon is dominated by oil refineries, had something new to be known for. In 1998, *Sports Illustrated* published a lengthy article on the growth of hockey in Texas. Entitled "Lone Star Skate," it used Odessa as the example of the new type of hockey hotbed in the Southwest. The hockey explosion eventually fizzled in many other southwestern cities, but the Odessa Jackalopes have survived. They were one of the teams included in the joint operating agreement the WPHL and Central Hockey League entered into in 2001.

MONDAY DECEMBER 5, 2005

Sunday had been a day off for the Jackalopes—sort of. On Saturday night, the team had played in Corpus Christi. After the game, the players climbed on the bus for the 769-mile trip home, disembarked in the parking lot north of Ector County Coliseum just after 10 on Sunday morning, lugged their gear into the locker room, stumbled into their cars and pickup trucks, and drove to their apartments. In less than 24 hours they were back at the arena, which local hockey fans called the "Jack-Shack," preparing for practice.

And they were all there on time. Clubhouse rules mandated a fine of five dollars for those who didn't arrive half an hour early for practice, with another dollar for each additional minute late. Other fines listed on the locker-room bulletin board included five dollars for a cell phone ringing during a meeting, a dollar for rookies failing to perform their

Jackalopes defenseman Jeff Ewasko protects his hand, broken during a fight, while he works out on an exercise bike. The 6-foot 7-inch native of Edmonton, Alberta, one of Odessa's "tough guys," counts working with children at hockey schools as one of his favorite hockey memories.

assigned duties and $50 for improper use of the washrooms on the bus. Fines could be appealed (usually unsuccessfully) at kangaroo court, and the money collected was put in the "fines jar." At the end of the season, the team voted on how to spend the accumulated cash.

The locker room and the area just outside it, where the stationary bikes were placed, were humming with activity by 9:30. Jeff Ewasko, the 6-foot 7-inch defenseman, strenuously pedaled one of the bikes, gently resting his taped right hand, which he'd broken in a Saturday night fight, on the handlebars; Josh Legge jammed his stick in the door and began a furious one-man tug-of-war as he worked to dislodge the blade from its shaft; Adam Loncan engaged in stretching exercises. Clothed in long black underwear, he resembled from a distance a silhouetted figure from the movie *Karate Kid*. In the trainer's room, Greg Andis carefully examined the blackened eyes and swollen nose of Jamie Lovell, who'd also mixed it up in Saturday's game.

Down the hall, coach Don McKee began what would be a 12-hour day. He'd been a school principal in Ontario, and his room resembled a school office on a busy Monday morning. He prepared his activities for the approaching practice while phoning secretary Claudia Jaquez to request that she arrange to have flowers sent to a medical technician who'd performed beyond the call of duty for the team. Then he acted on a request from a player who needed a hotel room for visiting parents, talked briefly to a visitor about the preceding week's games and the four upcoming games, and led the troops onto the ice.

Four spectators took in the practice. Two were sparrows, members of a resident flock, who seemed more intent on searching for bits of spilled popcorn than on the instruction taking place on the ice. Two were human and very interested. Pat Young, a fan and a dedicated member of the "Jack-Pack," the team's booster club, had taken the morning of one of her vacation days to check up on the players, whom she referred to as "my boys." She'd never seen hockey before the Jackalopes came to town, but now, she remarked, "I come to the practices whenever I can. I learn so much. My most favorite sounds," she continued, "are the sounds of skates on the ice and the puck hitting a stick."

The other spectator, Don Lassetter, was both the registrar of Odessa's youth hockey program, which had enrolled nearly 300 players of all ages, and a player himself. He'd never been on skates until the Jackalopes arrived in town, but then, at age 52, he made his first tentative strides on the ice, playing for what he called an "old folks' team." The Jackalopes had been instrumental in starting amateur hockey in the Odessa area, providing ice time, helping with instruction and, most important, giving novice players plenty of encouragement.

After an hour, the practice was over and the players skated off the ice. The day's instruction was not finished, however. Starting with the two goalies, Mike Gorman and Derek Dolson, the players headed in pairs to the principal's office. "They work in a buddy system," McKee later explained. "They talk with each other and to me about what they felt went well or not so well during the last week."

The meetings completed, most of the players left the arena for the world outside. For three of them, though, the hockey business of the day continued. Rookie defenseman Andrew Davis, sophomore defenseman Pascal Bedard and veteran goalie Mike Gorman accompanied Coach McKee as he drove 15 miles east to Chili's Restaurant in Midland. There they participated in the monthly media lunch coordinated by Odessa Sports, owners of the Jackalopes. With lunch and interviews completed, the workday was now over for Davis and Bedard. McKee and Gorman had one more duty: a seven o'clock appearance on *Hockey Talk*, a weekly radio show hosted by Bob Hards.

TUESDAY DECEMBER 6, 2005

Because it was game day, morning practice was fairly light. After 45 minutes of drills, the team proceeded to the dressing room, where Don McKee showed a five-minute video clip from the club's most recent game against the evening's opponent, the Lubbock Cotton Kings. "I wanted them to see some particularly effective forechecking that our players had done the last time we played them," McKee explained.

This would be the fifth meeting between the Southwest Division rivals, and the season's series stood at two wins apiece. Winning tonight's game would mean that the Jackalopes would gain sole possession of first place in the division, two points ahead of Lubbock, and because each divisional leader received an automatic playoff berth, every point in the standings was important. By the time the end of March arrived, they'd have faced each other a dozen times, nearly 20 percent of the season's 64-game schedule. There was one other team in the division, the Amarillo Gorillas, and they'd meet the Jacks a total of 14 times. By playing geographically close teams so often, the Jackalopes were able to limit travel expenses.

At 11:30, the players headed to Zucchi's Italian Restaurant to engage in their standard pre-game ritual of carb-loading. Long gone were the days when steak was the lunch of champions. In the player profiles included in the yearbook, only Josh Legge listed steak as his favorite pre-game meal. "But I can never afford it," he laughed. The players enjoyed not only the food—"The best Italian food in the Permian Basin," team captain and Odessa resident Donnie Margettie stated—but also the atmosphere. Owners Larry and Sandra Burdette dropped by to chat and wish the team good luck, and Tracey and Bill Nyborg, a local couple who'd recently purchased a minority share in the team, said hello and then quietly picked up the tab.

Game-day rituals are important for hockey players. For the Jackalopes, one of the most important is noontime carb-loading at Zucchi's Restaurant. Owner Larry Burdette (center) chats with players Dom Leveille (left) and Pascal Bedard.

Sixteen of the 18 Jackalopes were at the lunch—Jeff Ewasko was at the hospital having a pin placed in his broken hand, and Scott Hillman, at the tail end of a bout with the flu, had gone home—and they were a diverse group, ranging in age from 24 to 31; in experience from 1 to 10 years in professional hockey; in size from 5 foot 7 to 6 foot 8; and in weight from 160 to 235 pounds. All the players were from Canada; 12 had university degrees—three from U.S. schools, nine from Canadian; and 10 of them had been with the team the previous season.

They all loved playing in Odessa. Driving toward the town, passing the plains that appeared to be empty of everything but oil derricks and pumps, could be a depressing experience, one of the players remarked, but then you discovered the area's real attraction: the very friendly people. "I was talking to one of the members of the booster club," remarked Andrew Davis, who'd been traded early in the season from Memphis. "I mentioned that I liked to read Jack Higgins novels. The next day she brought me three she'd picked up at a local used bookstore." Four Jackalopes—Gorman, Margettie, Matt Cressman and Hillman—had purchased homes in Odessa. "The prices are unbelievably cheap," said Gorman, who bought his for $60,000. "And nearly all of the neighbors are great!" he added, implicitly teasing Margettie, who lived across the street.

During the meal the players chatted back and forth, occasionally shouting out good-natured insults to teammates a few seats away. For three—Dominic Leveille, Sebastien Thinel and Pascal Bedard—the conversations and insults were in French. The three had grown up in St. Jerome, a town north of Montreal. Thinel had come to Odessa four seasons earlier and had encouraged Bedard to join him two years later. Bedard, in turn, encouraged Leveille, a friend since the two had been eight years old.

Thinel left early to run errands, but Bedard and Leveille lingered to discuss their lives in hockey. Leveille, quiet and shy, had attended the training camp of the CHL's Laredo Bucks two seasons earlier and had then played 11 games for Oklahoma City, also of the CHL, before returning to Quebec. "But," interjected Bedard, "there was no way Sebbie [Thinel] and I were going to come back here without bringing our buddy Dom with us." The team's leading point-getter, with four goals and 18 assists—18th best in the league—Leveille had adapted to life in the Southwest. "I enjoy wherever I play. I'm a quiet guy, and I've got everything I need. The long bus rides aren't fun, but you do it. Hockey is what I do for work, but it's a lot of fun."

For Bedard, the road from St. Jerome to Odessa had passed through Anglet, a small city in the southwest of France, close to Basque country. "In September 2002, I figured my hockey life was over except for weekend play in senior leagues. I'd just entered the University of Montreal to study business. Then, at six in the morning of the first Monday of classes, a guy from France who I'd played junior with called me. 'We need a D-man,' he said. 'Can you come?'" Although his mother wasn't happy—she wanted him to stay in university—the offer appealed to Bedard's spirit of adventure. The friend called back at noon and received a positive answer. "The next day I went to the university and officially withdrew; then I renewed my passport. On Thursday I flew from Montreal to Paris and took a train to Anglet. On Friday I played in the season's opener."

The pay was good—better, he remarked, than in the CHL. "And I was cheap because I hadn't played major junior hockey." The schedule was light. "We played three games every two weeks." And because Anglet was far away from the other league cities, which included Rouen,

Grenoble, Amiens and Mont Blanc, he got to see a lot of France. "We sometimes had a couple of days off, so I'd travel to different places. My family came over at Christmas, and I took them to the Pyrenees, shopping in San Sebastian, Spain, to Paris and the French Alps."

He also played hockey. The arena was small, but for each game, 1,500 people jammed the place. "There was loud music playing all the time and that helped get the people into it. I liked it so much that I decided to go back for a second year. They sent me a contract in May and I signed it right away."

His roommate in Anglet had played in the CHL, and his description of his experiences intrigued Bedard. "I thought that I'd like to get a job there. It would certainly help my English. If I wanted to work in Montreal after I finished my degree, I'd have to be bilingual. So in April I called Sebbie and asked him if he thought I could cut it in Odessa. He talked to Don McKee, who was really great. The coach came to Montreal; we talked and played golf."

Bedard made another long trip to a new and different place. Early in October he loaded his white Cherokee and began the 3,000-mile drive south and west. The landscape changed drastically as he drove through southern Missouri. "When I hit west Texas," he said, "it was hard to believe. But I love to see new places and new cultures." He also had to adjust to a different brand of hockey. "It took me three weeks to adapt. The players were bigger and there was a lot more hitting and hooking. In France, the emphasis was more on finesse." Adjust he did, though. He was eventually named the Jackalopes' Defenseman of the Year. He liked his Odessa experience so much that he returned. "I like coming back to the same place; you know your team and the city."

Bedard had finished the second year of studies for his business degree, and he knew that in a few years he'd be settling down to a sales job in Montreal. But for now, the joy of traveling to new and different places to play hockey remained strong. "Adam Loncan has some contacts in Australia," he remarked. "Dom and I are thinking it would be fun to go down there in our summer to play hockey. The pay isn't great, but there aren't a lot of games, so we'd have a chance to travel around the country."

Four hours after lunch—nearly two hours before game time—activity at the Coliseum began to pick up. In the large area at the west end of the arena, a place used as a holding area during rodeos and for group picnics during hockey season, Harold Fuller, assistant general manager for corporate sales, stood by a brand-new all-terrain quad, in earnest conversation with Josh Firkins. By day, Firkins was a sales associate at Office Depot, but on hockey nights he became Slap-Jack, the team mascot. Tonight he was to ride the quad on the ice during the intermissions as part of a sponsored promotion. This was his first year in hockey, but for two years he had assumed the role of Juice the Moose, mascot for the RockHounds baseball club. "I'm just a normal human being," he remarked, "but as Slap-Jack, I've got to be a hockey-playing rabbit. I've studied the players and I try to imitate some of the things they do. I'm really here for the kids, signing autographs and hugging them. So even though I'm a hockey player, I'm a friendly one; I don't imitate the fights."

Slap-Jack, the Odessa mascot, gives a warm hug to six-month-old Zion Jessiah Hernandez. Mascots have become an increasingly popular way of attracting families with young children to hockey games.

At the other end of the arena, Donnie Davis, president of the Jack-Pack booster club, walked toward the club's display table carrying a large container filled with plastic carrots. He set them down beside a big pile of pucks, each of which had a player's picture laminated on it. The carrots would be sold for a dollar apiece, and fans would fling them onto the ice after each Odessa goal. Then a group of kids, members of the "Carrot Club," would collect them. The carrot sales, along with sales of the pucks and players' pictures, were the principal means by which the club financed its various activities. The main function of the Jack-Pack was to make both home and visiting players feel welcome in Odessa. At the beginning of the season, each Jackalope player was provided with a new set of bedroom and bathroom linens and such small appliances as he needed. The boosters also hosted welcoming parties and holiday dinners during the season. After each game, they provided a hot meal for the visiting team. And when funds were available, they would present a check to a local charity. Earlier this season, the Jack-Pack had made a ceremonial pre-game center-ice presentation of $2,200 to the Children's Miracle Network.

As the lineups were announced, a crowd of 2,585, a few hundred under the season's average, gave hearty cheers as the six Odessa starters skated through an inflated tunnel and onto the swirling patterns cast by spotlights. In a surprise move, Don McKee didn't send out the first line, but instead started with John Kozoriz, Mike Carter and Donnie Margettie, who between them had scored only six goals in the team's first 18 games. "I told Margettie that, as a team leader, he needed to show more aggressiveness on the ice, and I wanted Carter to strengthen his forechecking," McKee explained.

The home team quickly fell behind as Stacey Bauman's screen shot from the point eluded Mike Gorman 2 minutes and 47 seconds into the game. The Jackalopes could not capitalize on four power plays, and although they outshot the

Jack-Pack booster club president Donnie Davis holds a tub of plastic carrots. Sold for a dollar each, the carrots are thrown on the ice each time a Jackalope goal is scored. Proceeds help fund the booster club's activities.

Cotton Kings 16–8, they left the period trailing by a goal. In the second period, Odessa went on a scoring rampage, as it had frequently done in recent games, with four goals to the visitors' one. McKee's starting lineup strategy appeared to be working: Margettie had two goals and Kozoriz another. Two Odessa tallies in the third and one by Lubbock made the final score 6–3 for the Jackalopes. The crowd cheered loudly as adopted hometown boys Margettie and Scott Hillman were named first and second stars respectively.

In addition to giving the Jackalopes a two-point lead in division standings, the win also advanced what Bob Hards had described in the game-night program as "a hat trick of milestones" for three members of the team. Don McKee was two games shy of his 200th win as Odessa's coach; Scott Hillman needed six points to surpass the Jackalopes' all-time record point total of 279, held by John Bossio; and Mike Gorman was three short of becoming the team's first goalie to record 100 wins. Both McKee and Gorman moved a game closer to their targets; Hillman's three assists left him three away from the record.

After the game, Don McKee talked with *Odessa American* reporter Lee Scheide. He was pleased that changing the starting lineup had paid off, said he felt that the victory would give the team confidence as it prepared for three more pre-Christmas games against the Cotton Kings, and acknowledged that the visiting team appeared tired. "It's certainly understandable," he explained. "They flew to Youngstown [Ohio] Thursday, played there Friday and Saturday night, and then flew back to Texas on Sunday morning."

McKee returned to his office, showered and departed with his wife, Shirley. The Cotton Kings players headed for the picnic area and the hot meal served by Pat Young and other Jack-Pack members. Soon their bus chugged out of the parking lot, beginning its 145-mile journey back to Lubbock, and the lights of the Coliseum went dark.

WEDNESDAY DECEMBER 7, 2005

Although practice Wednesday morning didn't begin until eleven o'clock, four Jackalopes showed up at nine: Mike Rutter, Jamie Lovell, Jeff Ewasko and the most important of the quartet, Greg Andis, the athletic trainer. Rutter, who was suffering from a groin pull, was on the injured list, as was Ewasko. Andis would be taking Lovell to the doctor to see if the player, in addition to his black eyes, had suffered a broken nose during his weekend combat.

After checking on the state of Ewasko and Rutter, Andis sat down to relax and talk about his history in professional hockey. A native of Jal, a tiny community in southeastern New Mexico best known for staging cockfights, Andis had become involved in sports training in order to be with his friends. "They were all playing," he explained, "but I was too small. So I decided that I'd get into athletic training; I like helping people, and I'd be with my friends." He became his high school's student athletic trainer and attended classes for student trainers held at New Mexico State University. After finishing high school, he received a scholarship from Odessa College to study physical therapy, and, after two years at the junior college, he transferred to Southwest Texas State University to complete his degree.

When the Jackalopes came to town in 1996, he signed up to work for them. "I'd never even watched hockey on TV; it didn't interest me. I really liked football and basketball. When I came to the first practice, it was the first time I'd ever seen a hockey player." However, he quickly learned a great deal about hockey, hockey players and hockey injuries.

Although Andis was only seen by fans when there was an injury during a game and he had to slip-step his way across the ice to the side of the fallen player, a great deal of his work involved the prevention of injury and illness. He worked with Coach McKee on the team's conditioning program, and before every practice he placed 18 numbered water bottles on top of the boards in front of the players' bench. "We're very concerned with any virus spreading quickly through the team. With the players so often in confined spaces like the locker room and the bus, if one of the players gets something, the others could pick it up too. At least with 18 bottles, each player has his own, and that makes spreading any germs less likely."

Rehabilitation was another major component of the job. "And a lot of that," he said, "is psychological. Some players are afraid to come back into action, they think they might re-injure themselves; and sometimes they

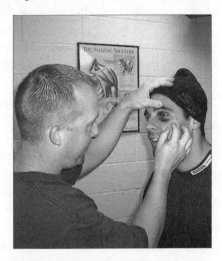

Jackalopes trainer Greg Andis inspects the black eye of defenseman Jamie Lovell. A rookie, who played the past four seasons at the university level, where fighting is outlawed, Lovell was rediscovering the rougher side of the game.

want to play before they're ready. Then you have to slow them down. I've found that hockey players are more willing to play through injuries than other athletes. I remember one of the Jackalopes telling me, 'If I can skate and hold a stick, I'll play.'"

Looking back on his tenure with the team, Andis proudly noted, "I've missed only four games since the team began. I've been to more games than anyone else in the organization. In fact, I didn't miss my first game until last year." He'd seen a lot of players and visited all the rinks in the history of the WPHL and all the CHL rinks since the WPHL merged with the CHL in 2001. "At the beginning," he laughed, "there were lots of fighters, and the fans loved them. There are still some fighters, but they can play hockey too. At first there were guys who couldn't skate as well as I could, and I was just learning. It was what you'd call a beer league."

The worst rink he'd visited was El Paso. He mentioned the leaking roof, which he said was so bad that one time the goal judge had to hold an umbrella over his head. "But the fans—the atmosphere was like being at a cockfight. I remember one game during the playoffs; they let people throw octopuses onto the ice. Then the attendants gathered them up and gave them back to the people to throw again." He'd also seen his share of bad ice. "In Waco it was so soft that the skate blades cut into the ice. The players were afraid of groin injures, and they had the equipment manager dull the skates so that they wouldn't sink in so deep."

As a trainer, Andis sometimes thought that he was serving as a "team mom." "They come to me with some of their problems. I don't let them play me off against the coach, but I respect their confidences. They just need someone to talk things out with." Looking back on his first nine years as a hockey trainer, he found it hard to pick a favorite memory. "I think the best part is the general relationships with the players. They're realistic; they know they won't make the NHL. But a lot of them have their university degrees. I was working on my masters at the University of Texas, Permian Basin, at the same time that some of the players were taking university courses. I feel that when I'm with the team, it's like having 18 brothers."

At this point, one of Andis's "brothers," Jeff Ewasko talked to him briefly about some physical therapy exercises for his right hand. The biggest Jackalope towered over the trainer. Ewasko later explained that he grew a foot in Grade 10. "I was really awkward, and I got cut from my midget team. I was devastated," the Sherwood Park, Alberta, native remembered. However, like his hero Mark Messier, and his father's hero Bobby

Clarke, whose number "16" he wears, Ewasko persevered and earned a spot for three years on his hometown Junior A team, the Crusaders.

In the autumn of 1997, Ewasko appeared to be about to make his first strides toward achieving the dream of so many Canadian boys: he received an invitation to attend the Washington Capitals' training camp. "But I dislocated my shoulder the first day of camp, got sent to Portland [Maine] of the American Hockey League, failed my physical, got sent to Hampton Roads of the ECHL, and after three games, when Washington sent a lot of their AHL players down to the East Coast Hockey League, I got traded to the Louisville RiverFrogs. I didn't like the experience, so I went back home and started taking classes at the University of Alberta."

For Ewasko, attending the university noted for having one of the best hockey programs in Canada was a turning point, both on and off the ice. "The hockey program made me a man. They taught us how to win, how to be humble and how to be thankful we were playing. We learned to work hard and to sacrifice for the team and for our education." It was a 14-hour day for Ewasko and his fellow Golden Bears: classes and studying from eight in the morning until practice began at five. After two hours on the ice, it was home for dinner and then back to the books. The hard work paid off as Ewasko earned two bachelor degrees—one in physical education, the other in education—and two national championship rings as a member of the hockey team.

"I think that the mental discipline of playing with a team that was system oriented really forced me to become a thinker. You had to learn to be a more rounded player; you couldn't just rely on one or two skills. We used to practice five or six breakout patterns each week and a number of penalty-kill systems. When the weekend arrived, you were really prepared for the team you'd be facing."

In fall 2001, when he finished his university studies, Ewasko returned to the professional ranks, putting in two seasons in the West Coast Hockey League with Long Beach and Idaho, and one in the United Hockey League with Adirondack, Rockford and Richmond. It was at this time that he began to develop a reputation as a hockey policeman, the tough guy who keeps the heavy hitters of the opposing team in line, thus allowing the smaller finesse players to do their jobs of setting up and scoring goals. In 161 games over three seasons, he amassed 964 minutes in penalties. He also scored 23 goals and assisted on 40 others—respectable numbers for a defenseman.

Like most Canadians, Ewasko saw fighting as an integral element of the game, not some kind of wrestling extravaganza laid on to entertain the fans. "Most people will tell you that the banning of fighting causes some nasty stickwork," he explained and then went on to outline aspects of his role as policeman: "Last night, a couple of Lubbock players took liberties with our small guys that they wouldn't have if I'd been on the ice. I think that when I'm out there, it helps our smaller players play bigger. I don't even have to get into anything. It just makes the opposition more honest. Then our players don't have to worry; it helps ease the fear and hesitancy and sets them free to skate, pass and shoot. A few days ago, Dom [Leveille] came over after a game and thanked me for what I was doing."

After his year in the UHL, Ewasko traveled to England to play for the Basingstoke Bison of the British Elite Ice Hockey League for the 2004–05 season. Because games were only played on weekends, he had time to indulge his other two interests: traveling and teaching. "One of the things I had liked when I was in the WCHL was that we flew to most cities and played two games there, so you had time to see places like Anchorage, Alaska, and San Diego—cities you'd probably never visit otherwise. In England, it was even better. They'd given me a Smart car; I was bigger than it was. I learned to drive on the wrong side of the street and visited interesting little villages whenever I could. When I had more time, I'd go to Europe: to Rome one time and Berlin another. Learning about new cultures always interests me."

He also taught chemistry, physics and biology two days a week at a school south of London. "It was a tough high school. A lot of the kids had no male adults in their lives, so I became a mentor, someone they could talk to. One of the other teachers and I started a science program for 10 kids. It was to help them pass at the basic level." But he admitted that Thursday afternoons were his favorite time at the school. "That was when what we'd call the Grade 12s had PE. They loved soccer, and they taught me a lot about it. I'm very competitive and I got in there and played with them."

The English season over, Ewasko returned to Sherwood Park and spent the spring teaching high school science as a replacement teacher. That summer he received a call from Jackalopes coach Don McKee. Donnie Margettie, who had been a teammate in Rockford, had recommended the big defenseman, and McKee was interested. "The coach said there'd be an opportunity for me to take classes toward a masters degree in business at the university here. It would be a chance to study, to see a new part of North America and to learn a new hockey role. He hoped I'd be a leader. I'd always been an unrecognized leader. Now I'd have the responsibility and accountability."

Looking back on his hockey career, Jeff Ewasko explained: "I'm in it for the experience. I love to play hockey and it's great that people want to watch. You know, I still get blown away when a little kid asks me for an autograph. And I love teaching. I remember at the University of Alberta hockey school when the kids were talking about what they'd most remember about their time there. One boy who'd been coming for three years said, 'I'll miss sitting with Jeff each morning, taping our sticks.' It brings a tear to my eye every time I think of it."

The Jackalopes' big, tough policeman was really a gentle giant. And now this gentle giant had more work to do and a big challenge: he had to study for a final exam that evening, and he had to figure out how he, a right-hander, was going to write it.

By the time Ewasko had settled down to study, the rest of the Jackalopes had finished their practice, showered, dressed and left the arena. One of the last to depart was Matt Cressman, who'd had a 15-minute meeting in Coach McKee's office. If Ewasko looked like a prototypical hockey player—big, strong and with a scar on his face—Cressman, over half a foot shorter, 80 pounds lighter and wearing glasses, seemed more like a mild-mannered accountant, someone who would smile politely and talk to clients about their income tax forms. In point of fact, he did have a degree in finance and economics from Western Michigan University, but his present jobs included being one of the best defensive forwards in the CHL and, since September 2004, assistant coach of the hockey club.

Cressman grew up in Cambridge, Ontario, in a family where education and hockey were both important. His dad, Dave, had played briefly for the Minnesota North Stars in the mid-1970s. "But he was also a teacher and didn't play in the National Hockey League until he'd finished university. My two brothers and I always played hockey, but Dad never pushed us; for him, education was very important." The two older Cressman brothers had played university hockey, and it seemed like the logical choice for Matt. "I wasn't very big, just 150 pounds at the time; the Ontario Hockey League wasn't interested in me, so I headed to Kalamazoo, Michigan, for school and hockey."

He found American university hockey very different from what he was used to. There were 30 players on the squad, and, because of his size, he had to work hard just to stay in the lineup. It was here that he developed his defensive skills. In addition, he said, "I learned to use my noodle!"

"After I'd graduated, my best friend and I thought it would be interesting to give pro hockey a shot, so we headed to Louisiana to play in the Whiffle [hockey players' name for the WPHL] for the Monroe Moccasins." His career nearly ended five games into the 1997–98 season. Because fighting was outlawed in American university hockey and because of his size, Cressman wasn't a fighter. "But in the early years of the WPHL, all the fans seemed to want were fights, so the league didn't want to discourage them. We were in El Paso and Jason Rose got into it with me. He was huge and he beat the daylights out of me. I was ready to quit playing hockey."

The Jack-Pack sells pucks, onto which are laminated photographs of players (in this case, playing assistant coach Matt Cressman), as a fund-raiser. (Photo by David Byerly.)

He called his lifelong mentor, his father, who recommended that he finish the road trip and make a decision then. Nine seasons and 493 games later, Cressman was still playing. When the Moccasins folded during the summer of 2001, Don McKee, whom he'd known all his life, invited him to come to Odessa. He agreed, and as he drove across west Texas, he had the experience that most players coming to the Jackalopes have had. "My wife and I looked at each other and said, 'What are we getting into?'" It was particularly a shock for his wife, who grew up in northern Michigan, with its lakes, rolling hills, and birch and maple forests.

Cressman didn't put up big numbers in Odessa—55 goals in 252 games—but he impressed his coach, his fellow players and the fans with his defensive skills, his work ethic and his team spirit. He served for three seasons as assistant captain, won the team's award for character and leadership, and was named the league's second-best defensive forward. The man who named Detroit's Steve Yzerman as his favorite player and role model—"He's quiet and always hardworking"—was recognized by his peers for his understated and very important role in the team.

It came as no surprise to most observers when, before the 2004–05 season, McKee named Cressman his assistant coach. "The league does not permit us to hire a full-time assistant," McKee said. "I knew Matt wanted to coach in the future, and I felt that with his temperament and his knowledge of the game, he'd be ideal as a player and coach." Cressman, who owned a house in Odessa, helped in recruiting during the off-season and was learning the many small details that made up the noninstructional aspects of his new position. "I guess it's in my blood. My dad coached Junior B and at the University of Waterloo. A few seasons ago, when Don McKee was having his heart surgery, my dad came down here and coached the Jackalopes for two or three weeks. I love the thinking part of the game; I couldn't play without thinking, and coaching is really helping me with that aspect of hockey."

Right now, home duties called. His one-and-a-half-year-old son had to be taken to the doctor. "I like to spend as much time with my family as I can and to give my wife a break. She's made a lot of sacrifices for my career. She and the kids have been very patient."

While he was talking, the Corpus Christi Rayz, the Jackalopes' Friday night opponent, took to the ice for practice. They'd arrived in Odessa two days early because no practice ice was available at home. The American Bank Center was booked all week for a college basketball tournament. Coach Ken McRae was not happy. "This happens two or three times a year. There's no other ice in the area. I think it might cost us a couple of wins a year, having to go on the road to practice, but it's part of the reality of playing hockey in the South."

THURSDAY DECEMBER 8, 2005

When Don McKee was briefly out of hockey in the fall of 1999, he nearly drove his wife, Shirley, and their daughter crazy. "I love Tim Hortons coffee," she laughed, "but not at 5:30 in the morning. Don always had to be up and doing things early, and so now that he was neither teaching nor coaching, he'd leave the house at five to get us all coffee and we had to be awake to drink it when he got home. Getting him back into coaching was a blessing—I got two hours more sleep each day and he was happy again."

Given McKee's self-confessed "type A" personality, it wasn't surprising that he arrived at his office long before any of his players. There was no chance he'd ever have to put money into the fines jar for not arriving at least half an hour before practice. His early morning pace wasn't frenetic: he watched a few minutes of video of a recent game played by Corpus Christi, made notes for some plays the team would work on during practice and chatted with a number of people who dropped in with questions, requests and observations.

McKee had been a teacher all his adult life and a hockey coach of young men for much of it. He discussed why, nine years earlier, when many of his colleagues in the teaching profession were taking

A gift from his children, Don McKee's vanity plates proclaim his occupation. The possessive pronoun refers not only to his relationship with his children, but also to the close ties he has with players and fans in Odessa.

early retirement packages and planning winter trips to southern golfing destinations, he began a full-time career as a minor-league hockey coach—a job as insecure as his educational situation was secure. "I'd been splitting my time between education and hockey coaching—juniors and then the University of Waterloo. During the 1970s, the NHL had been showing interest in university coaches for their minor-league teams. The idea intrigued me, but I didn't feel the time was right until the mid-1990s."

The minor leagues offered a challenge. "I wanted to find out what full-time coaching would be like and to explore new places. I knew that I'd be spending long hours and that I'd be facing new challenges as a coach and instructor. But because of my school pension, I wouldn't have to depend on being employed as a coach. It's nice to coach when you don't have to. I don't have the pressure that the young men in this league do; I can concentrate on helping the team achieve its potential."

McKee's work as a teacher, principal and instructor of coaches in Canada helped him make the adjustment with relative ease. "To coach, you need five traits," he explained, "strong communication ability, teaching skills, leadership skills, the ability to motivate and a knowledge of the game. So many of these related to what I did as a phys ed teacher, principal and educational consultant. And my work as chair of Hockey Canada's coaching committee helped me focus on my own role with my team."

His first challenge as a minor-league coach was to adapt to the differences between the lives of players in university, where he'd coached for a decade, and the lives of players at the lower professional levels. "The University of Waterloo had very high academic standards. Players had to be very good both on the ice and in the classroom. The coach had to accommodate the life of the team to the lives of individual students. But here in the pros, athletic output is the sole concern. It was my first experience working with players who had real fears that they'd be cut from the team. At the university, you had athletes who were most likely going to be with you for four years. Here, if they didn't make the grade in a couple of weeks, they'd be gone."

McKee drew on his knowledge of and connections with university hockey: two-thirds of the present Jackalopes roster was made up of college grads. "I still have a network of contacts, and I find that university players are looking for enriching experiences and that going to different places to play hockey appeals to them. They have good work habits because of their lives as students and, because there are only two college games a week and every game in the schedule counts, they know how to focus, how to prepare. The learning process continues for them at this level. This year we have five rookies and six second-year players. In a way, the team is overachieving, but that's because the players are constantly learning, progressing."

After a year coaching in England, McKee was approached by the WPHL. "The league told me in the fall of 1999 that they needed a coach in Odessa. I was impressed with the area for three reasons: there was a second ice surface in town that would be available for practice all year; the owners, who lived in Idaho and New York City, gave me freedom and only two instructions: win and don't cheat; and the city provided a friendly, supportive atmosphere, one that encouraged athletic competition." In 2000–01 and 2001–02 he was named the WPHL and, after the league merger, CHL Coach of the Year as he led the Jackalopes to 63 and 78 percent win-loss records.

For McKee, what should have been his first decade of retirement had been one of continuous learning. "First, I learned that Odessa has wonderful heart surgeons." Three years earlier, he'd had a heart bypass. Not only was the procedure successful, but he was able to return to his work much sooner than anyone expected. He also learned that he would never be able to contribute a chapter to a hypothetical book called *Life after Hockey*. "After 31 years of teaching hockey, I don't know if I can really retire. Last year Shirley and I took a three-week vacation in England with friends. If it hadn't been for golf, I wouldn't have made it through."

McKee noted that he didn't have a great turnover of players from year to year. Adam Doyle, who had played 302 games in six seasons for the Jackalopes and now worked in the team's front office, expressed the same idea more succinctly: "Players cry when they have to come here, and they cry when they have to leave."

One of the smaller Jackalopes, Donnie Margettie is also one of the feistiest and most popular.

After practice, when the other players headed to the furnished apartments the team rented for them, the four Odessian residents—Matt Cressman, Mike Gorman, Donnie Margettie and Scott Hillman—had household duties, family responsibilities, studies and, in the case of Hillman, a local business he owns to attend to.

Donnie Margettie, one of the most popular Jackalopes, spent the afternoon at home, studying for a final exam. When his hockey career was over, he hoped to remain in Odessa as a paramedic and firefighter, and he was working toward his certification in those professions by taking classes at Odessa College. "Next to hockey, that would be a great job. It's like hockey in a way because we work together so closely—there's a real team atmosphere." Some of Margettie's future teammates, in whose vehicles he'd been riding as part of his training, had attended Wednesday night's game and offered him loud verbal support, mixed in with a little good-natured heckling.

Margettie arrived in Odessa in the fall of 1997, at the beginning of his second professional season. The Niagara Falls, Ontario, native split his rookie year between Nashville and San Antonio of the CHL and scored 32 goals while amassing 154 minutes in penalties. "The CHL was hardnosed, with a lot of hitting. I'd been taught never to back down, and I didn't," said the Jackalopes' captain, still a fan of Doug Gilmour, the longtime NHL star who had, as Margettie explained it, "a little chip on his shoulder. He was tenacious; he always worked hard." Fighting became part of Margettie's game. "It was kind of silly; I looked for fights to thrill myself, and I liked to go after the big guys. That's a role now for the younger guys."

Although he left Odessa after one season, Margettie returned each summer to teach at hockey camps held in the west Texas town. In the fall of 2000, he was back with the Jackalopes for three seasons and then spent a year in the UHL, where he was involved in 28 fights. "I had to prove myself in a different league," he explained, but he returned to Odessa for the 2004–05 season. "I call it my home now." However, when he first drove across the flat plains, it was like nothing he'd seen before. "I was alone in the car and a tumbleweed bounced across the road. I thought that it was like a western movie—I'd never seen that before. Then I met the people. They're great. At first they didn't understand the game, but they wanted to learn and we taught them." A couple of seasons earlier he had met Leah Lang, an Odessian who didn't know a thing about hockey. "I'm so glad I stayed here, otherwise I'd probably never have met her," he remarked. The couple planned to marry after the current season.

By mid-afternoon, while Margettie was studying for his exam, another Jackalope was doing some teaching of his own. Scott Hillman had driven to Midland, where he'd opened up a second branch of his business, Next Level Sports, a fitness and training center. After he had finished explaining to a young woman the significance of the exercises in a program he'd developed for her, he talked about the road that took him from Windsor, Ontario, to west Texas.

At 5 feet 7 inches, Hillman had always been one of the smallest members of the teams he'd played for, and he knew that trying for an NHL career was a long shot. That's why, after graduating from the

University of Windsor with a degree in human kinetics, he headed to Germany to play for Duisburg. "I knew the coach, and I also had friends playing there. They felt that with my style and size, I'd enjoy playing there. But after three months I was disappointed and bored; there were so many weak teams in the league. I still wanted to play, so I contacted Todd Brost, who was coaching El Paso of the WPHL." Like so many players before him, Hillman discovered that playing in the Texas–Mexico border city was not fun. "Even though the rink was in shambles, in a way it was one of my favorites. I scored more points in El Paso than elsewhere. But I grew to dislike the city. Some of the guys said that their wives were afraid to go into town."

After nine games in El Paso, Brost gave Hillman news that the scrappy defenseman responded to with mixed emotions: he'd been traded to the Odessa Jackalopes. "I was glad to get out of El Paso, but I didn't particularly like Don McKee. It wasn't anything personal; it's just that he was the coach at the University of Waterloo, and we had a big rivalry with them when I was at Windsor." Hillman left El Paso that night, driving the car he'd bought a few months earlier. "I realized that I had a car payment coming due and that I couldn't make it without a job. So I decided to stay in Odessa." Six years and 403 games (including playoffs) later, Scott Hillman is still with the Jackalopes and is a permanent Odessa resident.

Scott Hillman, one of several Jackalopes who live permanently in Odessa, stands before a fitness machine at Next Level Sports, a business he owns with branches in Odessa and nearby Midland.

When he decided to return to the Jackalopes for a second season, he enrolled at the University of Texas, Permian Basin, to take a master's degree in kinesiology. "I was the first of the players to study here. I took classes for two semesters each year and earned my degree in 2003." Hillman soon found himself becoming an Odessian. Not only did he represent the city on the ice and study at the university, but he also became a local businessman and homeowner. "I found out that a lot of the local people who leave here come back. I think that the people make Odessa; they have a special sense of pride. At first I found it hard to adapt to the slower lifestyle, but it seems natural now."

It was while doing research on a skating treadmill that Hillman got to know the manufacturers, Frappier Acceleration. "I talked to them about opening a franchise in Odessa using their fitness equipment. The people of Odessa knew my work ethic in school and on the ice, and they supported me wholeheartedly."

He also met Dalyn, the woman who would become his wife, who at the time was living in Houston. She was an athlete, competing in women's rodeo events, and had a friend who was dating a hockey-playing acquaintance of Hillman. The hockey player from Windsor, who hadn't wanted to report to Odessa, soon became a family man in the city, attending church with his wife and his new stepson. Scott and Dalyn were expecting their first child later in the season.

Family and business responsibilities, along with several injuries, including a concussion, had Hillman contemplating retirement after the 2004–05 season. But Rick Gasser, a close friend who, during the season, had become a member of the team's ownership group, encouraged him to return to the ice for another year. "I couldn't turn my back on him; he'd been such a strong supporter of me, both on and off the ice. And Don McKee called regularly; he said that he'd really like me to return, and so would the rest of the guys." Two days after training camp began, Hillman did return to his first Odessa workplace, Ector County Coliseum. Team officials had been planning to have a ceremonial retirement of his number "6" jersey. However, Odessa's hockey fans would now have to wait to pay that tribute to one of their favorite adopted native sons.

FRIDAY DECEMBER 9, 2005

"You know," remarked Adam Doyle, a recently retired player who was now a member of the Jackalopes' sales staff, "there's so much to this business that you don't realize as a player." In minor-league sports, putting together a team to entertain the fans is less than half of the business. Acquiring the revenues necessary to cover on- and off-ice expenses and (with luck) make a modest profit requires a 12-months-a-year effort by a group of trained and hardworking sports business professionals.

The Odessa Jackalopes had the smallest market in the CHL—a quarter of a million people spread over two counties. "However," Monty Hoppel, general manager of both the baseball RockHounds and the Jackalopes, proudly stated, "we have the number one attendance and sales per capita in the league." That is in large part because of the experience possessed by Hoppel and his staff.

When the WPHL was searching for suitable franchise locations, it approached the Midland baseball team's senior management about operating a hockey team in Odessa. "We'd run the baseball club for over a decade, and the WPHL felt that, knowing this sports market as we did, we'd be ideal owners for the new league," said Hoppel. However, the WPHL had not secured a lease on Ector County Coliseum, and the baseball club's principal owners, Miles Prentice and Bob Richmond, decided they needed more time to study the league and the idea of running a professional hockey club in west Texas.

"They liked the overall developmental plan of the league, and, because of our contacts, they felt that it would be an advantage to have our business run a new team," Hoppel explained. "The novelty of the

Oil and high school football are the economic and social foundations on which Odessa rests. Just beside Ratliff Stadium, made famous by the movie *Friday Night Lights,* an oil pump works continuously. Just out of the range of the photograph is a large church, symbol of the area's strong spiritual foundations.

sport, combined with our experience and our extensive database of potential corporate sponsors and season-ticket holders, made us confident we could make it work." They marketed the new team in much the same way they did baseball—as enjoyable, affordable, family entertainment. "We scheduled promotions and special nights and stressed the tough, fast, physical nature of the game." They drew on the same fans who attended baseball games in the summer: business groups, amateur teams, church organizations and families. "We stressed that you didn't have to be a knowledgeable hockey fan to enjoy coming to a game," Hoppel continued. They also emphasized that this was Odessa's professional sports team. Midland had the professional baseball team in the summer; Odessa, the Jackalopes in the winter.

In the first two seasons the Jackalopes averaged just over 4,000 fans a game, but since then the numbers had leveled off at just over 3,000. The sport couldn't sell itself as a novelty anymore, and the sales staff worked hard year-round, selling advertising and promoting season-ticket renewals and group outings. "When the fans are enjoying a warm evening at the ball park, we're thinking hockey; and when they bundle up on a brisk December night to come to the arena, we're thinking baseball," one member of the sales staff laughed, adding that "80 percent of our sales work for hockey is done before the ice is laid at the arena in October."

The income from tickets, prices of which ranged from $13 to $23 a game for adults, was not enough to meet expenses. That was why corporate sponsorship—arena and program advertising—was so important and why the sales staff spent so many hot summer days visiting existing sponsors and contacting potential new ones. The 24 ads in the game-day program brought in $8,400 in revenue over the season. In addition, the Jackalopes sold programs for a dollar each, generating an estimated $16,000 of revenue over the 32-game season. Yearbooks, which sold for $3, contained $60,000 worth of advertising. Rink signage contributed $180,000 in revenue, while various promotions, giveaways, public address announcements and contests brought in another $80,000. Without lining up companies to purchase these sponsorships, the Jackalopes would be short more than $300,000 each season.

Fans didn't just spend money to watch the game, but also to park, to buy souvenirs and, especially, to buy food and drink. Jeff Corbett, executive director of Jack-Shack Entertainment, the food services arm of the parent company, estimated that per capita spending on food and beverages was $4.45 a game, which worked out to a total of more than $13,350 for a crowd of just over 3,000. Given an estimated markup of well over 50 percent on food and drink, Jack-Shack Entertainment could clear more than a quarter of a million dollars a year. Beer was a big seller; in fact, had Ector County not granted a beer license for the Jackalopes, the team might never have come into being. "We pay one dollar for a 16-ounce plastic bottle of beer and sell it for $3.25. If we didn't have beer, we wouldn't have hockey," Corbett remarked. "They didn't in Abilene and the team folded during its second season."

Group picnics, standard features at minor-league baseball parks, had become an increasingly important source of revenue for the Jackalopes. This Friday and Saturday night, Corbett announced, nearly

400 people would enjoy all-you-can-eat meals before watching the hockey games. Groups could choose from four different options ranging from $13 to $20 a person. "We can seat over 500 in one evening," Corbett said. "All of the profit from the food goes to us, and because the arena is seldom filled to capacity, the groups occupy seats in the Coliseum that would probably be vacant."

The Friday and Saturday night games would also be important for the merchandise department. It was the weekend of the Christmas jersey auction. Players would wear the specially designed white, green and red sweaters for Friday night's game, after which the jerseys would be sold to the highest bidders.

Before each home game, Jackalopes leftwinger Sebastien Thinel relaxes with a vigorous game of ping-pong. Behind him, Adam Loncan goes through his stretching exercises.

"Some of the sweaters of the very popular players will go for $800 or $900," said Ray Fieldhouse, director of merchandising. "In addition, we've got 12 more Christmas jerseys with players' names and numbers—

we'll sell them for $210. Fans will also be purchasing T-shirts, hats and replica uniforms for Christmas gifts. I expect that we'll gross between $10,000 and $12,000 in sales tonight and tomorrow."

Forty-five minutes after the gates opened on Friday night, Fieldhouse's prediction was well on its way to becoming a reality. Seven of the 12 extra Christmas jerseys had been sold.

A quarter of an hour before the game, Jeff Ewasko and Mike Rutter, the two injured Jackalopes, strolled through the concourse, stopping to talk with fans. Neatly dressed in suits and ties, they were fulfilling an important nonplaying role for the team by reaching out to their supporters in the community. These were the core fans, without whom a club could not survive and who, in their outgoing, friendly ways, had made the unlikely hockey destination of Odessa more and more attractive to players. For the front office, these actions were an important part of the outreach program that was not only designed to keep loyal fans happy, but also aimed to win back those who had drifted away and to attract new supporters.

Another important element of this program, Monty Hoppel explained, was to encourage Odessa residents to join the ownership group. "We knew that there were passionate, dedicated hockey fans who wanted to do all they could to make sure hockey thrived in Odessa. Having them as part of the organization would also help us meet more local people who might become sponsors

In the summer of 2005, Odessa residents Bill and Tracey Nyborg purchased a minority share of the Odessa Jackalopes. Local owners are becoming increasingly important in minor-league hockey as their ties to fans and businesses raise teams' profiles in their communities.

and season-ticket holders. They would help us become more responsive to the community's desires." Accordingly, the Jackalopes had invited Rick Gasser and Bill and Tracey Nyborg, three hockey fans who were also local business people, to become minority owners.

Bill Nyborg had been born in the small southwestern Minnesota town of Jackson; Tracey, in Odessa. Neither had been hockey fans

until the birth of the Jackalopes. Although he remembered watching a
Minnesota North Stars game when he was 12, Bill loved competitive
wrestling. Tracey grew up cheering for the Permian Panthers and Dallas
Cowboys football teams. "I came from a family of sports fanatics,"
she says. "We'd all watched a lot of sports on TV. But hockey wasn't
one of them."

When the Nyborgs came to the Coliseum to watch their first hockey
game, they became instant Jackalopes fans. "I'm so devoted," Tracey
laughed, "that when the rodeo is in town in January and there are no
home games for nearly a month, I go through withdrawal pains." Her
husband chuckled at her confession, but admitted that he was just as
bad. "I remember a couple of years ago, just before the Jackalopes'
training camp opened, I had an interesting dream. I was working in my
garage and needed a wrench. Someone was watching me and I asked him
to pass me the tool. I turned and it was Wayne Gretzky. He didn't say
anything, just gave it to me. I knew I was ready for hockey."

The couple became members and then directors of the Jack-Pack
booster club, then members of the hockey club's board of directors, a
volunteer group that provides input and, at times, advice to the team's
owners and management. Becoming part of the ownership group was
the next logical step. "We did it," Tracey explained, "because we love
the Jackalopes and we don't want them to leave town. We're here every
game and we know a lot of people. So we can get them on board; they'll
participate because they know us and Rick. That way we can help
reclaim some of the market that's slipped away. We're not in it to make
money; we're fans first and foremost."

The enthusiastic pre-holiday crowd of 2,894 enjoyed an evenly
played first period. The Jackalopes held an edge in the play for the first
10 minutes, but Corpus Christi scored the period's only two goals. As
they had on Tuesday, the Jackalopes came out strong in the second. Paul
Davies tucked in a wraparound shot at 3:31, and at 7:25 Dominic
Leveille and Sebastien Thinel combined to tie the game. In the third period, with just over two minutes to play, Leveille again took a pass from
Thinel and scored the winner for Odessa. It was Coach McKee's 200th
win; for Mike Gorman, in goal, his 99th.

After the game, Don McKee modestly accepted congratulations
on achieving his milestone victory, but, typically, he gave credit to the
members of his team who had made the victory possible, singling out

two hardworking forwards, Paul Davies and Matt Cressman, who had ended up getting credit for the third and winning goal. Leveille, who had originally been credited, made sure that Cressman received the point.

A larger than usual number of people stayed after the game. Many were there to bid on the Christmas sweaters, and as players returned to the dressing room, they received good-natured cheering or teasing when they reported the amount of the winning bids for their jerseys. Many talked with fans, particularly with younger kids who had been allowed to stay up late for the game, some of whom wore small Jackalopes sweaters with the names and numbers of favorite players on the backs. Gradually the crowds dispersed, and soon only a few women were sitting outside the dressing room: the wives and girlfriends for whom watching the games was an act of loyalty and support.

Finally, only Shirley McKee was left. Sitting in her husband's office, waiting for the coach to complete his many post-game duties, she chatted about her four decades as a hockey wife. "Don and I were both teachers in Kitchener; his school had been closed and the teachers were moving to ours. They all arrived while we were having our Hallowe'en party and I was dressed as a witch. I tell him all the time that I gave him fair warning."

Don was involved in minor hockey at the time, and so, from the beginning, Shirley was aware of his dual roles as educator and coach. "I'm a laid-back person, but my father was active like Don," she remembered, "so I knew what life would be like." She became a hockey mom, taking her son and other kids to their games and, when she could, watching Don's teams, becoming a kind of hockey mother to many of his players as well. "At times, Don would come home from a game and offer suggestions about how to do things around the house. I'd say, 'You let me run the power play, and I'll let you run the kitchen.'"

Since McKee's retirement into full-time coaching seven years earlier, she'd seen a lot more of her husband than she used to. "I do a lot of the office work, filling out immigration papers for players, sending daily reports to the league, helping to get apartments ready for new players. I'm very involved with the team. For many of them, I'm their mother away from home, and for others, the ones with kids, I'm a surrogate grandmother. Don sometimes tells me that he's going to fire me from my various hockey jobs, but I tell him that he can't because I'm a volunteer!"

Like the players, Shirley McKee had to adapt considerably when she entered the professional ranks and came to west Texas. "At first I thought the area was awful. We drove in at night, and when I woke up the next morning there was no green. Now I've come to appreciate the living desert." Her attitude to the landscape paralleled her response to the people. "I live the life of the people where I am. Moving to a culturally unfamiliar area, you have such a better time of it if you live life their way."

Shirley McKee, wife of Jackalopes coach Don, casts a critical eye over a bobblehead doll of her husband. "It's the only way I can keep him under control," she laughs as she holds the doll at arm's length.

As a hockey mom, one of her upcoming activities would be a Christmas dinner for the players and their families. "One of the French Canadian players told me about a sugar pie his mother made for Christmas and asked if I knew how to make it. I said I'd try, and since then I've been experimenting with different recipes on Don. When Adam Loncan heard about that, he asked if I could make some bannock. He's Métis and his grandmother used to make it for him. I found a recipe in a Canadian cookbook I brought down here, and I'm going to try it out on Don this week."

Much as she enjoys her life as a mom for professional hockey players, she says it has one major drawback: "It's too much of a meat market. I find it hard to see players leave; you make such good friends."

At this point, her "employer" and husband for four decades returned to the office. He good-naturedly asked her if she'd said anything controversial. "I wouldn't want to have to retract something tomorrow."

"I wouldn't dare," Shirley replied. "I don't want to be fired." The coach tidied the papers on his desk, turned off the computer and photocopier, and put on his coat. He switched off the lights, locked the office door and, with his wife, walked to the car. It bore the vanity plates "OURCOACH," a gift from his children. It was the last car to leave the parking lot. The next morning, as the sun rose above the west Texas plains, it would undoubtedly be the first one to return.

POSTSEASON POSTSCRIPT

The Jackalopes finished with 78 points, tops in the three-team Southwest Division, and faced second-place Amarillo in the best-of-seven quarter-final, which the Jackalopes won in six games. They lost the semi-finals four games to one against the Laredo Bucks, the eventual playoff champions. Although average attendance dropped to 3,047, nearly 200 less than in the previous season, the team's new minority owners, Rick Gasser and Bill and Tracey Nyborg, felt sufficiently optimistic about the Jackalopes' future to purchase controlling interest in the franchise. Jeff Ewasko returned to action on December 21 and finished the season with 268 minutes in penalties, eighth highest in the league. He also scored 10 goals, 14th best among defensemen. Scott Hillman finished the season as the first Odessa player with a career total of 300 points and 400 games. Sebastien Thinel's 91 points was tops on the team and fifth in the league. Dominic Leveille, with 81 points, was the second-highest-scoring rookie in the CHL. On January 29, Donnie Margettie injured his shoulder in a fight and spent the rest of the season on the disabled list.

3

CHARLESTON ON ICE

The South Carolina Stingrays of the ECHL

When construction first began on the 10,000-seat North Charleston Coliseum, there were no plans to include ice-making equipment. However, after an ECHL franchise was granted to the area, these plans changed, and the Stingrays became the arena's major tenant.

On a sunny, breezy holiday Monday in mid-January, tourists walked past the 300-year-old houses in Charleston, South Carolina, one of which had recently sold for over $6 million. Along the Battery, several of the strollers slipped quarters into power telescopes to gaze across the harbor to Fort Sumter, where the first battle of the American Civil War took place more than 140 years earlier. As the lunch hour approached, both visitors and locals headed to the many restaurants along East Bay Street to dine on Low Country cooking, a cuisine that was rapidly gaining international fame. There they sampled rich, creamy dishes, many of which featured local crab and shrimp.

In the early afternoon at Joe Riley Stadium, three miles west of

Charleston's historic downtown, the Citadel University baseball team took the field to practice for a season opener that was only three weeks away. Five miles upstream from the ballpark, on the other side of the Ashley River, visitors to Middleton Place, an 18th-century plantation, toured the historic home and strolled though acres of neoclassical and romantic gardens, where bushes of red camellia blossoms presaged the coming of spring. At Folley Beach, a half-hour drive from Middleton Place, couples walked along the hard-baked sand and children crept tentatively toward the water's edge, then retreated, laughing and shrieking, as a cold Atlantic wave rushed up the beach. From hotel rooms that rent for over $150 a night, even in the depths of the off-season, tourists gazed out their windows across the sparkling ocean. On the golf course beside the road leading back to town, foursomes walked over verdant fairways.

History, gracious homes and gardens, spectacular beaches, warm and sunny January weather, world-class cuisine—the Charleston area would seem to be an unlikely place to find a minor-league hockey team. And until the early 1990s, it was. The situation changed when the city of North Charleston decided that the rapidly expanding area outside the historical district needed a multipurpose arena. A site south of the Charleston International Airport was selected, and architects drew up plans for a 10,000-seat arena suitable for basketball, rodeo, trade shows and concerts—but not hockey.

At the same time as planning for the arena started, the East Coast Hockey League began to look for suitable but nontraditional hockey locations in which to place expansion franchises. Also at this time, Frank Milne of St. Catharines, Ontario, a former minor-league player who had gone on to a career as a hockey scout and coach, then owner and player agent, told his friend Pat Kelly, the ECHL commissioner, that he was interested in acquiring a team in the league. "Pat suggested I inquire in Greenville, South Carolina," Milne remembered, "and when I arrived there, people talked about the new complex being planned for North Charleston." However, he discovered that the North Charleston mayor and the majority of his council did not want ice in their soon-to-be-constructed building. They believed that basketball and other events would bring in more than enough revenue to cover expenses and make a small profit.

"It took a year to convince them how important an ice surface and a team could be for the project's success. I flooded them with information about how well the ECHL had done in the South," Milne continued. It was only after the major construction was well underway that the North Charleston council, now led by a new mayor, voted 4–3 to approve funds for the installation of an ice surface. Years later, one of the council members, now a devoted hockey fan, confessed, "I voted against the proposal two times; I never thought hockey would work here. I was very wrong." She certainly was. During the first season, 1993–94, the South Carolina Stingrays, as the team was known, averaged 9,151 spectators a game, one of the best averages in the minor leagues.

An event held a few days before the hockey team's first game helped to create interest. "They had a preview evening," Milne explained. "There was a stage at one end and ice on the other half of the arena. They put on a big show, and one of the events featured Marcel Dionne, who played for me a long time ago. He had a couple of young players on the ice with him, demonstrating the rules. Then he made some slap shots and they banged off the glass—the crowd loved it."

Just as the crowd quickly became interested in hockey, the Hall of Fame player became interested in the Low Country. He became the Stingrays' president and chief executive officer. The club made the playoffs on the final day of its first season and has been in the playoffs every year since then. In 1997 and 2001, the Stingrays won the Kelly Cup, which is presented to the ECHL playoff champions. After two years, Milne and Dionne sold the team to a mainly local ownership group. Although attendance never again reached the levels of the first season, the South Carolina Stingrays have always been in the top 10 in league attendance.

MONDAY JANUARY 16, 2006

The Stingrays did not have a practice scheduled on the Martin Luther King holiday Monday—for two reasons. First, the ice at the North Charleston Coliseum was not available during the morning, the Stingrays' usual practice time. On Friday and Saturday night, the stadium had been converted into a rodeo ground. A hundred tons of red dirt had been spread over the plastic and plywood that covered the ice, and crowds of 8,000 (much larger than the average of 4,500 people attending Stingrays' games this year) had come out to watch the fastest-growing spectator sport in the Southeast: bull riding. Crews had worked all day

Sunday and well into the evening, scraping off and then trucking away the dirt. At nine on Monday morning, Dick Barnfield, a semi-retired Chicago transplant who wore a Blackhawks jersey, began cleaning and repairing the ice, particularly a number of reddish brown spots where small amounts of dirt had leaked through the covering.

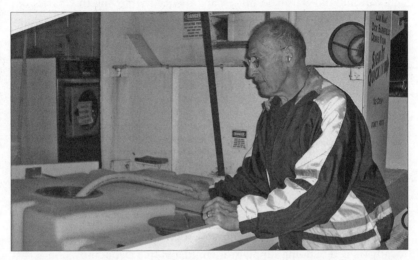

When ice-maker Dick Barnfield, a transplant from Chicago, began to work at North Charleston Coliseum, he had to tell building officials they needed to install a hot-water tap so that he could fill the Zamboni.

Barnfield, a retired postal employee, who over 30 years earlier had been the ice-maker and -keeper for the practice rink of the Chicago Cougars of the World Hockey Association, talked about the challenges of caring for an ice surface in a place where, during fall training camp, temperatures outside could be over 90° Fahrenheit. He and his wife had left Chicago because they wanted to escape the ice and snow. But when the Coliseum was built, it turned out that he was one of just two people in the area who knew anything about making arena ice. "The only ice people here knew about was for iced tea," he laughed. "When the other guy and I were hired, I asked them, 'Where's the hot-water tap?' They wanted to know why, and I explained that you needed to fill the Zamboni with hot water when you flooded the ice."

The biggest challenge to maintaining a good ice surface, Barnfield explained, was the humidity. "It should be between 40 or 50 percent, but here it's usually 80 to 90, and the building doesn't have any dehumidifying equipment. In addition, the building should be around 65 degrees, but that's too cold for people around here. The management keeps it at 75. Sometimes the ice won't dry after resurfacing; you have to use the water sparingly. It becomes a real challenge in the playoffs, especially when they go into May."

Not only did Barnfield not escape the ice by moving to Charleston; it turned out that he didn't escape the snow either. When the *Disney on Ice* show had come to town a few weeks earlier, one of the acts featured snow falling from the Coliseum ceiling. "It looked very pretty," Barnfield remarked. "And then I found out what it was made of. When I went to clean the ice between shows, there were bubbles everywhere, and when I dumped the Zamboni, it was filled with suds. One of the people from the show explained that they used soap flakes for the winter scene. It was like being trapped on the old Lawrence Welk show. I wanted someone to turn off the bubble machine! For the rest of the week I did dry cuts of the ice."

The second reason there was no practice for the Stingrays this Monday was that the two ice surfaces at the Carolina Ice Palace, four miles north of the Coliseum, were also in use. The Ice Palace had been a locally owned building supply store until a Home Depot moved in across the street and a Lowe's Hardware appeared down the block. One of the Stingrays' owners, Jerry Zucker, whose teenage son played hockey, bought the building, installed two regulation-sized ice surfaces, an outdoor skateboarding facility, a licensed lounge and a pro shop selling souvenir jerseys and a complete line of hockey equipment. Brandon Knight, who worked in the store as a floor manager, explained that it was the largest hockey store in the South. He proudly displayed a California Golden Seals replica jersey in a show window and a portrait of Rocket Richard. The legendary Montreal Canadien scowled intensely down on shelves of modern equipment. Knight then moved on to the Penalty Box Lounge, which was decorated in an "Original Six" theme—replica jerseys and photographs of players like Frank Mahovlich, Jean Béliveau and Bobby Hull evoked an era unknown to most native residents of the Low Country.

Since Friday, the Carolina Ice Palace had been the site of the Michael Lewandowski Memorial Hockey Tournament, a tribute to a local player who had died of cancer at age 14. Thirteen teams from four states, playing in five age classifications, had been competing for three days in round-robin and semi-final games. The finals were held on Monday morning. If you didn't look outside, you could have easily imagined you were watching an event in the Midwest, New England or anywhere across Canada rather than the U.S. South. Players whose games were finished slouched on benches, unlacing their skates and accepting snacks handed them by parents. They then shuffled into street shoes and trudged to the parking lot, lugging stuffed equipment bags. In the aluminum bleachers rising along one side of the rink, parents sat sipping coffee and shouting encouragement—and, in one or two cases, criticism—to their children.

The teams all had short benches; each club dressed two goalies and only two complete line changes. The players were of varying sizes and levels of skill—generally surprisingly good. On the Charleston Wol-verines, one of the finalists in the bantam division, the tallest player was a girl, 15-year-old Erin Mulligan. As the team skated toward a 4–1 victory over the Augusta (Georgia) Lynx, Erin's father, Mike, talked of his daughter's love of the sport. One of three or four girls playing high school hockey in the area, she also played on the Wolverines and a local women's team. When other parents were shuttling their athletically talented daughters to topflight soccer and basketball tournaments near and far, Mike and his wife, Mary, drove three or four times a month to Raleigh,

High school hockey player Erin Mulligan, flanked by her parents Mike and Mary, is one of a growing number of young hockey players in the Charleston area. The presence of the South Carolina Stingrays, along with the club's active involvement with amateur teams, is credited with the rise in popularity of this northern and Canadian sport.

North Carolina, over 200 miles away, so their daughter could play on an all-girl's hockey team. During the summer ahead, she'd be attending a tournament in Brampton, Ontario, and a summer camp for women players at Dartmouth College in New Hampshire. After the game, Erin proudly displayed her first-place medal. Mike and Mary looked on proudly—like hockey parents everywhere.

TUESDAY, JANUARY 17, 2006

By Tuesday morning, the ice at the Coliseum was clear, hard and clean. Few signs of the rodeo remained. There was a little red dirt in the driveway to the service entrance and—to the distress of Stingrays trainer D.J. Church—some scattered on the rubber matting around the players' benches. "That's going to play havoc with the skates," he grumbled.

Before nine, coach Jason Fitzsimmons and his assistant Jared Bednar attended to the business side of their hockey jobs. Bednar was in conversation with officials of the Charlotte Checkers, against whom the Stingrays would play on Sunday. Because the National Football League's Carolina Panthers were in a playoff game that would be on television at 6:30 p.m., the Checkers wanted to move the starting time of their home game to 3:00 p.m., two hours earlier than scheduled. "I guess that means we'll have to get up a couple of hours earlier to catch the bus," muttered a player who'd come into the coaches' office to drop off some paperwork.

Fitzsimmons chatted with veteran Cail MacLean about some paycheck juggling that would be necessary to keep the team under the ECHL's weekly team payroll cap of $10,500. Then he helped the team's newest member, Likit Andersson, a Thai-born Swede who had just been acquired from the Stockton Thunder, fill out required forms. Fitzie, as he was known to the players, telephoned office manager Julie Thoennes to report recent roster changes that she would fax to the ECHL office.

Down the hall from the coaches' office, players wandered in and began to prepare for practice. When rookie Ty Morris arrived, several people asked about his wife, who was expecting their first child soon. In one corner, hoots of good-natured derision greeted Robin Gomez's announcement that he had both an exceptionally high IQ and the hardest, most accurate shot in the league. "Yeah, sure," retorted one cynic. "But a 100 IQ doesn't mean 100 percent, and how come your hardest shot is always very wide of the net?" Team captain Trevor Johnson, now on the injury reserve list, retreated to the trainer's room for a bag of ice to apply to a groin injury. The kidding stopped only briefly when Fitzsimmons entered the locker room and announced that the week's practices would be fairly long and strenuous. "There's things we need to get down if we want to do well this weekend and go into the all-star break [the next week] on a high note."

In their baker's dozen years of existence, the South Carolina Stingrays have had a large turnover of on- and off-ice personnel. In addition to ice-maker Dick Barnfield, who is employed by the Coliseum, only two people currently associated with the team were around when the unfamiliar northern sport was introduced to curious sports fans in the Low Country: D.J. Church and Julie Thoennes. Jason Fitzsimmons, the Stingrays' third coach, joined the club as a goaltender in the second season.

As he tidied the training room, preparing it for the players' return after practice, Church remembered the fall of 1993. "I'd finished two years of college and was interested in sports medicine. I'd been talking with the Stingrays' trainer before camp opened, and he said that the club needed an equipment manager. I got the job and on the first day was told I'd need to order a skate sharpener. 'What the heck is that?' I asked. I'd never heard of a skate sharpener. In fact, I'd only seen one hockey game in my life; when I was a kid growing up in Maryland, we went to see the Flyers play. But I learned as camp went on—simple things like what an offside was and icing. And I liked working beside the ice instead of next to a football field. It was a lot cooler."

Church left the club after two seasons, completing his degree at the College of Charleston and then working in sports medicine, including four years as trainer of the Charleston Battery, the local minor-league soccer team. "Then a couple of years ago, the Rays' trainer quit with six weeks left in the season, so Trident Sports Medicine, who supplies the athletic trainers, asked me to come back. I was the only one they had with any hockey experience."

As he remembered his and the team's first two seasons, Church offered explanations for hockey's instant and phenomenal success in the area.

Stingrays trainer D.J. Church receives a head massage from Rob Concannon, who played eight seasons with the club and now sells real estate in the Charleston area.

"The community really took to the team and treated the players like celebrities. They packed the barn every night. There were a lot of northerners who came, including guys from the military bases, who used to watch games back home. The others who came had a NASCAR mindset—they liked the hitting and the noise. And when you added the fights, that was a bonus. The first year we had a little guy, Andy Bezeau, who'd fight anyone. He was the number one star to the fans—they loved him. But I remember the players shaking their heads because people kept cheering at the wrong times."

When Church returned to the Stingrays after seven years, he found that not only had the quality of play in the ECHL improved, but the fans' knowledge had also increased. He noted that "at first you had to explain everything over the PA and the program had three or four pages of rules. They still cheer for the fights, but now they applaud for the little things as well. A lot of season-ticket holders have been coming since the first year, and now they know what to watch for."

On the ice, Jason Fitzsimmons reminded his players that they were expected to show up at the Life Quest gym after the practice for an hour of conditioning work. They'd been there on Monday, their day off from skating, and would be in again on Wednesday. "I show up too," he remarked back in his office. "I think the coach needs to lead by example, and besides, I need the exercise. But first I need lunch." He drove to California Dreaming, a restaurant next to a marina filled with expensive pleasure boats. On the way in, Fitzsimmons stopped to chat with two longtime fans. Then, as he waited for his "California Dreaming" salad, he discussed his life in hockey.

Although he'd been in the sport as a player and then a coach for 29 of his 34 years, the Regina native's career very nearly didn't get started. He was enrolled in beginners' hockey when he was five, but after two weeks he decided to quit. "The practices were on Saturday mornings, and I wanted to stay at home to watch cartoons," he laughed. A year later he returned to the ice, and when the coach asked the players what positions they wanted, he emphatically announced, "I wanna play net."

When he was 15, Fitzsimmons realized that making a career of hockey was a possibility. "I was at the rink one day when a scout asked me if I knew where Jason Fitzsimmons was. I said that I was Jason, and he told me that Weyburn of the Saskatchewan Junior Hockey League wanted me for the next season." After a year at Weyburn, he moved to Moose Jaw of the Western Hockey League. In June 1991, after his third season there, he was barbecuing in the backyard when the phone rang inside the house. It was the Vancouver Canucks of the National Hockey League calling to let him know they were interested in drafting him. "I was so excited that by the time I got back to the grill, the burgers were like hockey pucks!"

On draft day, he watched the first round on TV and saw Quebec City select Eric Lindros as the first pick. Then he headed out to play softball. "It was a beer tournament. Someone told me that my friend Paul Dyck had been drafted. So I figured I'd call my dad to see if it was true. When he answered the phone, he was really excited. 'The Canucks phoned; they've drafted you.' But he was so excited that he'd forgotten what round it was, and we had to call the radio station to find out." He had gone in the 11th round. Fitzsimmons finished another year of junior and then, with his $40,000 signing bonus and a three-year contract, turned pro.

He split his first pro year between Columbus of the ECHL and Hamilton of the American Hockey League and returned to Hamilton the next season. At the end of training camp in the fall of 1994, just when he thought he was about to begin his third AHL season, the Canucks sent him to their new ECHL affiliate in Charleston, South Carolina. "I thought the place was in West Virginia, and then I found out it was in the South. I packed my trunk and drove 15 hours straight to get there. Rick Vaive [the coach] met me and took me to see the rink. It was October 1, and the temperature was 90 degrees Fahrenheit. I wondered how the ice could hold, and I didn't see how hockey would ever make it here."

Former Stingrays player Mike Jickling (left) transacts some business with his former coach, Jason Fitzsimmons. Jickling, now a mortgage officer, is one of nearly two dozen players who live in the Charleston area.

When over 9,000 showed up for the opening game of the Stingrays' second season, Fitzsimmons was amazed—both at the size of the crowd and its reactions to events on the ice. "In the first period, the other team lobbed a long shot from just over center and I made an easy glove save; but the people stood up and really cheered. After that, whenever I made a glove save, I quickly raised the glove over my head. They loved it!"

After the season, Fitzsimmons signed with the Edmonton Oilers and spent a season with their AHL club in Cape Breton. But he returned a year later to the Canucks' organization, spending the fall of 1996 in Syracuse before heading south again to Charleston, where he has been ever since. The Stingrays won the Kelly Cup, the ECHL playoff trophy, and Fitzsimmons, who'd played with a bad back, was named the playoff MVP. However, he struggled the next season and then retired.

Rick Vaive asked him if he'd like to stay in Charleston as an assistant coach. "I still had the passion, probably because my parents had never pushed me but had always been supportive. I was only 26, and I wasn't ready to leave the game. I didn't have a future on the ice, but I was young and would get a lot of good coaching experience that would help me move up in the profession. By the time I'd be 30, I'd have a real head start over guys who were just beginning their coaching careers." It was a difficult transition, however. Fitzsimmons had to separate himself from his former teammates; he had to earn respect rather than keep friends.

As he described his job, Fitzsimmons, who became the head coach in the fall of 2002, listed a series of opposites or contrasts that he constantly worked to balance. On one hand, he worked with players just out of the college ranks; on the other were veterans who had a decade or so of experience. He had to teach the young players while not boring the older ones, and he had to encourage veterans to mentor rookies. He also had to make sure the players knew he was in their corner.

Fitzsimmons had to balance his roles as developer of young players and coach of a winning team. Like most clubs in the ECHL, South Carolina had affiliations with an AHL team, the Hershey Bears, and their NHL parent, the Washington Capitals. Each year the Rays were sent four or five players under contract to either the Bears or Capitals, usually young prospects in need of more instruction and experience. The difficulty was that should the development process go well, players who were making contributions to the Stingrays would be lost and the rest of the team would have to readjust to accommodate replacements. The Rays also sold a few of their own players to AHL teams that needed to fill roster vacancies. "I'm really happy for them when they move up, but this isn't like the AHL, where the focus mostly is on development. Winning is important here; it brings in the fans."

Fitzsimmons went on to explain that the affiliation with Washington was a good one. "They had me and Bruce Boudreau, Hershey's coach, at their training camp this fall. We ran some of the practices and were with the NHL team for exhibition games. It helped us learn their system so that there was continuity in the organization, and it was certainly a nice perk. I had fun and I learned a lot. I always want to keep learning."

While Fitzsimmons, the Stingrays employee with the second-longest record of service, headed to the gym, Julie Thoennes, the only remaining original staff member, was busy at work at the team's offices. The woman who has been called "the one who holds this organization together" was answering phones, responding to queries from a steady stream of co-workers and filling out several forms that had to go to the league headquarters.

Like the original fans, she had known virtually nothing about hockey when she began to work for the team before its first season. She remembered the franchise's opening months. "It was tough to get fans out at first because, in the fall, everyone was interested in high school football. But there were lots of northern transplants, and they bought season tickets. There was a huge media blitz with a regular countdown of hours, minutes and seconds until the opening game. We told guys buying tickets to bring their girlfriends, and we did give away free tickets. We knew that if we got people out to see a game, they'd be back." It worked. A large number of the more than 9,000 people who showed up for the first game kept coming back. In fact, as Julie explained, going to the hockey game soon became the thing to do in the Low Country, a social event for the 20-somethings.

Asked to choose a favorite player and memory, Julie paused and then replied, "There have been so many really nice people. In fact, one of the hardest parts of the job at first was seeing players leave—especially being released. I had to learn that this was the reality of professional sports." She found it easier to name her most memorable and, as it turned out, most frightening event. "The front-office staff had gone to Lafayette, Louisiana, for the final game of the 1997 playoffs. The fans were pretty rowdy, and when we started cheering because the Stingrays won the cup, the people around us became very nasty. We got nervous, and we headed down the stairs right away so that we would be near the dressing room. They were swearing and throwing things at us. We felt happy when we got to where our players were; then we could really celebrate!"

WEDNESDAY, JANUARY 18, 2006

In some ways, the office that Jason Fitzsimmons and Jared Bednar shared could be seen as the Tim Hortons of the North Charleston Coliseum. Like the Canadian restaurant chain, or the cafés in the small Saskatchewan towns where the two coaches played hockey, people were constantly dropping by and sitting down over coffee to chat about sports news, a game they'd seen on TV the night before or family events. On this day the visitor was Keith Vorhis, a retired college administrator and a transplanted northerner, who had watched college hockey in upstate New York several decades earlier. He was showing the others pictures he'd taken at a recent practice, and as he produced each photograph, he provided knowledgeable comments about the pictured player's recent on-ice performance. As practice time approached, the coaches excused themselves, and Keith and another visitor wandered out to the seats behind the players' bench, where they watched the Rays go through their drills.

A glance at the Stingrays' roster quickly revealed the major difference between ECHL teams and those in the Central or United hockey leagues. Seven of the Stingrays had been selected in the NHL amateur draft, with the highest pick, goalie Maxime Daigneault, going to Washington in the second round in 2002. Fourteen players had appeared in a combined total of 617 AHL games. This year, six had been called up to the AHL. For four players, the stay was brief; two others remained in the higher-level league. Five Stingrays were contract players assigned to the team by NHL clubs. Fourteen players had come into the professional ranks from major Junior A teams in Canada, and six were from U.S. colleges. The Stingrays were a young team, with an average age of just under 24. Only five men were over 28. Five players were rookies and four were sophomores. With nine pro seasons each, Marty Clapton and Cail MacLean were the graybeards.

Unlike player moves in the CHL and UHL, movement in the ECHL, of which there is a great deal, is usually vertical rather than lateral and involves shuttles to and from teams in the AHL or Southern Professional Hockey League. ECHL clubs usually call on the lower-level SPHL when they need what are referred to as "warm bodies," roster fillers who spend two or three games with the ECHL team when other players have been injured or have gone briefly to the AHL. South Carolina had used five such replacements already this season.

However, not all the upward mobility from the Stingrays involved a trip to the AHL, and occasionally a player called up from the SPHL became more than a warm body. Such were the cases for two Stingrays who spent the early afternoon at the Life Quest gym, chatting with each other as they pedaled their stationary bikes. Nick Harloff, a 21-year-old defenseman, had been called up from the Columbus Cottonmouths of the SPHL in early December and was still taking regular shifts with the Stingrays. At the end of December, Maxime Daigneault, also 21, spent a weekend with the Washington Capitals as their backup goaltender. The two were a study in contrasts: the shy Harloff had played for a virtually unheard-of lower-level junior team in Georgetown, Ontario; the more outgoing Daigneault was a much-heralded prospect with Val-d'Or of the Quebec Major Junior Hockey League (QMJHL), a team that had gone to the finals of the Memorial Cup.

Nick Harloff (left) and Maxime Daigneault work out on the stationary bikes after a Stingrays practice. Rookie Harloff began the season in the lower-level Southern Professional Hockey League before being called up to the Stingrays. In mid-season, Daigneault was called up to the Washington Capitals, where, for two games, he served as the NHL team's backup goalie.

Harloff had spent long hours during his childhood on outdoor rinks playing one-on-one games with buddies. "I liked Mario Lemieux," he remarked, "but I didn't pretend to be anyone, just myself. It wasn't until I was 18 that I thought I could pursue hockey, that I could keep doing something that I love to do. We used to talk about pro hockey, and Cindy Bowers, a power-skating instructor, encouraged me." As his junior eligibility wound down, he was contacted by the Columbus Cottonmouths' assistant coach Ryan Aikia, who'd seen him play junior. Harloff opted to try out with the Trenton Titans of the ECHL, but when he was cut late in training camp, he called Aikia and made the trip to Georgia.

"I knew it would be a big jump from Tier II to the pros, but I'd trained hard all summer, lifting weights and working on power skating, so I thought I had a chance." By the late fall, Harloff found himself taking long bus rides to such unlikely hockey destinations as Huntsville, Alabama; Kissimmee, Florida; and Florence, South Carolina, playing in a league where the weekly salary cap for each team was $5,600 and virtually no one had a chance to make it to the higher minors. "Some of the teams didn't treat their players too well—they gave them poor housing and there were no perks. But the Columbus organization was very good to us. Even if they hadn't been, I was just happy to be playing, to have a chance to prove my skills and hopefully to get noticed. The fans loved the fights and the hits. One of the guys told me that if you scored 50 goals, they'd think you were okay; but if you got into 30 fights, they figured you were the man." He also commented on the hot weather; it was great for golfing, but the ice got badly chewed up.

On the morning of December 9, 2005, he got word that his hard work had paid off. The team was in Kissimmee and had just boarded the bus to go back to the motel after the morning skate. Coach Jerome Bechard came up to Harloff and told him to head to the airport. Jason Fitzsimmons, short a defenseman, needed an emergency replacement. "I took my morning skate in Florida, got to the Orlando airport and flew to Charlotte, where the Stingrays were playing, and took my pre-game skate 700 miles from where I was in the morning."

Harloff was surprised, happy and nervous when he arrived at Charlotte's new Bobcats Arena. "I thought I'd had a good camp at Trenton, but I wasn't sure. They play a more physical game, and they move the puck a lot quicker in the ECHL than they do in the SPHL. But I learned to keep it simple and to be sure to keep my head up." He spoke enthusiastically about his new team, about going to the rink every day, playing in front of 6,000 people, and every night feeling the pressure of being in games that counted. "You play with and against such incredible talents." And then Harloff, who had yet to score a goal as a professional, looked over at Daigneault. "In practice, if I score against Max, it feels really great. If anyone had told me this time last year that I'd be here now, I wouldn't have believed them."

Maxime Daigneault, who had become a goalie at age six because his father was one and because he liked the equipment, especially the decorated masks, began to attract attention when he was 15 years old and a Quebec newspaper predicted that he'd be the first person chosen in the QMJHL draft. The prediction came true, making

Daigneault the first goalie ever to be the number one choice. In the fall of 2000, the now 16-year-old started in goal for the Val-d'Or Foreurs. His rookie year went well; he appeared in 28 games and posted a 3.55 goals-against average. Although the Foreurs lost the Memorial Cup final game, Daigneault was named the top goaltender of the tournament. His second and third seasons were stronger; his average dropped and he recorded five shutouts, no small accomplishment in the very offensive QMJHL.

With his improved statistics and on-ice performance, Daigneault became a top prospect and a likely first- or second-round pick in the NHL's June 2002 amateur draft. He, his parents and his agent traveled to Toronto, and on June 20 the quartet gathered close to the stage of the Air Canada Centre, waiting for the proceedings to begin. His was not among the 30 names announced in the first round. The second round proceeded; another 28 names were called. Then he heard his name, the 59th selection. He'd been chosen by the Washington Capitals. "Everyone shook my hand; my father hugged me; my mother kissed me. Then I walked to the podium, and they put a Capitals sweater on me."

That fall, Daigneault attended the Washington training camp. "It was awesome; I stopped Jaromir Jagr on a breakaway. But most important, I learned what I had to do to improve." The young goalie returned to Val-d'Or for two more seasons and honed his craft. "The Q is more offensive than either the Ontario or Western junior leagues. A goalie needs to be good to survive." Asked if he had ever faced Sidney Crosby, the 2005 number one draft choice, he replied, with a slight note of pleasure in his voice, "Two games, and he didn't score a goal."

Daigneault turned professional in the fall of 2004, starting the season with the Portland Pirates of the AHL and playing in 11 games before being sent to South Carolina. The young goalie's steady performance in both the AHL and the ECHL led some to predict that he would begin the current season in the AHL. Such was not the case; Washington assigned him to the Stingrays. After a slow start, in which he won only 2 of his first 12 games, he had a streak that saw him win 8 of 11 games.

On December 30, he got the call he had long hoped for. "We'd finished our morning skate and were getting ready to go to Augusta for a game that night. Fitzie came into the dressing room and said, 'Congratulations!' I thought I was being moved to the 'A,' but he said no, I was going to Washington to be the backup goalie for the weekend. So instead of taking the bus to Augusta, I took the plane to Washington."

Daigneault didn't appear in either of the Capitals' two games—one against Philadelphia, the other against Atlanta—and he returned to the Stingrays on January 2. However, the experience filled him with awe. It began when a limousine took him to what he described as a "great hotel." Later, he passed by the White House on the way to the MCI Center. "When I got to the dressing rooms, they were huge. The training facilities were incredible and the hot tub was really big."

Sitting on the bench during the games opened his eyes. "When you see these people for real, it's so much different from TV," he explained, and he rattled off names: Alexander Ovechkin, the first choice in the 2004 draft, and goalie Olaf Kölzig, a veteran of 544 NHL games—both of them Capitals—as well as Atlanta's high-scoring young left-winger Ilya Kovalchuk. Daigneault spoke of how hard Kovalchuk worked and the quickness of his hands. Ovechkin seemed much bigger than on TV and was "very skilled." Kölzig took time to talk with the young goalie. "He told me that I had to be patient, that goalies usually took a lot longer to make it to the NHL than position players." Daigneault would have loved to have had some ice time, "even one minute. But just being there was a dream come true. I learned so much; now I know what I have to do to improve and get back."

After the players had finished their individual workouts, several of them went to a room at the back of the fitness center where a volleyball court had been set up. Nate Kiser and Craig Olynick declared themselves captains and, amid much hooting and ridicule, picked sides. It was clear from the game that followed that the volleyball players could have used coaching from Christy Jickling, the wife of recently retired Stingrays player Mike. Christy coached volleyball at a local high school.

Unfortunately, Christy wasn't there. Serves sailed into the net, attempted spikes ricocheted off walls and a spectator had his glasses knocked off when a setup traveled in an unintended direction. Jason Fitzsimmons, who had wandered in, laughed when someone yelled, "Don't quit your night jobs, guys." He thought the game was an important part of the workout. "It really helps the guys relax and get together as a team." It wasn't clear whether the contest had a victor or whether the game just petered out. Players strolled to the exits, discussing plans for the rest of the day.

THURSDAY JANUARY 19, 2006

Mike Jickling, husband of volleyball coach Christy, showed up at the next morning's coffee gathering. The retired player, who was now a local mortgage broker, grew up in the small Alberta town of Eckville and had made many hockey stops on a road that finally brought him to the Low Country, passing through Washington state, Alberta, California, New Mexico, Florida, Sweden, Italy and Scotland. In 1992, he'd been an eighth-round draft pick of the Quebec Nordiques and faced a choice. "I decided that if I didn't get a contract after training camp, I'd go to university. I ended up at the University of Alberta, a real adjustment after major junior hockey. In junior we played three or four games a week; at the university we spent Monday through Thursday getting ready for two weekend games. It took me until my second year in school to buy the philosophy of combining study and athletics."

After five seasons with the Golden Bears, Jickling graduated with a degree in biology and psychology; however, he decided to try professional hockey, signing a contract with the Long Beach Ice Dogs of the International Hockey League. "I expected that they'd assign me to their West Coast Hockey League team in San Diego, but instead I landed in New Mexico of the Western Professional Hockey League. It was quite a surprise. I wondered if pro hockey was worth it. Some of the players didn't seem to have much of a commitment; it was more like a senior beer league. I remember some of the rinks we visited. In Austin, we changed in a trailer outside the rink. One time we had to walk through the rain to get to the ice. I ended the season in Fort Myers with the Florida Everblades of the ECHL. I loved it and decided to keep playing."

Keeping playing involved moving to Europe. "We were in Sweden and then Italy; my wife and I loved both places. Sweden was like Canada; they loved hockey. In Italy, the level of hockey was lower than in Sweden. But the quality of life was excellent—the food, the wine, the mountains. We'd go hiking on our off days." The Jicklings returned to Fort Myers for the 2000–01 season and then spent the next year with the Ayr Scottish Eagles.

Jickling had intended to return to Ayr for a second season, but the team went bankrupt. He'd played with the Stingrays' assistant coach Jared Bednar during his junior days and gave the South Carolina team a call. "They needed a centerman, and Christy was able to get a job teaching. We both loved the area and so, after a year, we applied for green cards." These arrived near the end of the 2004–05 season. Jickling, who'd suffered several injuries in recent seasons, retired. "A Charleston businessman whom I'd met through hockey offered me a job in his mortgage company. We've settled into this area. We've made good friends, the food is wonderful and we're 10 minutes from the ocean. It's another example of how good hockey's been to me. I haven't made a lot of money, but Christy and I have seen a lot of the world, and we've experienced a lot of different cultures."

Before he left for his day job, Jickling and Jason Fitzsimmons talked briefly about players from the University of Alberta. Jickling had kept in close touch with the school's hockey program, and because he knew the style of play and the personnel needs of the Stingrays, he was able to suggest a couple of Golden Bears who might be able to help South Carolina, possibly after the Bears' current season ended in March or in the next season.

Down the hall, several players were teasing the team's tough guy, Steve "Spinner" Spencer. He had acquired the name while playing junior hockey in Saskatchewan. "During the first couple of games, I was running around on the ice and the coach called out, 'Atta boy, Spinner.' I didn't know why, except maybe for my style of play. They finally told me that it was the nickname of Brian Spencer, who played for the Toronto Maple Leafs and was pretty flaky. It's followed me around. Usually it's old guys who start it up again. When I was at the New Jersey camp a couple of years ago, Larry Robinson and Jacques Laperriere called me that."

Spencer, who grew up playing on natural ice rinks in small Saskatchewan towns, is one of the team's enforcers and the only Stingray who has had a special fine created for him. On the fines list on the team's bulletin board, there's a line that reads "Telling Meadow Lake Stories … $1.00," a recognition of his penchant for talking about his hometown. Spencer's love of playing tough was born when he reached the peewee level and learned that it was now legal to hit other teams' players. "When I saw someone coming through center ice with their head down, the bells and whistles would go off. Now that I'm in the pros, I have to pick my spots more carefully, but when I get a chance to hit someone, my eyes still get as big as saucepans. They eat up that style of play here in the South. If they see a physical game, they're sure to come back. The people here watch for me to come on the ice; they're hoping for a big hit."

Spencer had seriously considered winding down his hockey career after midget, but decided to play Tier II Junior A hockey in the Saskatchewan Junior Hockey League in hopes of earning a scholarship to an American college. Instead of college, his play earned him a spot with the Swift Current Broncos of the major junior Western Hockey League. "They told me they wanted me to be a hard-hitting, stay-at-home defenseman," Spencer remembered. However, six games into the season the

team's fighter suffered a major injury, so "Spinner" assumed an additional role. "And so," he laughed, "37 major penalties later ... " By the end of his first season with the Broncos, his versatility had attracted the attention of scouts from the Nashville Predators. On Saturday, June 22, 2002, his mother woke him up early. "I was sleeping off the effects of the night before, and it was hard to realize what she was telling me at first," he explained. He'd been selected by Nashville at the end of the eighth round, a long time after the top defen-

Hard-hitting Stingray defenseman Steve "Spinner" Spencer signs his name on a Valentine heart that will be sold in a booster club fund-raiser.

seman to go in the draft, Jay Bouwmeester, had been picked. "I was happy. If someone had given me a contract right then, I'd have said, 'Where do I sign?'"

It was neither that quick nor that easy. When Spencer arrived at the Predators' camp in the fall of 2002, he was overweight and, he admits, "I was amazed at how good they were and how hard they worked. They sent me back to Swift Current to work on my skating and puck handling." He did, and he also cut back on his role as a fighter. "I only had 13 or 14 majors that season. It was like a vacation." The Predators didn't offer him a contract, but the next season he was invited to the New Jersey Devils' camp, where he was mentored by Laperriere, who'd been an all-star defenseman for the Montreal Canadiens in the 1960s. "He thought of me as a player, more than as a fighter. That made me think that I had more to offer on the ice than to hit people or fight them."

Spencer spent his first professional season in South Carolina, and the next year he split time between the Stingrays and Albany of the AHL. He felt that his performance for that season would earn him a berth in the AHL for 2005–06. "But they were overloaded with defensemen, and there was no room for me in the 'A.'" His fortune took a turn for the better early in the season. He was part of a multiplayer trade between the New Jersey Devils and the Phoenix Coyotes, and because the Coyotes were thin on defensemen, he knew there was a good chance he'd receive a call-up from the Stingrays to Phoenix's AHL team, the San Antonio Rampage.

The call came in late November. "They said they had a plane ticket for me at the Charleston Airport, but they didn't know I'd broken my thumb in a fight. South Carolina still needed me because they'd lost a couple of defensemen. I could play with a cast, but I couldn't fight. Then last week the Coyotes called again. I told them that I was still wearing a cast, but they told me that I wouldn't need to fight. The next day my wife and I had packed my suitcases and I went to the airport. Then they called me on my cell phone and said they didn't want me just yet." Spencer drove home disappointed, but encouraged. He'd been only a few minutes away from taking the trip to the highest level of minor-league hockey. Only the cast had stopped him. When the next call came, he'd be ready—to hit, to fight or just to be a stay-at-home defenseman.

After practice, Spinner and the rest of the team had the afternoon off. Fitzsimmons had decided that another trip to the gym would be counter-productive. Three days of exercises and four mornings on ice should be enough to prepare the team for its upcoming three-game weekend.

FRIDAY JANUARY 20, 2006

The first sound an early morning visitor to the Coliseum heard while walking down the hall toward the Stingrays' dressing room was the zinging of a skate being sharpened. Rounding a curve in the hall, the visitor saw a shower of sparks and a young man in goggles holding a skate blade against the rotating wheel. He pulled the skate back, pushed the protective eyewear up onto his forehead and inspected his work. Satisfied, he placed the skate on the worktable and reached for another.

He was Heath Kaufman, generally the first Stingray to arrive for work in the morning and the last to leave. Although unnoticed by virtually all the fans who came to the games, he was a very important member of the hockey team. As the biographical sketch in the program stated, his duties were many: "Heath holds responsibility for all of the players' equipment, including skates, sticks, helmets, etc. He is in charge of the locker-room facilities, he supervises the stick boys, and he also sharpens the players' skates."

On a normal morning, Heath arrived at the rink shortly after 7:30. "First I straighten the room up and hang the practice jerseys in each player's stall; then I begin to work on the skates and get the coffee going. When the players arrive, they post their requests for equipment repairs on the bulletin board." During practice, he would retire to his workroom, which contained, among other things, a heavy-duty sewing machine. "I fix gloves and pads and then work on sweaters. There are usually a couple with tears, and when a new player arrives, I have to sew a name on the back of his sweater." After the players left, usually around noon, he would do the laundry, clean the dressing room and get things ready for the next day's practice or, as he did on this day, the upcoming game. He took inventory, made new orders and checked on the status of recent ones. "When the new stuff comes in, I have to hide it from the players until they need it," he laughed. "Otherwise it would be gone in no time."

The next day would be even busier for Kaufman. In addition to his usual game-day duties, which included preparing the visiting team's

Stingrays equipment manager Heath Kaufman checks a newly sharpened blade while Cam McCaffrey, the skate's owner, looks on. As hockey equipment has become increasingly more complex and sophisticated, the position of equipment manager has grown in importance.

dressing room and supervising his four game-day assistants—Brendon Duncan, Willie Williams, Justin Lindgren and Joey Abate—he would have to get ready for the team's early Sunday morning departure for Charlotte. "Basically, I have to be prepared for anything that could happen at a game. On the road I have a skate sharpener and a portable sewing machine, along with extra sticks and game uniforms."

For Heath, the present season was his eighth in professional hockey. "I started as a stick boy during my senior year in high school. I had no knowledge of anything related to the game; in fact, until the Stingrays came to town, I'd never heard about hockey." In 2003 he'd left town to take the job of equipment manager for the Columbus (Georgia) Cottonmouths. But when that team left the ECHL, he returned to the Rays. "My wife, who, by the way, can't sew, wonders why I spend so much time at the arena. I tell her that I love the job, the environment, the players. And I can even play hockey now—a little bit."

His skate-sharpening duties finished, Kaufman checked on the coffee-maker and then took a freshly brewed pot to Jason Fitzsimmons's office. Two new people had joined the coffee gathering: Rob Concannon, who'd played with the Stingrays for several seasons and then remained in the Low Country, and Dave Prior, goalie coach for the Washington Capitals, who'd come to observe his young prospect, Maxime Daigneault. Concannon, who had earned the nickname "Kookie" because of his antics both on and off the ice, carried on a conversation that resembled the ad libs of comedian Robin Williams at his most frenetic. He talked about his career, the beautiful women of Charleston, tonight's game and his belief that the 20 or more former Stingrays living in Charleston could ice a team that would beat most old-timer squads in the country.

Dave Prior, in contrast to Concannon, sat quietly, and when he spoke, he did so in a soft voice. Now in his seventh season with the Capitals, the Guelph, Ontario, resident had previously worked for several other NHL clubs and for the NHL's Central Scouting Bureau. His trip to South Carolina had occurred early in an incredibly busy nine-day itinerary. On Tuesday, he'd been in Ottawa to watch a game featuring top prospects in the Canadian major junior leagues. Back home in Guelph on Wednesday, he'd watched the Capitals on TV; had they won their game, he'd have headed to Washington. Because they lost, he'd made hasty arrangements to come to South Carolina. "The airlines lost my bags and so I won't be able to get on the ice with Max today—my skates haven't arrived." It also turned out that Daigneault wasn't scheduled to start either Friday's or Saturday's game. Prior would have to make the bus trip to Charlotte to watch him. On Monday he would go back to Guelph. Tuesday, he'd drive to Pittsburgh to join the Capitals for their Wednesday game against the Penguins, and after the game he'd fly with the team to Boston for a Thursday night game.

Concannon drained his coffee cup and left for his day job, selling real estate. Prior moved to the stands to watch the goalies work out, and Fitzsimmons took to the ice to lead his team in its final preparation for the evening's game.

Two blocks from the Coliseum, the Stingrays' off-ice team was also busy preparing. The hockey team needed to turn its season around; the front-office team needed to turn the attendance around—at 4,448 people a game, it was down nearly 500 from the previous season.

The eight people in the front office had two main jobs: to sell tickets and to sell sponsorships in the form of rink, program and radio advertising. The two were linked. When more people came to games, the various types of advertising received greater exposure. Thus, when attendance dropped, advertisers were slower to sign up. In the Stingrays' early years, both sources of revenue had been very good. The novelty of the facility and of the sport sold the team. "But," as Stingrays president Taylor Lee explained, "once the novelty wore off, you couldn't just sell hockey. You had to sell the total experience of coming to a game at the Coliseum."

A Charleston native, Lee had been one of the local people who, in the early 1990s, wondered why the North Charleston council was considering putting ice in the partly constructed Coliseum. He attended games and became a fan. Lee was an active member of the area's business community and had been involved in organizing several major local sporting events. It was because of this background that, in the fall of 2003, the hockey team's owners invited him to apply for the position of president. When he began to work with the Stingrays in the fall of 2003, he faced a daunting task: to halt, or at least slow, the decline in attendance and to increase sponsorship revenues. He began by increasing the team's visibility in the community, telling players that they would be required to spend 25 percent of their time appearing in public, and also scheduling mascot appearances throughout the year. He assembled a trained and hardworking front-office staff to spend 12 months a year selling what he called "the Stingrays experience."

One of these people was Chris George, a graduate of West Virginia University who had grown up playing hockey in Erie, Pennsylvania. He said that he had really learned about sports marketing when he worked for the Roanoke Express of the ECHL. "When the Express owners let go of all the office staff except me," he explained, "I had to work hard just to generate enough money for people to be paid." Now the Stingrays' vice-president of sales and marketing, George was already preparing for the next season. "In February we'll begin working on season-ticket renewals. People who renew by mid-March are eligible to win a week's vacation." In April the Stingrays would begin to solicit potential new season-ticket holders, and during the spring and summer they'd work heavily at promoting group sales. "We also will focus on ticket sales for opening day; we need a large crowd to begin the season."

"You have to send invitations if you want people to come to your party," George added, explaining that at each home game the team organized a number of raffles and contests that required people to fill out and deposit ballots that included a brief questionnaire along with spaces for their names, addresses and phone numbers. This information provided the basis for a data bank that the sales staff drew on during the off-season campaign to increase sales for group outings, ticket mini-packs and season tickets.

When the Stingrays had three home games scheduled on a weekend, which would happen twice later in the season, the front office faced a particular challenge: the third game was usually poorly attended. This season, George had been working on a solution. He'd scheduled a home fair for the three-game weekend in late February. "For $300, a merchant is given 40 tickets that can be distributed to customers and is assigned a display table on the arena concourse. We have the possibility of attracting over a thousand people who might not otherwise come to a game; some of them may return to another game. Our goal is to increase the Stingray Nation."

Down the hall from Chris George's office, Steve Fraser, game-day operations and promotions manager, sat in front of his computer as he prepared an important document for the "game-day experience." He was working on the script—31 pages that contained instructions and PA commentary for all the events that would be part of the evening at the Coliseum. "My job," he explained, "is not to entertain them with hockey, but with everything else." Everything else included video shots of fans displayed on the center-ice matrix board, a remote-controlled blimp that dropped merchant coupons into the crowd, T-shirt tosses and a screaming contest with a pizza as the prize. In addition, the script included short commercials for area businesses and an appeal from the ECHL for donations to the Hurricane Katrina relief fund.

That evening, 5,973 fans turned out to scream, shriek and cheer. They began their cheering when the announcer asked them, "Are you ready to make noise for your boys?" They roared when the home team opened the scoring with a power-play goal at 19:22 of the first period, a Marty Clapton tip-in of a rebound. The Augusta Lynx evened the score in the second, and midway through the third period, Brad Parsons scored the winner for the Stingrays, another rebound shot. The star of the game was goalie Davis Parley, who made 32 saves, 17 of them in the first period when the Lynx dominated play.

After the game, the coaches' office was more crowded than usual. Andrew Miller, the *Post and Courier* hockey writer, gathered quotes from Fitzsimmons, and Christy Jickling chatted with Chantel Fitzsimmons, Jason's wife, who was expecting her first child in late February.

Although, like her husband, Mike, Christy Jickling was now just a Stingrays fan, when she had been a hockey wife, she hadn't been a typical one. That's because, like her husband, she had been both a university and professional athlete, and for the three and a half years that the couple had lived in Charleston, she had followed her career as a high school English teacher and girls' volleyball coach. The two had met in the mid-1990s at the University of Alberta in, of all places, a doctor's waiting room. Christy, a member of the university volleyball team that would win three consecutive national championships while she played, had back problems; Mike's knee was bothering him. The two went on to enjoy post-university professional sports careers in Europe. Mike played hockey and Christy played volleyball in Switzerland and Sweden. "But neither of us were making much money," she said, explaining her retirement from pro sports, "and I realized that if Mike was going to stay in Europe, I needed a job that would pay." She returned to the University of Alberta to take the 18-month post-degree teacher certification program.

When the Jicklings decided to return to North America in 2002, it was important that they find a place where Christy could teach. "The owners of the Stingrays had contacts. I became an English teacher in the Charleston County School District." She also became the girls' volleyball coach at West Ashley High School and was named the conference coach of the year. "I am," she remarked, with a touch of pride in her voice, "the only English teacher in the system who coaches a varsity sport."

For Christy, being in a two-athlete household, one where both big games and injuries were basic elements of life, meant that "both partners have a real understanding of what the other is going through. It also helps you to understand each other's sport. Because you've studied your own sport so deeply, you apply these techniques of learning to the other sport. You try to understand the intricacies of technique and the complexities of team strategy."

Having her own profession, a nonathletic one, was also important to Christy. "I couldn't have been a stay-at-home wife, living vicariously through my husband's sport; nor could I have been only a physical education teacher. My undergraduate degree was in English and comparative literature, and now I'm working on a master's degree in English at the Citadel [the Military College of South Carolina]. It was a conscious choice to teach an academic subject. I love the coaching and I enjoy mentoring the girls on the team, but my teaching life isn't just athletics."

As the gathering in the coaches' office broke up, Christy and Mike declined an invitation to join the group for a late-night snack. Reminded that the next day was Saturday, Christy replied, as she frequently had when Mike was a player, "Yes—but I have a set of student essays to mark over the weekend."

SATURDAY JANUARY 21, 2006

On Saturday morning, the atmosphere in both the coaches' office and the Rays' locker room was subdued. The previous night's game had been a tough one, and, although the team had been training hard for five days, the players couldn't let up yet. Tonight's game would be against the relatively weak Columbia Inferno, but the Rays would have to be up early Sunday for the three-hour bus ride to face the Checkers, who'd beaten the Stingrays in the teams' first five meetings.

There was only a single visitor—a very young one—in the office: Cruz Bednar, assistant coach Bednar's six-year-old son. Like thousands of parents in North America who were with their children at hockey rinks that morning, Bednar knelt before the boy, lacing on his skates. Then he led him out of the office and along the padded mats that made a pathway to the rink and stood watching as Cruz took some tentative steps onto the ice. The boy looked small—the only person skating, with no one in the 10,000 seats of the Coliseum. His father flipped a puck out in front of his son, and the child reached his stick out, controlled the disk and skated toward the goal. He shot wide and then turned toward one of the large faceoff circles, amusing himself by skating around its circumference.

He was still circling a few minutes later when Dominic Soucy, the Rays' 6-foot 4-inch right-winger skated onto the ice. He called a hello to the child and then skated into the crease, where he assumed a goalie's

crouch. Cruz abandoned the face-off circle, retrieved the puck from behind the net, moved in front, shot and scored. Soucy's goaltending abilities remained deficient as the young Bednar put the puck in the net on five consecutive shots.

Back in the trainer's room, Marty Clapton, who, with that week's arrival of 32-year-old Likit Andersson, was no longer the old man of the team, eyed the breakfast snacks spread out on a counter. He chose a bagel, spread strawberry cream cheese over both halves and retired to a folding chair where he munched and answered questions about his hockey career. Now in his ninth professional year, he'd played all but 20 of his games in

Six-year-old Cruz Bednar, son of the Stingrays' assistant coach Jared Bednar, skates in on Dominic Soucy, who was unable to make a save on the youngster's shot.

the ECHL, first for the Hampton Roads Admirals and then, since the fall of 2000, for the Stingrays. He'd had three brief call-ups to the AHL, and the previous season he had spent 10 games with the ECHL's Long Beach Ice Dogs. He'd never had a 20-goal season, but he'd distinguished himself for his steadiness and his work ethic. As the cliché goes, "He came to play every day."

A native of Newton, Massachusetts, Marty came from a hockey family. "Even though he was born in England, my dad played hockey," Clapton explained. "He played at the University of Massachusetts, and he began to coach me when I was four years old." Marty grew up admiring Wayne Gretzky and, because his family loved the Boston Celtics basketball team, Larry Bird. "I think that these players made the players around them much better." It wasn't until Clapton received a hockey scholarship from Brown University that he realized he might have a chance to play hockey professionally.

His break came at the end of his senior year at college. He'd played in a U.S.–Canadian college all-star game that had been attended by John Brophy, the coach at Hampton Roads. "At Brown, academics were very important; it was hard to maintain your competitive level for hockey. When Brophy offered me a contract to play in the ECHL, it gave me a chance to focus on hockey," Clapton remembered. Brophy was legendary for being a hardnosed, "take no prisoners" coach, and his teams were always among the league leaders in penalty minutes. "But I liked his being hardnosed. He was a real motivator—I needed that. He demanded the most out of his players."

Veteran Stingray Marty Clapton enjoys a snack before a Saturday morning practice.

Moving from college to professional hockey and from New England to Virginia was a shock. "I was amazed at all the promotional things going on during stoppages of play. And then there was the idea of being paid to play—that was amazing to me as well. It wasn't much money, but I was delighted. Going from 30 games or so a year to 90 was a real challenge. During my first season, we won the ECHL championship—nothing like that had happened at Brown." He also discovered fighting. "I made the mistake of fighting the other team's tough guy. He got in the first punch and then I got mad and threw a couple. I found out that it wasn't too bad."

When the Hampton Roads franchise shifted to the AHL, Clapton realized that he'd better begin working the telephones. "I liked Charleston when we'd gone there to play, and I had a good friend who'd studied at the College of Charleston. I attended the Admirals' training camp and was their last cut." His calls to the Stingrays paid off, and he made the trip south. In addition to a new lifestyle, he had to adapt to a new type of hockey fan. "In Hampton Roads they had a very large naval community, and it included a lot of hockey fans from the North. Down here, the game is just part of the evening's event; hockey is developing into an entertainment type of sport. People enjoy the games, but they don't always have a great understanding of what they're seeing. I think the game's greatest success in the South will be in smaller cities like Charleston."

The Stingrays won the Kelly Cup championship in Clapton's first year with the team. During his second season, his steady play earned him a 25-game contract with the AHL's Rochester Americans. "I only got into 12 games, and then I was on the fourth line. It was tough. When you don't get that much ice time, you don't get the chance to put up the numbers that will keep you around. But the experience did improve my game, and the money in the AHL was pretty good."

Clapton had not been back to the AHL for the past three and a half seasons, and as he became surrounded by younger players on the Stingrays, he adapted to a changed role. "Over the past three seasons I've played both forward and defense. As an older player, you want to be as useful as you can—being a utility man does this." He also realized that his career could be over relatively soon. "I play each season as if it may be my last. Hockey's been my life for the past nine years. But I realize that it won't last forever."

By eleven o'clock, the practice was over. The players had showered and changed, and were walking to their vehicles in the west parking lot. From there they prepared to drive to their pre-game lunches and then naps. It was a warm, sunny day and several wore shorts. One, Cail MacLean, had also donned a pair of work gloves. He stood between two pickup trucks, transferring campfire wood from one to the other. "We have a fire pit in our backyard and my friend brought this wood for me. My wife and I sit out on warm evenings, and the fire's nice. I couldn't do that back home at this time of year." Home was Middleton, Nova Scotia, a small town just over 100 miles west of Halifax.

For the past 13 years, MacLean had spent virtually no time in Middleton during the winter. In the fall of 1992, he had joined the Ottawa Junior Senators of the Tier II Junior A Central Ontario Junior Hockey

League. After a year he moved to Kingston, playing major junior with the Frontenacs for four seasons. Then he began a professional career that saw him play for 15 teams in three different leagues—the ECHL, the IHL and the AHL. He signed with the Stingrays, his fourth ECHL team, in the summer of 2005.

MacLean had discovered hockey at age four, when his parents took him along to his older brother's practice. "I told them I wasn't going to a rink again until I had a stick of my own, and that was the beginning. Hockey's been a big part of my existence ever since then." On Saturday nights he watched the Toronto Maple Leafs with his father, and his father used to point out people like Gretzky and Steve Yzerman. "My dad told me that they were good because they were hard workers. I wasn't that big, and I was often the youngest player on my team when I was growing up—so I knew that I'd have to work hard."

After his junior year in Ottawa, MacLean had a decision to make: major junior hockey in the Ontario Hockey League or college. "I didn't play much in Tier II, so I didn't get any offers from U.S. colleges. I thought the OHL would be a direct route to the NHL, so I signed with the Frontenacs and enrolled as a part-time student at Queen's University. Now I'm studying by correspondence from Athabasca University in Alberta."

Playing with the Frontenacs didn't provide MacLean with a direct route to the NHL. Instead, he earned a tryout with Cleveland of the IHL. When that didn't work out, he signed with the Jacksonville Lizard Kings of the ECHL. The coach, Bruce Cassidy, had seen him during a Team Canada summer tryout, and he later invited MacLean to be a member of teams he coached in Trenton, Indianapolis and Grand Rapids. MacLean loved the Florida weather, which he said energized him, but he didn't care for Jacksonville's aging arena, which players referred to as the "Reptilian Pavilion."

Between his rookie season in 1997–98 and the 2004–05 season, MacLean had played for 11 IHL and AHL teams, but with the exception of 2002–03, when he appeared in 74 games for the Hershey Bears, and the next season, when the Bridgeport Sound Tigers dressed him for 61 games, his stays in the highest levels of the minor leagues were short, ranging from one to 35 games. "It was month to month," he commented. "Somebody joked to me, 'Don't buy too many groceries; you might not be here long enough to eat them all.' When I'd get assigned to an AHL team, I knew and they knew that I was a filler. But it was still discouraging when I got sent back. I'd never been drafted, so that's the way it was. My job was to keep my mouth shut, work hard and do my job. I didn't get a great deal of playing time."

Why, then, did he keep playing? "I love the game, the lifestyle of professional hockey. I love coming to the rink. It's what I've been since I was four." He, like Clapton, saw a new role for himself as one of the team's veterans. He wanted to offer leadership. "None of us in the 'E' is that good that we can afford not to help younger players. I like to teach and to help the younger players develop pride in their profession." Moreover, he enjoyed living in Charleston. "This summer, when my wife and I were thinking of where I'd play, the Stingrays were very high on our list. The team had a reputation of being a good organization, and my wife, who's from Jacksonville, likes living near the ocean."

MacLean remarked that, since his first season in Jacksonville, southern fans have become more knowledgeable. "They are growing with the game," he explained. "They still clap at times that seem strange for us, but now it's not just for the fights, the banging and crashing, or the goals. They're beginning to notice things like blocked shots and the strategies of a penalty

For Cail MacLean, one of the most enjoyable bonuses of playing for the Stingrays is the chance to enjoy the gorgeous January weather. After practice, wearing only shorts and a T-shirt, he loads wood for use in his backyard fire pit.

kill." He also admitted to being both amazed and pleased when he saw fans, both young and old, wearing uniform jerseys with his name and number on the back. "It's humbling; you're an ordinary person. It's like we used to do when we wore Gretzky's sweater."

Saturday's game had been advertised as "Pack the House Night." Parking was free and upper bowl tickets were on sale for five dollars. The Stingrays didn't pack the house, but a crowd of 8,092, the season's largest, did show up. The first period ended with no score, as did the first 10 minutes of the second. Then at 10:05, with two Columbia Inferno players in the penalty box, Cail MacLean tipped in a long shot by Brad Parsons. Less than two minutes later, the Stingrays, now shorthanded themselves, went ahead by two, as Brad Parsons scored on a breakaway.

After each of the goals, the crowd cheered loudly, looked up at the matrix board and then cheered again. They weren't applauding a video replay of the goals; they were applauding the picture of four women wearing white Stingrays' sweatshirts, each of them holding up a sign bearing a letter. Taken together, the signs read GOAL. Then each woman flipped the letter over, revealing a new one that was part of the word RAYS. As the game went on, the quartet formed new words: TREV, ROBN, MATT, JOEL. Three were abbreviations of the names of current players. The fourth was for departed Ray Joel Irving. ("We still keep his name because we hope he'll come back here," one of the women later reported.)

Between the second and third periods, the Rays Ladies, as they called themselves, discussed their history as hockey fans. Betty Morgan and her daughter Donna had moved from Hartford, Connecticut, to the Low Country at about the same time that the Whalers left the North. "We thought that we were leaving hockey behind," Donna remembered. "When I heard about the Rays, I yelled, 'Yeah!' We were so glad to be able to watch hockey again, no matter what the level."

Joan Stanko had been a hockey fan in Pittsburgh and also thought she was leaving hockey behind when she came to Charleston. "When I heard that they were bringing pro hockey to Charleston, I was tickled pink. I'd missed it so much since we'd left the North. The Rays have been so good for Charleston. Now there's kids' hockey, high school hockey and women's hockey."

Stanko brought her friend Joan (pronounced Jo-Ann) Ward to a game five or six years earlier. The West Virginia native had never seen hockey before, but "I was hooked right away," she remarked. "I'm amazed by their skating skills, but I'm really here to see them fight. Robin Gomez is my favorite. But he's calming down. You know, it's like going to your grandchildren's games and cheering for them."

The Rays Ladies had been in the sign business for four or five years. "At first we just had handheld signs that spelled GOAL," Joan Stanko explained. "The team management noticed us and encouraged us to make signs with players' names. That's when we started to make the flip cards on sticks."

Donna Morgan, Betty Morgan, Joan Stanko and Joan Ward (left to right) are the Rays Ladies. Several times each game they hold up their signs, which celebrate goals and favorite players. Their images are displayed on the large scoreboard and are always greeted with applause from the other fans.

"We like to entertain the other fans," Joan Ward added. "And we also like to see ourselves on the screen."

The Rays Ladies had one more occasion to flash their GOAL sign, as Matt Reid scored an empty-net goal in the last minute of the game to seal the Stingrays' victory. Goalie Davis Parley, who made 26 saves to earn his first shutout of the season, received the first star. Brad Parsons and Cail MacLean were the second and third. The 3–0 victory did not move the club out of fifth place in the South Division standings as both Charlotte, ahead of them, and Augusta, below, earned wins as well.

There was little time for celebration. The players quickly left the arena—in just over 10 hours, they'd be back again, packing their equipment onto the bus, and in 16 they'd be playing their third game in less than three days.

POSTSEASON POSTSCRIPT

The Stingrays finished the season in fourth place in the eight-team southern division and thus earned a playoff berth for the 13th consecutive season. They defeated the Charlotte Checkers two games to one in the first round of the playoffs, but lost the second round to the Gwinnett (Georgia) Gladiators in three straight games. During the season, their attendance increased to an even 5,000 a game, slightly above the previous year's total. During the last two months of the season, the roster was in a constant state of flux. At the end of January, Brad Parsons, then the team's leading scorer, signed to play in Finland at a salary three times what he'd earned in the ECHL. Ty Morris, Marty Clapton, Steve Spencer and Matt Reid all spent time on the injured reserve list. One weekend in February, the roster was so depleted that Mike Jickling was called out of retirement for a game. At the end of March, the team had only 13 healthy skaters. Deryk Engelland, Cam McCaffrey, Matt Reid, Robin Gomez and Maxime Daigneault all received brief call-ups from the AHL. In March, Nick Harloff, Ty Morris, Dominic Soucy and Jeff Legue were traded to other ECHL teams as coach Jason Fitzsimmons worked to strengthen his club for the playoffs. Bergen Fitzsimmons was born in late February. There have been no reports yet of his father assigning him duty as a practice goalie. As the season ended, team president Taylor Lee announced that he was resigning in order to take a position as chief operating officer of Health First of Charleston.

4

NOTHING COULD BE FINAH

The Fayetteville FireAntz of the Southern Professional Hockey League

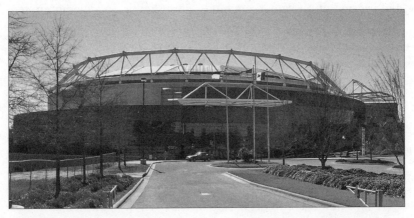

During the early stages of its construction, Fayetteville's Crown Coliseum was mentioned as a possible temporary home for the NHL's Carolina Hurricanes. However, because minor-league hockey executive Bill Coffey had already signed an exclusive lease agreement, the facility became home to, first, the Central Hockey League's Force and, later, the FireAntz.

In 1996, when the Central Hockey League decided to expand eastward, adding privately owned teams for the first time, Bill Coffey, one of the founders of the East Coast Hockey League, applied for a franchise in Fayetteville, North Carolina. With a population of close to a quarter of a million people, the Cape Fear region, as it is called, was the home of Fort Bragg, one of the largest military posts in the world and residence for a large number of soldiers who'd grown up watching hockey in their northern hometowns. "In 1995, before they'd even broken ground for the building, I'd signed a lease for hockey," Coffey remembered.

Although Coffey had begun his quest for a team with a choice of leagues, the choices soon dwindled. The Southern Hockey League disbanded after the 1996–97 season, and the American Hockey League had moved out of the South after the Hartford Whalers came to North Carolina in 1997. On June 17, 1997, the CHL announced that Fayetteville would become a member. Although the Force, as the team was named in honor of the military base, did poorly on the ice during the first season, it was a financial success and drew an average of almost 4,000 people a game. While northern servicemen and other transplants came because they were overjoyed to again be watching a game they loved, others came because of the novelty of the new Crown Coliseum (named for its resemblance to a royal headpiece), because the sport featured fights and because of the zany promotions. For example, in a modification of the between-periods contest of shooting the puck at a tiny opening in the goal, contestants aimed at empty beer cartons placed along the goal line. For each carton hit, the shooter took home a full case of beer.

After two years, Coffey sold the club. Without his experienced and innovative leadership, the team faltered financially. The honeymoon between fans and the new sport and its arena was over. The new ownership group lacked knowledge of the business of minor-league sports, and the travel to places as distant as San Antonio, Texas, became increasingly more expensive. The brightest moment of the Force's last two seasons occurred on January 25, 2000, when the Coliseum hosted the CHL all-star game. Although eight inches of snow had fallen during the day, 6,128 people showed up.

In the late spring of 2001, the CHL announced that, as part of its amalgamation with the Western Professional Hockey League, its eastern franchises would be dropped. During the summer of 2001, rumors circulated that the chronically dollar-stressed Roanoke club of the East Coast Hockey League might relocate to Fayetteville. That did not happen, and there was no professional hockey at Crown Coliseum for the 2001–02 season.

Meanwhile, Bill Coffey had begun to organize the Atlantic Coast Hockey League, and Fayetteville figured largely in his plans. "It wasn't easy," said Kevin McNaught, now the FireAntz' president, who set about approaching Cape Fear–area investors who might support a new team. "We needed to raise $300,000 so that we could secure a lease, and many people felt leery about minor-league sports. When the Force folded, it left a lot of debts." McNaught gathered together eight local business people. "It was essential to have home-town ownership. They had the contacts with local businesses." Their presence gave potential sponsors and fans the assurance that the new club was not an operation that would last one or two years and then disappear. "One of the most important things they did," McNaught said, "was to honor the debts that the Force left behind. Our owners didn't have to do that, but it gave people faith in our organization."

A key element of marketing the newly formed hockey club was selecting a nickname. Although the military remained an important part of the fan base, the new owners did not, because of the off-ice difficulties of the CHL club, want to use the term "Force." After a name-the-team contest, FireAntz was selected because it was different, cute and, at the same time, feisty. The fire ant is known for its aggressiveness and its sharp bite (one of the early marketing slogans was "Get Bit").

Since the team started playing in fall 2003, the goodwill and hard work of the FireAntz' ownership group and front-office team have paid off. In the first season, 3,100 fans attended each game; the next year, after the ACHL had split into two leagues, the Antz of the South East Hockey League drew 200 fewer fans a game. In the third year, playing in what was now called the Southern Professional Hockey League, attendance returned to its first-year level. In the 2005–06 season, the FireAntz led the league with a 3,702 per-game attendance average. In early January it set a league attendance record for a single game when 7,750 people showed up. That occurred on a Tuesday night, a traditionally poor night for attendance, but the club promoted it as "Two Dollar Tuesday," offering groups 25 tickets for $50, and selling all concession items for $2. "It was a very low price for tickets," assistant general manager Lane Cody remarked, "but we generated $12,000 more income than the team usually did in midweek."

TUESDAY JANUARY 24, 2006

When visitors dropped in at the FireAntz' business offices on McPherson Church Road to buy tickets for a hockey game, there was a good chance they'd be greeted by a member of a dance team, a former major-league baseball umpire or a man who had once scored 25 points, seven of them goals, in a single British Hockey League game. Annie Taylor, Dallas

Parks and Kevin McNaught brought unusual backgrounds to the business of running the FireAntz.

Kevin McNaught, president and general manager, had had his astonishing night while playing for the Medway Bears in England. After playing Junior A with the Ottawa 67s of the Ontario Hockey League and college hockey at the University of Saskatchewan, he had packed his skates and moved to Europe, playing hockey there for 14 years. "In England, each team was allowed two imports; the rest were locals and they had pretty limited experience. The imports played 50 minutes a game, and you didn't like to take off your imports because when you did, the other team's imports would really go to town."

It was on a golf outing at Myrtle Beach at the end of one European season that McNaught met his future wife, a resident of the South Carolina resort town. He was back in England a few seasons later when his mother-in-law, no doubt wanting her daughter and grandchildren closer to home, sent him a clipping from the *Fayetteville Observer* that announced the arrival of a professional hockey team. After the 1996–97 English hockey season, he traveled to Fayetteville to visit the offices of the Force. "I said I wanted to work for them. I told them to just give me a desk and a cell phone and I'd work for commission." McNaught began to work for them soon after, and he said, with pride, "I'm also the only person who has seen every professional hockey game played at Crown Coliseum."

After the CHL left, McNaught, with his experience and contacts, was the logical choice to lead the effort to bring hockey back to town. He put together a group whose members had enjoyed success in real estate, retail sales, contracting, medicine and restaurant management. They had the necessary capital, as well as the contacts with local businesses that would insure the club acquired the requisite advertising sponsorships. Moreover, they inspired confidence in the club, which was vital if it were to survive, let alone thrive.

Even with the local corporate support, the FireAntz' continuing success depended on getting new people to come to a game and then making them repeat customers. "We've got to reach and keep a wider audience," McNaught said. "Some Canadians who have come to our games shake their heads; they think some of our promotions are hokey. But down here, you've got to entertain all the time—loud music, contests, giveaways, dancers and mascots—we have three mascots." The team put on special events such as Military Appreciation Nights, when the players wore camouflage-type jerseys that were auctioned off after the game. Recently, the FireAntz had given goalie-type masks made of foam to the first 1,000 children through the doors, and all children's seats were only five dollars for every game. "Nearly all of them are accompanied by at least one adult, who buys a full-priced ticket," McNaught explained. "And the adults buy lots of concessions."

He admitted that, although the fans' knowledge of the game was increasing, the aspect of hockey that a large number of the people who came to Crown Coliseum most enjoyed was the fighting. He noted that in many southern cities, when the fights decreased, so did the number of people who came to the games. "Earlier this year we won 13 straight home games, and a season-ticket holder complained to me that there weren't enough fights. Some people think that it's like the WWE; they don't understand that the fights are real, that it takes real courage to get involved. You risk humiliation if you lose and, more important, you risk injury."

On a table outside the office next to McNaught's lay a pile of posters that bore the caption "Ice Hockey Just Got a Little Hotter." The oxymoron wasn't another marketing slogan, like the previous season's "Fire on Ice," but a statement about the Sting Dancers, a local troupe that performed during the hockey games and at various club functions in the area. When fans arrived at a game, the Sting Dancers were there passing out giveaways and game notes. During the intermissions they did

The Sting Dancers—from left to right, Annie Taylor, Kristy Feltis, Danielle Gooden, Kim Sublett, Ashley Brookhouse, Brittany Edwards and Winter Jojola—perform regularly at FireAntz games. For some fans, coming to Crown Coliseum isn't just about hockey.

a dance routine on the ice, threw out T-shirts and helped with the other promotions. They also performed on a stage beside the rink during short stoppages of play.

Third from the left on the poster, posing in her black dance garb, was Annie Taylor, the FireAntz' public relations coordinator, who had joined the dance group two years earlier. As a member of the hockey team's front office, Annie spent much of her time arranging the public appearances of the players. "We've taken a hockey net out to a local mall, and one of our goalies lets kids take shots with a foam puck. We've helped one of our local sponsors, the Saturn dealership, with their safety program of fingerprinting children."

This week the major public appearances involved players and front-office staff visiting Teresa C. Berrien Elementary School to participate in Celebrity Reading Week. Today the reader was Jason Fleming, FireAntz vice-president of communications, who'd grown up in Orange County, California, an avid booster of the Los Angeles Kings. In fact, when he'd lived on the West Coast, his car bore a vanity license plate: "Grets 99." "I'd seen a plate that said 'Luuuk,' which was what the fans used to call out when Luc Robitaille came out onto the ice, and I thought one about Gretzky would be cool. I had to go through three or four variations before I found one that wasn't taken."

Before he began reading Chris Van Allsburg's *Jumanji* to the Grade 3 class assembled in the school library, Fleming captured the children's attention by rolling up his left pant leg and showing them a scar just below his knee—a souvenir from a hockey injury. The boys

Jason Fleming visits a Fayetteville elementary school during Celebrity Reading Week. School librarian Carla Brooks looks on as he answers questions. Most of the boys wanted to talk about hockey injuries, not about the importance of reading in his work.

gasped in awe and admiration; only the gentle reminders from librarian Carla Brooks about listening manners returned their focus to the book. Fleming led the children through the story like an experienced reading teacher, inviting their responses to details in the plot and illustrations. The follow-up question-and-answer period, which was supposed to be related to the value of reading and writing in Fleming's work, quickly turned to queries about cars and sports. Again Carla Brooks refocused the children. The hour closed with each child receiving a team poster and a program containing a picture of Fleming, which he autographed. "I'm going to be a hockey player when I grow up," one boy proudly announced.

When he returned to the team office, Fleming conferred briefly with Dallas Parks, director of sales, who had umpired in the American League for 15 years and had also been an important factor in the FireAntz' off-ice success. Parks compared his current job to the one in which he wore a navy blue uniform. "I've always said that if you're going to succeed as an umpire, you have to be able to sell every call you make. That requires people skills and confidence in what you're doing." Although his father groomed him to become a major-league baseball player, those plans came to an end when Parks was attending Florida State University and tore an Achilles tendon while playing a pickup basketball game at his fraternity.

A decade later he returned to the baseball diamond, this time as a minor-league umpire. He moved quickly up the ranks and by 1979 was officiating in the American League. "I was involved in a lot of historic games," Parks remembered, including Disco Demolition Night, a notorious promotion in which vinyl records were burned at Chicago's Comiskey Park. When fans stormed onto the field during the event, which was being staged between games of a doubleheader, the second game was canceled and the home team, the White Sox, lost by a forfeit.

A few years after he retired as a major-league umpire, Parks moved to Fayetteville, where he began working with the Fayetteville Swampdogs, an amateur baseball team, selling fence and program advertising. It was here that he met one of the FireAntz' owners, Howard Bullard, who invited Parks to join the hockey operation as director of sales. When he accepted the job, he had a rudimentary knowledge of the game, but after seeing a few contests he came to the conclusion that "hockey players are the greatest athletes in the world; they have to be. As soon as the puck is dropped, they go full blast for a minute or two. It's no wonder they need a rest; it's as if they were sprinters going at 100-yard-dash speed for 45 seconds."

Although his appreciation of the sport and its players grew with every game he watched, Parks didn't believe that a knowledge of hockey was necessary to sell the corporate sponsorships that generated well over one-third of the team's revenue. "It's common knowledge that sports advertising is one of the largest forms of marketing in America. Advertisers get the biggest bang for their buck there, and because hockey fans are among the most affluent sports spectators and because we outdraw minor-league basketball, football and baseball in this area, sponsors are attracted to us. We found that sponsors get a strong revenue return when they invest with us. And we try to make them as happy as we can so that they'll come back." The ice and the boards at the Crown Coliseum were adorned with over six dozen advertisements. During games, an additional 46 banners were hung around the concourse, and the names of area businesses that sponsored starting lineups, power plays, penalty kills and post-period and game summaries were flashed on the large center-ice scoreboard.

Parks was very appreciative of the players' contributions to the community. On a shelf beside his desk was a stack of five or six wall clocks, each with a picture of a FireAntz player on the clock face. Every year, Parks made one for each member of the team. "I want them to know how much we appreciate their coming to Fayetteville. They're not paid much, but they give so much of their time to the community."

WEDNESDAY, JANUARY 25, 2006

Because FireAntz coach Derek Booth wanted B.J. Stephens, a newly acquired forward who had arrived in town at noon, to skate with the team, morning practice had been moved to three in the afternoon. However, by one o'clock the ice surface was occupied. Shut out of their home rink by the arrival of the rodeo, the SPHL's Pee Dee Cyclones had had to make the 83-mile drive from Florence, South Carolina. "By the time the hockey team had been formed in the summer, the arena had booked a lot of events," coach Mark Richards explained. "In fact, we go 24 days without a home game later this season." Fortunately, the FireAntz did not face these difficulties over practice ice. There was an ice rink at nearby Fort Bragg. It had been built so that there would be a large cold-storage area that could be transformed into a morgue should a major disaster occur.

As the Cyclones skated, Derek Booth sat high in the stands, observing his team's Friday night opponent and reminiscing about his life in hockey. Growing up in Niagara Falls, Ontario, he had had a picture of Bobby Orr on his bedroom wall and admired Edmonton Oiler defenseman Paul Coffey. "I loved watching offensive defensemen," he remarked. Booth played four years in the Ontario Hockey League and, in the fall of 1991, attended the Detroit Red Wings' camp. He turned professional with Toledo of the ECHL that same year and, after recovering from an early season knee injury, finished the year with the Phoenix Roadrunners of the International Hockey League. "It was a great year for learning," he said, "playing with experienced skaters who stressed positional play. From the ECHL, the IHL, to the National Hockey League, I saw how players became smarter and faster. And I realized how important it was to develop a good work ethic."

Booth got his first taste of southern hockey in South Carolina when he became the first player to sign a Stingrays contract. "My fiancée, Brenda, and I loved to travel, and this seemed like a great place to spend a winter. But the irony was that I got called up to Rochester of the American Hockey League before the season started and spent the whole

FireAntz coach Derek Booth (left) shares a joke with assistant coach Kory Baker before he begins to diagram a drill to be worked on during practice.

year there." He did spend the next year in South Carolina, but then the
travel bug hit. A friend suggested that he come to play in Austria. "I told
him not to tell Brenda, but he did, and so we went. They only play 40
games a season over there, so we had lots of opportunity to travel."

After four years, Booth found that he missed the North American
style of play. "I was getting older. I realized that if I wanted to stay
in the game, coaching would give me that opportunity. And I would
have to refamiliarize myself with hockey back home." In the summer
of 2003, Ray Edwards offered him the role of playing assistant coach
with the San Angelo Saints of the CHL. The 2003–04 season marked
the culmination of what had been many years of an almost unconscious
apprenticeship. "I'd always been very interested in coaches' approaches
to the game. When I was with Ray Edwards, I really understood that,
no matter how much you know about hockey, the most important thing
was to respect the game and the players."

Asked to describe his own coaching style, Booth quickly replied,
"I'm a systems man. That means the players have to know their roles
on the ice and as members of the team. It's important to have intelligent
players, ones who can learn systems and who like to use them." For
example, he continued, when the FireAntz acquired Kory Baker in the
middle of the 2004–05 season, Booth recognized that, even though
the new acquisition was only 24, he had a keen knowledge of the game
and had quickly gained the respect of his new teammates. "I saw that he
had the potential to become a coach in the future, and after the season I
asked him if he'd like to be a playing assistant coach."

Booth went on to stress that he believed it was important for a coach
in the lower levels of professional hockey to be sensitive to the situation
of the players. "They're not making very much money at all, and they
have some pretty grueling bus trips. I'm only a year and a half away
from my playing days, so I know what it's like. I think that helps me a
lot on this job."

How did Booth put together a team, seeing that the FireAntz did
not have an affiliation with a higher-level club that could send younger
players to him for seasoning? "First," he explained, "I start with a core
group returning from last season." Nine members of the current roster
played in Fayetteville in 2004–05. "Then Kory and I talked about the
kind of club we wanted to create—one that focused on puck control
and hard hitting. We got some names from coaches and GMs I know

and from agents. But our players are our best recruiters. When they like our program, they tell their friends, and those players get in contact with us. Over the summer, Dean Jackson told us about Mike Clarke, whom he'd played with at Elmira College. Mike made the team, and now he's the top-scoring defenseman in the league."

Booth did not agree with the idea that motivation must be a problem in a league where the chances of moving to the AHL and then to the NHL were very slight. "The kids aren't prospects, but they want to prove themselves because, if they do, there's a possibility of landing a regular job in the CHL or the United Hockey League. Every year, two or three guys from each club in the league move up. And the veterans motivate themselves. Some of them hope that they can move into coaching. They love the competition, and they still have the passion."

"The passion"—the phrase Booth applied to the veterans—was a term that players frequently used to describe their relationship with the sport; it seemed to be the emotional, almost spiritual energy that kept them return-ing in spite of the long bus rides and small paychecks. For himself, Booth said, "It's knowing every day that I can get up, go to my job at the rink and love it. The hockey team is like a sec-ond family. I work with 18 younger brothers and chil-dren. I think when you don't have hockey, it's like having a dark hole in your heart."

The memory of the Great One lives on in Fayette-ville, North Carolina. Jason Fleming, FireAntz vice-president of communications, purchased this Gretzky license plate when he lived in south-ern California.

About the leader of his first family, his wife Brenda, he added, "She's my 13-year veteran, my road warrior. She has stuck with me through all the highs and lows. And thank goodness she loves to travel."

Booth's team, which took the ice for what would be a very strenuous, demanding, nearly two-hour practice, was less experienced than teams in the CHL, UHL and ECHL. The players ranged in age from 23 to 29 and had played an average of just under three and a half seasons. Nine had spent time in the ECHL—periods ranging from brief three- or four-game call-ups to Mike Clarke's 43 games and Scott Corbett's 67. Four players—Corbett, Tim Schneider, Gavin Hodgson and Mark Phenow—had played briefly in the ECHL during the present season, but none of the FireAntz had appeared in the IHL or the AHL, and no members of the current roster had been selected in an NHL draft.

The team included three players who had not been with the club a week earlier, and it was without an equal number who had been either traded or released. The FireAntz, who had opened the season with 13 consecutive home victories, had slumped in recent weeks, winning only 2 of their last 10 games, and Booth had made personnel moves in an attempt to reverse the team's fortunes. In addition, he was trying to find healthy bodies for his struggling team: two players had suffered season-ending injuries and two others were questionable starters for the weekend's games.

As the practice wound down, a new player, one who looked considerably older than all of the others at the practice, stepped onto the ice and began to skate with George Nistas and Nick Kormanyos. He was 39-year-old Jimmy Diamantopoulos, the owner of Miami Subs and a major corporate sponsor of the FireAntz. He'd played hockey as a boy in Montreal and had been a devoted fan of Guy Lafleur and later,

Fayetteville restaurant owner Jimmy Diamantopoulos lines up between FireAntz players Nick Kormanyos (left) and George Nistas to form the "Greek Connection." Diamantopoulos was preparing for a 30-second shift with the pair as part of a promotion saluting local businesses.

when he lived in Pittsburgh, of Mario Lemieux. A few months after he'd moved to Fayetteville, a customer entered his restaurant wearing a FireAntz jersey. "I didn't know there was a professional team in town; I thought it was a high school team," Diamantopoulos remembered. He soon bought season tickets, purchased rink and program advertising, and made his restaurant a gathering place for players.

Kevin McNaught had come up with the idea of having a local businessman play a 30-second shift with the club at the beginning of a game and, knowing of the restaurateur's on-ice experience, invited him to be that businessman-player. Asked what kind of a signing bonus he received, Diamantopoulos laughed and said that his agent was still working on it. He had acquired a nickname, "The Secret Weapon," and said that, after he appeared briefly on the evening television news, he'd signed dozens of autographs. As a businessman, he saw the value of the promotion. "More people know about my restaurant, and the Greek community is going to show up at the arena on February 12, the day I play. Already they've bought nearly 400 tickets." Jimmy would be on a line with Nistas and Kormanyos. "We've had the French Connection," he remarked, referring to the famous Buffalo Sabres line of the 1970s. "Now we have the Greek Connection."

By six o'clock, only one player remained at the rink. Team captain Mike Fournier had showered and donned his sweat suit and was waiting for 6:30 to arrive. At that time, he'd begin his volunteer duties as an instructor in youth hockey and learn-to-skate classes.

Although he grew up in Charlton, a small eastern Massachusetts town, none of the Boston Bruins were his heroes. Instead he looked up to his cousin, who played at Boston College, and his own little brother. "He played Triple A hockey," Fournier explained, "and I only made it to Double A." It was when he moved to the Moncton Wildcats of the Quebec Major Junior Hockey League, where he became a teammate of Kory Baker, that his hockey education really began. "It was a tough league, and the players worked long hours on and off the ice. I had to learn to move the puck quickly and to skate better. I didn't realize before how passionate Canadians were about training."

At the end of the 2000–01 season, Fournier earned a one-game try-out with the Jackson (Mississippi) Bandits of the ECHL. "They picked me up at the Jackson airport and took me to the team bus. We drove to Lafayette, Louisiana, and I played on the fourth line. I'd dump the puck in and chase it." He also experienced, for the first time, the nature of hockey fans in the South. "They were enthusiastic," he remembered, "but not too knowledgeable." In the fall, he received an invitation to attend the South Carolina Stingrays' camp. Although he was cut and sent to Fayetteville, he discovered in Charleston another important element of professional hockey in the South: the close bond that develops between a team and the fans. "I met Brett Marietti (one of the Stingrays' veterans), and I thought it was awesome how he'd established himself in the town and started a business. He'd created a life after hockey in Charleston."

Fournier split his first two professional seasons between Cape Fear (as Fayetteville was then known) FireAntz, St. Petersburg/Winston-Salem Parrots, Knoxville Ice Bears and Orlando Seals—all of them teams in the ACHL and its various successors. At 20, the youngest player in the ACHL during his rookie season, he considered retiring during his second season. However, in Orlando he became a forward as well as a stay-at-home defenseman and found he enjoyed the freedom of skating in deep and having the chance to score. His six goals in 48 games were a personal season high.

Fournier found himself back in Fayetteville at the beginning of the 2004–05 season, playing for a new coach, Derek Booth, who named the 22-year-old his team captain. "I had to grow up quickly; it took at least until Christmas." In addition to assigning him the role of captain, Booth gave him the responsibility of being the team's tough guy. "Derek said that he wanted me to find my role. My job is to protect my guys." He'd been doing this so well in the 2005–06 season that he had already accumulated 108 minutes in penalties.

His efforts had certainly been appreciated by the Fayetteville fans. "They love goals and fights," Fournier remarked. "If you do one or the other, they'll love you. They're always asking me if the fights are staged, and I explain that there's always a purpose to them, to protect the smaller players or to get the team going." However, he was not above embellishment. "If this is my role," Fournier laughed, "I might as well have a little fun. When I fight in home games, I skate to center ice and they play my fight song, 'The Big Show' from WWE. For a while this season I had a Mohawk and wore a handlebar moustache. Some little kids wore Mohawks after they saw me at the games."

Fournier viewed his situation in the SPHL realistically. "I'm like the rest of the guys; we know we won't ever make it to the NHL, but we love to play.

I only bring home $185 a week, and I have a part-time job, but I still have the passion. It's great to get up in the morning, go to the rink and strap on the skates." His interaction with the people of the town was also important to him. "You get to know people very quickly here; they love to talk with you when they see you in town."

One of the most important fan relationships came when he saw children wearing hockey sweaters with his number, "34," on them. "It's tough to describe. The first time it happened, I felt a little giddy. You don't realize how much of an effect you have on children." At this point, one

FireAntz captain Mike Fournier regularly returns to Crown Coliseum on weeknights to volunteer as an instructor in the youth learn-to-skate and hockey programs. Here he enjoys a turn around the ice with one of his fans, seven-year-old Anthony Lane.

of Fournier's biggest fans, seven-year-old Anthony Lane, clomped down to the player's bench, dressed in a FireAntz jersey with the number "34" on the back. The FireAntz' captain helped him lace up his skates, and together they stepped on the deserted ice and, passing the puck between them, skated toward the goal.

THURSDAY, JANUARY 26, 2006

The first FireAnt to arrive at Crown Coliseum each morning was equipment manager Clay Roffer; the second was frequently Kory Baker, the assistant coach, who suited up before meeting with Derek Booth. On this day, Baker and Booth planned to go over the ways they could make the shortened practice an effective preparation for that night's opponent, the Florida Seals. The FireAntz were tied for second place with the Columbus (Georgia) Cottonmouths and were only two points ahead of the Seals. It was important they win because, while the chances of not making the playoffs were slim—six of the league's seven clubs qualify— the top three teams would have home-ice advantage for the first round, a two-out-of-three-games series. Moreover, a victory would end a streak of four consecutive home losses, which would please the fans and, quite possibly, increase attendance for Friday night's contest.

The practice over, the 25-year-old from Miramichi, New Brunswick, who as a young player admired the gritty play of the Toronto Maple Leafs' Wendel Clark, sank deeply into one of the very old couches that furnished the players' lounge. He gently flexed his recently dislocated right shoulder, an injury that would not prevent him from appearing in the evening's contest, but would certainly limit his playing time.

When he was 17, Baker traveled from the Maritimes to the tiny town of Wilcox, in southern Saskatchewan, in order to enroll in the Athol Murray College of Notre Dame, a school that attracted hockey players from across Canada and around the world. The institution balanced time for studies with time for playing on one of its 17 teams. "It was an unbelievable experience. I really grew up—they taught you about life." Teachers and coaches frequently invoked the spirit of Father Athol Murray, the school's legendary leader, a man whose influence on both the place and its young charges was so great that, Baker noted, "There have apparently been sightings of his ghost."

At Notre Dame, Baker learned to play a sound defensive game. For the two years after graduation, he skated as a member of Moncton and then Val-d'Or of the Quebec Major Junior Hockey League, where he learned offense. When he was traded to Val-d'Or early in his second season, he was reluctant to leave his teammates and the loyal Moncton fans. However, he found that the small town embraced the team. "They all loved us," he remarked. The Foreurs, whose goalie Maxime Daigneault was now a member of the South Carolina Stingrays, earned a berth in the Memorial Cup and traveled to Regina, less than an hour's drive from Notre Dame, for the tournament. "We lost the final game to Red Deer in overtime," Baker remembered. "It still hurts when I think about it."

Baker's performance as a junior earned him a tryout the next fall at the training camp of the AHL's Wilkes-Barre (Pennsylvania) Penguins. He was assigned to Wheeling, West Virginia, of the ECHL, but elected instead to play with El Paso of the CHL, where he knew the assistant coach, also from Miramichi.

Like so many players who toiled for the Buzzards in far western Texas, Baker experienced culture shock. "We drove into the parking lot one morning, and on a vacant field beside it there must have been a hundred kids chasing a soccer ball. It was like being in a Third World country." He recalled the Buzzards' narrow rink—"It gave us a real advantage over visiting teams"—the rickety boards and the brown spots on the ice created by leaks coming through the rusty roof. "Going to the locker room between periods was terrible," he continued. "We had to go through an area behind the ice surface that was a holding area for rodeo animals. Even if there weren't cows there, it really smelled awful. Then we had to climb a flight of 20 stairs to get to the locker room." He also remembered Mexican Night, when the arena was jammed with close to 8,000 singing, whistling and clapping fans. "I think most of them were from Juarez. I'm sure they didn't know what was happening on the ice. But they seemed to be having fun—they sure were noisy."

In the early part of the 2002–03 season, Baker skated for Arkansas and then Cincinnati of the ECHL and learned about the politics of minor-league hockey. "If you're not a contract player [owned by an NHL or AHL team], you don't have much control of your destiny. I think your jobs are more secure here in the SPHL than in the ECHL. It's much more of a developmental league. Younger players who aren't under contract get much more ice time than they would in the ECHL." Baker finished the season with the Jacksonville Barracudas and played with them until the middle of the 2004–05 season, when he was traded to the FireAntz.

During the off-season, Coach Booth invited him to become a playing assistant coach. "I've thought about coaching for a long time," Baker remarked. "I feel that I really know the game within the game and that I can communicate. I think it's something you're born with. Derek is more defensive-minded and I'm more offensive, so we complement each other. I help a lot with the power play. I'm vocal in the locker room, and I try to lead by example on and off the ice. I think the key is developing a mutual respect with the other players." When his playing career ends, Baker would definitely like to coach. "In fact, if Derek moved to another club, I'd certainly like to follow him and be his assistant."

While Baker was leading the FireAntz through a power-play drill, the evening's opponents, the Florida Seals, entered their dressing room. They'd arrived in town early Wednesday evening after a nine-hour bus ride from Kissimmee. Immediately following that night's game, they'd make a seven-hour trip to Knoxville, and on Friday night the team would travel five or six hours to Columbus, Georgia. Saturday night it would be back on the bus for the eight-hour drive home. The following Monday, they'd have a 40-mile bus trip to Cocoa Beach for practice, something they'd do for home practices throughout February. "Our ice isn't available, and other arenas nearby are very expensive. It's cheaper to go out of town," explained coach Tommy Stewart.

At five o'clock, the FireAntz players, neatly groomed and wearing suits and ties, as required on game day, returned to the arena and began their various activities. Because he would not be starting that evening's game, goalie Glenn Ridler did not have to undergo what was, as he explained it, a very complicated ritual. "I'm pretty normal for half an hour when I arrive for a game, and then I stop talking to everyone. I run two laps of the concourse below the upper bowl, do stretching exercises and then put on the gear for the lower half of my body, grab a squeezable ball and go to the ice." He would hand the ball to a security woman standing by the players' box, perform 10 stretches to his glove side and 10 butterfly kneels, leave the ice, retrieve the ball and proceed to a wall

behind the dressing room. "I lean the stick and blocker glove against the wall and throw the ball 10 times so that it bounces to my stomach, and twice so that I have to make glove saves. Then I go back to my stall and finish dressing."

Growing up in Guelph, Ontario, Ridler began playing as a forward because his father, a goalie himself, insisted that his son first learn to become a good skater. "He said it would make me a better goalie. He was always my goalie hero, so I did. Then one day, our regular goalie had to miss a game and I

Goalie Glenn Ridler compares two different masks: his ornately decorated game equipment and the foam rubber masks given out to children at a recent game.

filled in." His dad's advice paid off; Ridler played for two seasons in the Ontario Hockey League, first with Kingston, then London and finally Belleville. He spent another year in Junior B, but found it difficult at that level to get noticed by scouts. That is why, when he heard of a new independent professional league starting up in the American Midwest, he decided to try out, hoping that exposure there would attract the notice of coaches in higher leagues.

He joined the Lansing (Michigan) Ice Nuts of the International Independent Hockey League, which began play in the fall of 2003 with teams in Michigan, Ohio and Indiana. The number of teams constantly fluctuated, the schedule was in a state of continuous revision and various minor-league hockey forums on the Internet were filled with tales of alleged underhanded dealings and poor treatment of players. The league suspended operations shortly after Christmas, promising first a restructured league and, later, a spring tournament, neither of which came to pass. "The horror stories were true," Ridler remarked. "Some people I knew had to pay for ice time to practice, and I heard that a bus driver left players from an Ohio team on the side of the road because he hadn't been paid."

However, his eight games for the Ice Nuts, played before two-figure "crowds" in Michigan State University's huge arena, accomplished what Ridler desired. "We went eight and nothing in the games I started, and that opened some eyes in the SPHL." The Lansing coach knew Scott Rex, then coach of the FireAntz, who offered the goalie a tryout. "It was going from No Man's Land to a shaky league. But the SPHL has become a lot more stable since then." Ridler appeared in 15 games, posting a respectable 3.58 goals-against average. "I'd faced some strong shooters in the OHL, so that adjustment wasn't too great."

The next year he played four games for the Dundee Stars of the British National League. "I had a very good time there; it was a lot of fun. Each team was allowed seven imports, so there were two good lines. The other players were of Junior B caliber. I had to slow the speed of my reaction time to their shots. Otherwise, it was like swinging at a knuckleball in baseball." He returned to Fayetteville late in the 2004–05 season and rejoined the club this year, playing a large part in its early season success. He enjoyed the wins the club earned while he was in the goal, but it made his diet a little monotonous. "When we're on a winning streak," he explained, "I never change my pre-game meal."

As the players began their pre-game warm-ups, the two members of the media took their places at two banquet tables located on risers behind the final row of seats. Brett Friedlander, hockey beat reporter for the *Fayetteville Observer*, explained the origin of what, after eight seasons of pro hockey at Crown Coliseum, was still a makeshift press box. "The day before the official opening, the arena manager gave me a complete tour of the facility. When it was over, I asked him where the press box was. His jaw dropped and his face went white," the reporter remembered. "It turned out that during the planning stages, no one had thought about the media. At least now the tables are on risers. At first there were just tables behind the seats. When there were big crowds and people stood up, it was hard to see the action."

As various FireAntz are traded or removed from the active roster because of injury, their names are taken from their lockers and placed on a bulletin board in a storage room.

Friedlander remembered the comedy of errors that marked opening night: long lines at the main box office when other ticket windows around the arena had no lines at all; long-winded speeches by dignitaries and an invocation so extended that fans became restless; a Zamboni that didn't work. "They sent an emergency call to Fort Bragg to borrow theirs. It arrived on a flatbed truck and got the ice ready for the second period. The driver of Fort Bragg's Zamboni looked at the broken one and discovered the problem: the Coliseum's driver had forgotten to turn on an important switch!" As the game was winding down, around 11:30 p.m., the announcer apologized to fans, explaining that games weren't usually this long. But by that time, most of the crowd of 4,100 had gone home.

At the second table, Adam Minnick, the Seals' director of media relations and broadcasting, set up his radio equipment. Now in his fourth year of broadcasting play-by-play in the South, he'd worked for the FireAntz until management decided to discontinue radio broadcasts, then moved to Macon to do the games for the Trax. However, midway through the season, with the team losing money, the ownership decided to cut costs by canceling the broadcasts. This year, Minnick, along with former Macon coach Tommy Stewart and several players, had joined the expansion Seals franchise.

"Radio broadcasts in the South," Minnick explained, "provide a service to the diehard fans and a three-hour commercial for the team." Doing play-by-play for fans who may not be familiar with the rules and certainly do not know the intricacies of the game required a different approach than the one he would use if he were in the upper Midwest or New England. "It's like writing a newspaper article on a subject most readers are not familiar with. You talk to them at a lower level. In a way, you're a teacher, not just explaining the rules, but explaining why, for example, a power play was successful or not, or maybe why certain lineups are put on the ice." Minnick admitted that he always wanted the Seals to win, but he strove to be honest and to be critical of the team when it deserved it. "It's tough to call a losing game, especially during a losing streak. And I really dislike a road loss: it makes the bus trip after the game long, quiet and gloomy."

The game started slowly before a subdued weeknight crowd of just over 2,000. However, the fans rose to their feet at 8:30 of the first period when Andrew Katzberg of the Seals charged FireAntz goalie Chad Collins. Fayetteville newcomer Chris Ferguson came to his fallen comrade's defense, dropping his gloves and, to the spectators' delight, scoring an obvious victory over Katzberg. "Ferguson's fight endeared him to the team right away," Derek Booth later remarked.

The FireAntz scored the game's only goal 55 seconds into the second period, when Scott Corbett broke through the defense to put the puck behind Seals goalie Terry Denike. Chad Collins, who had joined the Fayetteville team a week earlier, made 27 saves to earn the win. After the match was over, Corbett was named the player of the game, while Ferguson received the Glass Rattler of the Game award, which was sponsored by Metz Auto Glass, a local firm.

An hour after the game, as the Florida Seals began their long, quiet and gloomy bus ride to Knoxville, Johnathan Peterson and Jeremi Del-Campo, the evening's referee and linesman respectively, settled down to a post-game snack at a local restaurant. Peterson, from Waupara, Wisconsin, and DelCampo, who grew up in Spokane, Washington, faced traveling schedules more daunting than those of the players. A member of USA Hockey's officials development program, Peterson had flown to the Southeast on Wednesday, and the next week he would fly to Alaska. DelCampo had driven from his present residence in Charlotte, North Carolina, and would remain in town for the next night's game. He'd return home Friday night so that he and his wife could shop for new furniture, but in the middle of the next week he'd head to western Virginia for a UHL game, and on the weekend he'd go to northern Florida.

Both had begun to officiate at an early age. Peterson, now 23, was involved in youth hockey as a player and referee. "Refereeing was a way to earn some money on the weekend." Later, as a student at Harvard, majoring in economics and Spanish, he played junior varsity and officiated games in the eastern Massachusetts area. "After graduation I thought about law school, but I realized that I wanted to referee more than anything." The 2005–06 season marked his first year in professional hockey. "The players here are smarter and the play is quicker," he observed. "When you work the games, you realize that you're dealing with men, not boys."

DelCampo became an official because he broke a cardinal rule of hockey when he was 12 years old. "In a game I was playing, I got knocked down pretty hard," he recalled, "and when I looked up, the referee was standing over me. I don't know why, but I hit him." He was given a three-game suspension and had planned to spend the next weekend away from the rink. "But I got a phone call from the league administrator saying that they were short a linesman on Saturday. She knew I wouldn't be playing and wondered if I could help out. When I showed up at the rink, the referee was the guy I'd hit." DelCampo officiated youth games in Spokane and went on to work games in the North American Hockey League, Western Hockey League and CHL. Like Peterson, he spent time with USA Hockey's officials development program.

At this point, a young man sipping a beer at a nearby table approached the officials and asked if they were players from the Florida team. When they identified themselves, he introduced himself as Chris Ferguson, the FireAnt to whom Peterson had given a fighting penalty in the first period. The three talked briefly about their travels in hockey, comparing notes on arenas and cities they'd been to, until a young waitress, anxious to close the restaurant, presented her remaining patrons with their bills. They paid and walked across the parking lot to the motel where they were all staying, ready for a well-earned night's rest. Meanwhile, in the hills of western North Carolina, the Seals' bus moved through the night, bringing its now-sleeping passengers closer to their next game.

FRIDAY JANUARY 27, 2006

On his second morning as a member of the FireAntz, forward Scott Zwiers missed practice. But he would not be assessed the $100 fine usually imposed for absence, because he had a very good excuse. At ten o'clock, when the other players were taking the ice, he was piloting a C-130 Hercules cargo plane for his other employer, the United States Air Force.

It had been an exciting few days for the forward from suburban Chicago. Earlier in the week he'd called FireAntz coach Derek Booth to ask if he could skate for him. He'd heard that the club occasionally needed emergency short-term replacements and figured he might as well let the coach know he was around. After all, for four seasons he'd been a member of the Air Force Academy team in the top-level Western Collegiate Hockey Association. He hadn't played competitively for two and a half years, but he had nothing to lose by making the six-mile drive from Pope Air Force Base to Crown Coliseum. What he didn't realize was that three of the team's forwards had injuries.

Zwiers had showed up at the arena just after eight in the morning, even before Clay Roffer. When Coach Booth showed up, he didn't ask the newcomer to take a solitary skate and shoot a few pucks at the net; he asked him to dress in full equipment and join the team in practice. After the workout was over, Zwiers got news that was both good and bad. Booth offered him a five-game professional tryout, beginning with that evening's contest against the Florida Seals. But that meant he'd have to cancel a dinner engagement with his wife's parents, who were coming to town later in the afternoon. Instead, he left two tickets for them and another for his wife at the will-call window. He didn't have a shift during Thursday's game, but he had acquired three more tickets for the Friday game, and his family would see him take two shifts late in the third period.

While the players were skating, Roffer and Lee Fowler, director of hockey operations, met in the equipment room to check on the team's stick supply and order however many more would be needed to see the team through the rest of the season and the playoffs. It wasn't a simple matter of ordering a number of left- or right-handed sticks of specific lies; they had to consider the composition of the stick shafts and blades. In addition to the old-fashioned one-piece wooden sticks, players could now choose between one-piece composite alloy sticks and a number of combinations of composite shafts or shafts with wooden cores, as well as wooden or composite blades.

Roffer explained that the team made four or five orders a season and that the stick budget for an SPHL team could run up to $15,000 a year.

He noted that some players liked the composite sticks because of their lightness, but others preferred sticks whose composition better transferred the feel of the puck. Jeff Coulter used very few sticks, while Scott Corbett and Dean Jackson could go through two or three in a given week. Some players thought they needed a new blade each game; others felt that a stick only had a certain number of good shots in it and got rid of it when that total had been reached. Roffer recalled that when he worked for the Orlando Seals, one of the goalies insisted on retaping his stick before every game, while another would never use the same stick for both a practice and a game.

Equipment manager Clay Roffer carries a basket of stick blades into the FireAntz' locker room. Players mix and match wooden and composite alloy shafts and blades to suit their personal preferences.

After the brief practice, Rob Meanchoff, one of the players still using a one-piece wooden blade, remarked, "They feel right, and I like the weight and the ability to feel the puck through the stick. How could thousands and thousands of players who used wooden sticks for so many years be wrong?"

Meanchoff, who grew up admiring Wendel Clark and Rick Tocchet for their grittiness, played Tier II junior hockey in the hope of earning an athletic scholarship at an American university. When no scholarships were forthcoming, he enrolled at the University of Ottawa, only to find he couldn't get a dorm room. "The coach wanted me to try out for the hockey team, and I said that I would if I could get a dorm room. I got the room and made the team. Playing there rekindled my relationship with the game. I had decided to play to get accommodations on campus; now it was hockey that kept me in school."

After graduation, Meanchoff wanted to play at the highest level he could, and he accepted a tryout with the Tulsa Oilers of the CHL. Asked what it was like playing in the South, he answered, "For the first time in my playing career there were fans coming out to watch games I was playing in" and went on to explain that initially he was surprised to find out how little they understood the game. "They tried to equate an off-side with offsides in football, and they couldn't make sense of our rules. But they were very supportive. I've played my three professional years in the South, and I've made friends that I'll have for all my life."

Moving from Canadian university hockey to the CHL and then, in the fall of 2004, to the SPHL, Meanchoff had to make many adjustments. "In college hockey, we worked all week on perfecting systems. When I came to the CHL, I expected more Xs and Os, but I found that there was a lot of improvisation. I had to learn to think quickly on the ice. When I came to the SPHL, I found that our best lines were about equal to the CHL's second lines. If you take away their top three or four players and best goalie, an SPHL team could give them a good game."

Meanchoff admitted that he'd frequently thought about a question many people have asked him: Why, with a university degree and very little chance of playing even one NHL game, is he playing for under $200 a week? "Why?" he replied. "It's because we can. Hockey guys are the best guys in the world. We don't want to be like some players who didn't try pro and look back with regret, saying, 'I should have done that.'" He added that he still had "the passion" and noted that, at the University of Ottawa, they were told that "passion" was one of the five pillars of the game. "It's about the game, about the people around you. It's much more than just what happens on the ice."

Meanchoff was a realist; he knew his playing career could not last forever. Already he was preparing for life after hockey. The previous summer he had worked for Banks and Dean, a Toronto-based business-consulting firm, and this season, after each practice, he would go back to his apartment and, with the aid of his computer and telephone, do consulting work for the company. That night at the press table, Brett Friedlander explained that because Meanchoff received paychecks for this work, he took the minimum salary from the hockey team, which meant Derek Booth had extra cash he could use to attract much-needed replacements for his injury-riddled team.

By 5:30, the players had changed out of their suits and were donning the black undergarments over which, in an hour or so, they'd be strapping their pads and pulling on socks, hockey pants and jerseys. A few minutes away from entering his ritualistic cone of silence, Glenn Ridler, who would be the starting goalie, fiddled with his mask, which he'd decorated with pictures of the Riddler from *Batman* comics and on which he'd printed the question "Can you solve this riddle?" Several other players carrying stick blades and shafts wandered over to a long table just outside the equipment room.

The table was marked with scratches and gouges and scarred with burn marks. Attached at one end was a vise, and scattered on the top were a blowtorch, a couple of hacksaws and vise-grips, scissors and rolls of white and black tape. For the next half-hour, players sawed shafts to the desired lengths; applied flames to the bottom ends of shafts, heating them so that they'd expand enough for the short shafts of blades to be inserted; placed blades in the vise and gently heated them to create the desired curves. Finished sticks were then tightly taped and inspected. More than one player, after looking at the finished product, shook his head, reached for a pair of scissors, cut and then ripped the tape off and started over again. Like a warrior preparing implements for battle, making sure each weapon was exactly as he desired, each player had to be satisfied with his stick, knowing that otherwise he'd lack the confidence in the passes and shots he'd be making during the game.

As he worked on a stick blade, gently twisting it and then securing it in a shaft, Rob Whidden, a 25-year-old rookie from Coquitlam, B.C., remembered when he was a child, showing up bleary-eyed for early Saturday morning practices and games and, in the evening, watching games on TV that featured his heroes Trevor Linden, Jeremy Roenick and Mark Recchi. He admired their gritty play, their hard work every game. "They had a passion for the game and did a lot for it. They were very inspiring for a young player."

"At each level I played," Whidden remembered, "I hoped that I'd make the next level and maybe, some day, become a pro." He took a major step forward when he began attending the Athol Murray College of Notre Dame, where he met Kory Baker. "Awesome" was the word Whidden used to describe his Notre Dame experience. "They develop you as a player and a person." His learning experiences on and off the ice earned him a spot on the hockey team at the University of Wisconsin-Superior, a Division III school that was the alma mater of another Fire-Ant, Tim Schneider. "I got into a fight in my first game and was suspended for the next one. I only missed one more game in the four years." He was also part of the squad that won an NCAA Division III championship.

As Whidden's university years wound down, former classmate Kory Baker contacted him, suggesting that he might enjoy playing for Derek Booth at Fayetteville. "Turning pro," he remembered, "was a bit intimidating. Particularly because I was the only rookie on the team. But the guys welcomed me. They made a tough step much easier. I remember the first game: as the only rookie, I was really nervous. But after my first shift, it was okay." It was another learning experience for Whidden. "I found out that you couldn't get away with the stuff you could in college. Because fighting is allowed in pro hockey, there wasn't the stickwork you saw in college."

However, adapting to the pressure of the pro game proved to be more difficult than Whidden anticipated. Although he'd scored eight goals, including a four-goal hat trick, he left the team at the end of November and went home to British Columbia to sort out his priorities. Five weeks later he returned to the FireAntz, and although he'd made a contribution in each of the games he'd been in, he hadn't scored since his hat trick. Perhaps the stick he was now working on for the evening's game would be the one to turn his fortunes around.

As 7:30 approached, the pace of activity quickened behind the north goal. Three people lugged fire extinguishers to the edge of the rubber carpet the FireAntz would walk on as they headed to the ice. When the names of the starting lineup were announced, the extinguishers would be activated and players would emerge from the rising "smoke" into the spotlights trained on the entrance to the ice.

Before the players made their appearance, three strangely costumed individuals cavorted between the blue line and the end of the rink. Mascot performances were as important a part of the game here as they are throughout minor-league hockey. The difference was that in Fayetteville, there were three mascots: Slapshot, a large bear wearing a hockey helmet and missing its front teeth; Puck Head, a man dressed in what looked like a matador's costume and wearing a hat that was a giant puck; and Anthony Ant, who wore a hockey sweater and whose head was covered by a large red turban. His face was smeared with red paint. When the mascots saw the Sting Dancers form two rows between which the FireAntz would skate, the trio slid, lurched and staggered off the ice.

During the first and second period and the first intermission, Anthony Ant entertained the crowd with reckless abandon. One of the few sports mascots that talk, he raced up and down the aisles, exhorting the fans to cheer loudly; he threw himself against the glass, shaking his red fists and hurling insults at visiting players and the referee. During the first intermission, he turned himself into a puck, sliding from the blue line into the goal. But in the second intermission, the ant overreached. The Sting Dancers set up a picnic blanket at center ice and Anthony, true to his insect nature, intruded. The young women were well prepared; one of them produced a giant can of ant killer, and Anthony was exterminated. To the cheers of the audience, the late-lamented was removed from the ice.

In the three seasons that he'd performed at Crown Coliseum, Anthony had never made it alive to the third period; the second intermission always ended with the ritual of his extermination. Each time his death had been different. Once, for example, he'd unwittingly wandered into a giant refrigerator carton decorated as an ant trap. His certain demise

Fans at FireAntz games are entertained by the antics of three energetic and zany mascots: Puck Head (left), Slapshot (center) and Anthony Ant (right).

was appropriate: the mascot was sponsored by Master Exterminators. The deaths were humorous: like Wile E. Coyote or Kenny of *South Park*, he'd be back to suffer another death at the next home game. Unlike the characters in *South Park*, however, no one cried out, "You bastards, you've killed Anthony!" It was, after all, Faith and Family Night.

On the ice, the FireAntz started the third period with a 3–1 lead. Rob Whidden must have performed the right operations on his game-day stick, because he'd given Fayetteville a 2–1 lead over Pee Dee at 13:23 of the first period, scoring his first goal since returning to the team. Pee Dee narrowed the gap to one with a power-play goal at 11:55 of the third. Then Whidden struck twice, with a short-handed tally at 12:11 and a full-strength goal at 17:11, to earn his second hat trick of the season. Baseball caps sailed down from the stands in celebration of the achievement. Named the player of the game, Whidden modestly accepted congratulations, but was most happy for the "W"—the win that kept Fayetteville tied with Columbus for second place, three points behind Knoxville.

As the players showered, four young women sat on the ancient couches outside the FireAntz equipment room. Three were players' girl-friends; one was the wife of Dean Jackson, who'd won the Glass Rattler award for a resounding body check he'd thrown in the second period. Christina, who was expecting the couple's first child in March, had met Dean when he was playing for the Elmira Jackals of the UHL. "A friend made the date for us. I wasn't really interested in him at first," she laughed. "I was a very casual fan, but my sister had season tickets. She made me keep going out with him so that she'd be able to hang around the hockey players. I guess you could say that I took one for the team."

Christina remarked that being a hockey wife was probably some-thing no fan could really understand. "It's an all-consuming lifestyle. A player's wife usually can't work during the season because you never know if he'll be traded or moved up. And you worry a lot, particularly when they're on the road. Last year, Dean had a concussion in a road game. I heard about it on the radio, and I wondered if it was as bad as the announcer was making it seem. It was an hour and a half before I heard anything—Dean called me and he was okay."

Christina and her friends were discussing the Jacksons' expected baby—it would be a boy and his name would be Henry—when Dean and three other players joined them. The four couples left for the "Meet

Ladies in waiting: Christina Jackson, Savannah Molina, Taylor Duffy and Nikki Miller wait for the players in the loosely named "players' lounge."

and Greet" function the club was holding for players and fans at a nearby sports bar. One of the other FireAntz would be spending a very short time at the event. Tim Schneider had to drive to Columbia, South Carolina, that night for his weekend job. The next two days he'd be skating, as he had done the previous Saturday, as an emergency call-up for the ECHL's Inferno. Columbia had offered him a long-term contract, but he still hadn't made a decision. The possibility of moving up was attractive, but because the FireAntz had a good chance of doing well in the SPHL playoffs, finishing the season in Fayetteville was also attractive.

Down the hall from the lounge, Jeremi DelCampo prepared for the four-hour drive back home to Charlotte. Somewhere in eastern Tennessee, the Florida Seals' bus was in the early stages of the long trip to Columbus, Georgia.

POSTSEASON POSTSCRIPT

The FireAntz finished in fourth place with 68 points in 56 games, but lost the first round of the playoffs, two games to one, to the Florida Seals. During the season, the club averaged 3,684 people a game, a record for the SPHL and its predecessors, the South East Hockey League, World Hockey Association 2 and ACHL. Mike Clarke and Dean Jackson, who had been teammates at Elmira College, a Division III American college, both received league honors. Jackson, whose 76 points were fifth best in the league, was named to the second all-star team. Clarke, whose 67 points was best among defensemen, was named defenseman of the year and a member of the first all-star team. Jackson's son Henry was born on March 10. Mike Fournier finished the season with 169 minutes in penalties, ninth highest in the league. On March 7, Glenn Ridler left the FireAntz to sign a contract with the Roanoke Valley Vipers of the UHL. Although the Vipers had already been all but eliminated from the play-offs, the UHL's weekly salary cap was nearly double that of the SPHL. In early July, Derek Booth was named head coach of the United Hockey League's expansion team, the Bloomington Prairie Thunder.

PART TWO

AN ICE AGE IN DIXIE

Southern Minor-League Hockey
1988-2005

BEGINNINGS

1988-92

Three minor leagues operated during the 1988–89 season: the long-established American Hockey League (AHL) and International Hockey League (IHL) and the new East Coast Hockey League (ECHL). Founded in 1936, the AHL's teams played in Ontario, Quebec, the Maritime provinces and the northeastern United States. Because each team was affiliated with a National Hockey League (NHL) club, the AHL enjoyed the reputation of being the premier minor league and frequently applied the term Triple A (used for a century to designate the top level of minor-league baseball) to itself. During this period, the Baltimore (Maryland) Skipjacks were the league's only southern team.

INTERNATIONAL HOCKEY LEAGUE: DELUSIONS OF GRANDEUR

The IHL began play in 1945 with teams in Windsor (Ontario) and Detroit, expanded to include a number of small and medium-sized cities in the upper Midwest, and later added larger cities such as Milwaukee, Indianapolis and Salt Lake City. In 1988 the league began an ambitious expansion program aimed at increasing the number of larger cities hosting member clubs. Within a few seasons, Denver, Phoenix, Albany (New York), San Diego and Kansas City had joined the league, making it almost continent-wide. The "I" had ambitions of occupying those major markets that did not have NHL franchises and of becoming an alternative major league.

These plans ultimately failed, and even in the early stages, weaknesses appeared. In Denver, a city with teams in three major-league sports, the Rangers folded after one year, averaging only 2,086 fans a game.

The Albany Choppers were intended to be the anchor tenants for the Knickerbocker Arena—a luxurious new 15,000-seat entertainment center for New York's rapidly expanding capital district—but they folded on Valentine's Day 1991, partway through their first season.

EAST COAST HOCKEY LEAGUE: CREATING CREDIBILITY

The East Coast Hockey League began, essentially, because Henry Brabham needed opponents for the Virginia Lancers, the club that played in the Vinton, Virginia, arena he had built. The Lancers had played in the now-defunct Atlantic Coast Hockey League (ACHL) and the All-America

Hockey League. "There I was again," Brabham laughed when he spoke to me many years later, referring to the loss of two leagues in successive seasons. "I had a building and no games to put in it. I didn't want to quit and neither did Bill Coffey, who owned a team in Winston-Salem, North Carolina. So we got in our cars and traveled all over, looking at buildings that had ice." The two settled on Erie and Johnstown, Pennsylvania; Roanoke Valley, Virginia; Winston-Salem, North Carolina; and Knoxville, Tennessee—cities that not only had buildings with ice, but also had a history of minor-league hockey. Finding owners was no problem—Brabham would run Roanoke Valley (which played first

Ed Lowe of the Elmira Jackals spends a few quiet minutes catching up on his reading. Outfitted with bunks and a galley, the team bus is the players' home for a total of nearly six weeks each season.

in Vinton and later in Roanoke, where it was known as Roanoke Valley), Johnstown and Erie; Coffey, Knoxville; and John Baker, an associate of Coffey, Winston-Salem (which played the first season as Carolina).

In "Celebrating 10 Years," an article about the East Coast Hockey League's first decade, Coffey recalled the summer of 1988: "I couldn't believe it ... [In one place] Henry just pulled out his check book and

wrote a check for a year's rent."[1] Brabham himself later explained that
the owner of the Erie arena had recently been cheated by unscrupulous
tenants. Not only did he write that check, which was for $80,000, but
he also provided money for Coffey to confirm a lease in Knoxville.

One of the first orders of business for the newly formed league was
to appoint a commissioner to run the hockey operations. Brabham
contacted Pat Kelly, a long-time minor-league coach he had met in the
1960s. "The team I was coaching in Peoria, Illinois, had just won the
IHL championship," Kelly explained when he talked to me in 2005,
"and I figured that after 24 years behind the bench, this would be a
good time to bow out." He had just returned to his home in Charlotte,
North Carolina, and begun making plans to start a hardware business
when Brabham phoned. "He told me all about this new league he and
Coffey were starting up and said that he wanted me to be involved. I
let him know that I was through with coaching, and he explained he
needed a commissioner."

Kelly drove up to Vinton (just outside Roanoke), and after some
strong salesmanship by Brabham, he accepted the position, along with
that of manager of Brabham's LancerLot Arena. "The commissioner's
pay wasn't enough to get by on, so he threw in the other job as well.
There were nights," he laughed, "when I'd be in my jacket and tie driving
the Zamboni around the ice, and sometimes, instead of watching the
game, I'd be fixing the toilets."

When he accepted the position, Kelly was keenly aware that the
league's predecessors had the reputation of being havens for goons. "I
told Henry and Bill that the best way of succeeding was to market the
teams as family entertainment. And that wouldn't happen if bench-
clearing brawls broke out every night. That meant that when I suspended
players, they had to stay suspended. That hadn't happened in the ACHL.
It was also important if we wanted the NHL teams to send us younger
players. They wouldn't if they felt that their prospects could be injured
by the goons." Kelly stuck to his guns. In the league finals, the Carolina
Thunderbirds from Winston-Salem traveled to Johnstown for the seventh
and deciding game with only 13 players, including two goalies. Three
others were still serving suspensions. Nevertheless, they defeated the
Johnstown Chiefs 7–4 to win the first ECHL championship.

During that first season (1988–89), clubs began a trend of building
their teams around younger players, not the lifers who had characterized

the lower minor leagues of the past. There were 49 holdovers from the ACHL and All-America League, and 18 other players had had IHL and AHL experience. However, 20 arrived from major Junior A Canadian leagues, and there were an amazing 40 from U.S. universities—most of them from smaller eastern colleges. Only 10 of these younger players had been picked by NHL clubs in the first 10 rounds of recent amateur drafts. Not surprisingly, just a few of the players from the ECHL's first season advanced to the IHL or AHL, and only four went on to the National Hockey League. Scott Gordon of the Johnston Chiefs became the first ECHL alumnus to reach the NHL, playing 10 games for the Quebec Nordiques during the 1989–90 season. In 2003, 13 years later, John Torchetti, a member of the victorious 1989 Carolina Thunderbirds, became the head coach of the Florida Panthers. None of the players in the ECHL's first year became rich; the average salary was $250 a week.

The inaugural season ended successfully—average per-game attendance was 2,512 for the regular season and 2,774 for the playoffs, and all five teams planned to return for the second season—so the ECHL began a program of expansion that would continue for a decade and see league membership increase to 28. Expansion fees for the 1989–90 season were set at $25,000, and owners from Greensboro (North Carolina), Hampton Roads (Virginia) and Nashville (Tennessee) paid up to bring league membership to eight clubs in four states. Average attendance increased by over 900 a game. The average Hampton Roads audience of 7,107 people exceeded the average for all but one team in the AHL. This success enhanced the status of the ECHL, increasing its credibility in the eyes not only of future investors, but also of hockey people, particularly those in the NHL. During the 1989–90 season, 53 NHL draft picks played in the ECHL, and 21 of the league's players later appeared in at least one NHL game.

Jeff Brubaker, a journeyman NHL player who began his coaching career with the 1989–90 Greensboro Generals, commented to me on the surprisingly high caliber of play in the league. "Nobody in the hockey business thought it was *Slap Shot*. The players looked forward to being there. We had the draft choices who weren't ready for the AHL and some really very good undrafted players. You have to remember that after the IHL and the AHL, we were the only pro league. And we had only eight teams. A lot of strong players couldn't get a job; it was a buyers' market. With the NHL talking about expansion, people saw playing in the league as a chance to get noticed." Brubaker's Greensboro Generals defeated the Winston-Salem Thunderbirds four games to one to win the ECHL's second championship.

The league added three new teams in 1991–92 (Cincinnati, Ohio; Richmond, Virginia; and Louisville, Kentucky) and another four the next season (Toledo, Dayton and Columbus, Ohio; and Raleigh, North Carolina). With the exception of Louisville, the expansion franchises were located in established hockey towns. Cincinnati, which averaged 7,696 fans a game in its first season and 9,473 in the second, had been a member of the World Hockey Association; Toledo, Dayton and Columbus had iced teams in the IHL. Miles Wolff, who had made the Durham Bulls one of the most successful minor-league baseball franchises of the 1980s, ran the Greensboro club. Average league attendance increased in each of the two years—to 4,072 and then 4,591.

In spite of the increasing success of the ECHL, both on and off the ice, there were problems. Many people wondered if the league was dividing into "have" and "have-not" cities; they worried that larger cities would be able to acquire the revenues that would bring successes not possible in small cities. In 1992, Henry Brabham announced that his Roanoke Valley team, which had averaged 2,000 people a game in only one season, was for sale. At the end of the 1991–92 season, the Winston-Salem club announced that it would move to West Virginia, and the highly successful Cincinnati Cyclones prepared to move to the higher-level IHL.

COLONIAL HOCKEY LEAGUE: NORTHERN BEGINNINGS

In the fall of 1991, the Colonial Hockey League began play with teams in Thunder Bay, Brantford and St. Thomas, Ontario, and in Flint and Fraser (a Detroit suburb), Michigan. With the exception of Flint, which had had an IHL team until 1990, none of the cities had hosted professional hockey for several years. The makeup of the clubs for the first season was much different from that of the ECHL teams. In the first year, 28 players had been picked in the first 10 rounds of the NHL draft; 14 had seen limited NHL action. A large number of players were older, had had their chance at advancement and were now playing out the string. With a weekly salary cap of $7,000, most players earned around $400 a week. No attendance figures were kept during the first season; however, the league was sufficiently successful that all five clubs returned the following season, along with expansion franchises in Muskegon (Michigan) and Chatham (Ontario).

EXPANSION

1992-96

From the beginning of the 1992–93 season to the close of the 1995–96 season, minor-league hockey expanded rapidly. The 1991–92 season ended with 45 teams, 11 in the South; by the fall of 1995 there were 85 teams, 34 in the South. Three new leagues began to play during this period—the Central Hockey League and the Sunshine Hockey League (which later became the Southern Hockey League) in 1992 and the West Coast Hockey League in 1995. Much of this activity was influenced either directly or indirectly by the NHL's four-club expansion: Ottawa and Tampa Bay joined in 1992, with Anaheim and Florida coming in a year later. The addition of these clubs opened jobs for approximately 100 players in the American and International Leagues and an equal number at the lower professional ranks. The formation of the two Florida clubs created new levels of awareness of hockey in the American Southeast, as did the Dallas Stars' arrival in the Southwest from Minnesota after the 1992–93 season.

AMERICAN HOCKEY LEAGUE: CAROLINA DREAMING

The American Hockey League (AHL) remained in the north and in the border state of Maryland until the 1995–96 season. However, when it noticed the success of the ECHL in southern markets, the league expressed a willingness to receive applications for expansion franchises from several southern cities. Although Greensboro, Hampton Roads, Charlotte, Raleigh and Charleston appeared regularly on rumor lists, the owners of the Greensboro Generals were the only ones to pay the

$1 million expansion fee. They left the ECHL to become the Carolina Monarchs in the fall of 1995.

The move was disastrous. During the 1995–96 season, attendance dropped by 1,500 fans a game. Jeff Brubaker, the extremely popular coach of the ECHL team, was not hired to coach the AHL club, a fact that angered long-time hockey fans. He later suggested that the AHL players, while offering a superior brand of hockey, did not have the attachment to the city that their predecessors had. "A lot of the ECHL players stayed in Greensboro, married local girls and became a part of the community. The fans felt that they were their own. The AHL players were in town to get out—their goal was to make the NHL as quickly as possible. The fans couldn't connect with them," he explained. The club struggled through a second season, which saw another 500-person drop in per-game attendance. In the spring of 1997, when the NHL's Hartford Whalers announced that they would play in Greensboro for two years (becoming the Carolina Hurricanes), the dethroned Monarchs headed north, slinking into Connecticut as the Beast of New Haven.

INTERNATIONAL HOCKEY LEAGUE: NOT CONTENT TO BE A MINOR LEAGUE

The International Hockey League continued its rapid expansion, all of it into large markets, growing from 10 to 19 clubs over four seasons. Two clubs relocated: Muskegon to Cleveland in the fall of 1992, and San Diego to Los Angeles in the fall of 1995. Cincinnati and Atlanta received expansion franchises in 1992, and Las Vegas got its franchise in 1993. Detroit, Houston, Chicago and Denver (which moved after a year to Salt Lake City) joined the league in 1994, and San Francisco in 1995. Expansion fees reached $6 million.

Attendance increased steadily for three years, reaching a peak per-game average of 8,261 for the 1994–95 season. Expansion into the South initially proved successful. Houston and Phoenix averaged over 8,000 in attendance per game; Atlanta and Las Vegas between 6,000 and 8,000. Players were delighted: salaries averaged over $70,000 a year, with teams' yearly payrolls ranging from $700,000 to $1.2 million.

By the end of the 1994–95 season, the IHL appeared to have established itself as the premier minor league. In January 1995, Commissioner Bob Ufer stated: "We want to build this league to unprecedented heights."[1] He also announced that the league would form a European division to begin play in the fall of 1995, with each new club paying a $1 million entry fee. The date was pushed back a year and then abandoned when the International Ice Hockey Federation refused to sanction the plans.

In the fall of 1994, as the NHL began what would be a nearly four-month lockout, *Sports Illustrated* ran an article about the IHL. Entitled "Putting on a Show," it focused on the popularity and prosperity of IHL teams and quoted Detroit Vipers president Tom Wilson, who told writer Michael Farber, "Maybe one day we won't be content to be a minor league."[2] He was ecstatic about the Vipers' opening-day crowd of 21,182 at the Palace at Auburn Hills, in the northern suburbs of Detroit.

However, the 1995–96 season began what would prove to be the IHL's six-year slide into oblivion. A sampling of newspaper headlines from that season provides glimpses of the problems:

ICE DOGS DUMP HIGH-PRICED PLAYER;
COULD BE FOLDING
—*Las Vegas Review-Journal*, November 5, 1995

CROWDS FALL AS STAKES RISE IN CHANGING IHL
—Peoria *Journal Star*, November 17, 1995

"I" FIZZLES INSTEAD OF SIZZLES IN COMPETITION
WITH BIG BOYS
—*Tampa Tribune*, February 11, 1996

During the season it quickly became evident that the two new California teams, the Los Angeles Ice Dogs and the San Francisco Spiders, were in trouble. The Ice Dogs were reported to be on track to lose well over $2 million. The Spiders, playing in the aging Cow Palace, attracted 5,000 fans a game, 3,000 below the break-even number. Las Vegas, Minnesota and Milwaukee expected to lose close to $2 million each.

Why did what seemed to be such a bright future for the league prove so quickly to be a mirage? There were several factors. One was that owners failed to account for the fact that when they expanded into major markets that hosted major-league teams in other sports, the IHL would be perceived as minor and supported accordingly. Another factor was that by 1995, with the league extending from Orlando to San Francisco and from St. Paul to Houston, travel costs, the majority by air, increased dramatically. Costs were further increased by the league's desire to sign high-priced free agents with NHL experience. However, the greatest problem most of the IHL teams faced was their increasing dependence on their share of the league's expansion fees to meet operating expenses. When these disappeared, as they did over the next two seasons, several teams were in considerable trouble.

EAST COAST HOCKEY LEAGUE: HOCKEY ON INTERSTATE 10

While the IHL's expansion plan was beginning to show the cracks that would eventually bring down the league, the East Coast Hockey League became steadily more prosperous, growing from 14 to 21 teams between 1992 and 1996. There were some relocations. The Winston-Salem team moved to Wheeling, West Virginia, and the Cincinnati club to Birmingham, Alabama, for the 1992–93 season. The Virginia Lancers, now called the Roanoke Valley Rampage, moved to Huntsville, Alabama, for the 1993–94 season. A year later they relocated to Tallahassee, Florida. Roanoke received an expansion franchise in 1993–94, and the Louisville franchise, which had been dormant for a year, moved to Jacksonville, Florida.

Much more significant than the relocations was the granting of expansion franchises to nontraditional markets: Charleston (South Carolina), Mobile (Alabama) and Lafayette (Louisiana). The latter two teams' location on Interstate 10, the southernmost transcontinental highway, symbolized hockey's move into unusual, uncharted, new territory. In fact, during the 1995–96 season, nine minor-league teams in four different leagues played in cities located on the highway that stretched from Jacksonville to Los Angeles (compared to seven minor-league teams playing in Canada at the time).

The ECHL's southern expansion—it now had teams in eight southern states—proved successful far beyond the optimistic expectations of league officials. From 1992–93 to 1995–96, 16 teams had seasons in which they averaged over 6,000 fans a game. The most amazing success story occurred in 1995–96 when the first-year Louisiana IceGators attracted an average of 9,775 fans (fourth highest in the minors) to the Cajun Dome, their Lafayette, Louisiana, home. The club had a sellout crowd of over 11,026 for opening night; a season-ticket base of almost 2,000; and a total season attendance of 342,154—a league record and a figure exceeded that year by only nine minor-league teams.

The Louisiana IceGators' Phenomenon, a book published after the inaugural season, offered explanations as to why the team was so successful.[3] General manager Dave Berryman and his brother Tim, the director of marketing—transplanted Canadians who had worked with the very successful South Carolina Stingrays—developed a strong marketing campaign to bring the new club to the attention of families, as well as sports fans, in southern Louisiana. An extensive ticket-selling campaign emphasized not just the speed and physicality of this strange northern sport, but also the concept that a night at the Cajun Dome would be an inexpensive family entertainment experience.

And it was. The festivities at a home game began as the team, led by team mascot Alfonse the Alligator, skated onto the ice through the smoking jaws of an inflated alligator head. Attendants slung hotdogs and T-shirts into the stands during breaks in the play. The "Horn Dudes," two green-faced fans, wandered through the stands inciting the crowd to noisy excitement as they blasted on their plastic instruments. People had many opportunities to take "stuff" home, including red pucks

Looking like a metallic hydra, the glove-drying machine is found outside most professional hockey dressing rooms.

on Valentine's Day and green ones on St. Patrick's Day. The product on the ice was good; the expansion IceGators finished two points ahead of Nashville to win the seven-team Southern Division crown. The club lost in the first round of the playoffs, but drew 28,795 fans in three games.

During this four-year period, the standard of hockey in ECHL arenas continued to improve steadily. The 1995 media guide stated that "the league has evolved into one of the top minor league systems in professional hockey with 45 players having moved up to the American and

International Hockey Leagues."[4] A year later, 16 of 21 clubs had NHL affiliations. Eric Cairns, whom the New York Rangers had picked in the third round of the 1992 draft, began his second pro season playing 14 games for the Charlotte Checkers before the Rangers promoted him to Binghamton of the AHL. A year later, he donned a Rangers uniform to play in what would be the first of 406 NHL games.

Although some players advanced to higher-level leagues, some became lifers in the lower minor leagues. One such player was Trevor Jobe, a seventh-round draft pick of the Toronto Maple Leafs in 1987, who entered the professional ranks with what most predicted to be a bright future. In 73 games with the Newmarket Saints of the AHL, he scored 23 goals, a good start to a professional career. However, over the next 15 seasons he played only 16 AHL and NHL games—this in spite of the fact that during the 1992–93 season, playing for the ECHL's Nashville Knights, he scored an amazing 85 goals, still a minor-league single-season record. After that record year, Jobe never played a complete season with one team. He was a gifted scorer, but it seems he didn't get along well with his teammates, who felt he played for himself. Plagued as well by off-ice problems, he was either traded from or chose to leave clubs during subsequent seasons. In the early 1990s and beyond, newspaper stories about fall training camps often reported that he had arrived overweight and was wondering whether he should retire. Much traveled, Trevor Jobe seems to have arrived at each new destination with considerable baggage.

The ECHL had become largely successful by the end of the 1995–96 season, but there were trouble spots. The relocation of four franchises and the fact that in 1995–96 four teams had per-game attendance averages of under 3,000 indicated that not all of the league's markets could support professional hockey. The ECHL also faced competition for desirable new territories from the Sunshine Hockey League in Florida and the Central Hockey League in the Southwest. Both these leagues sought to establish charter or expansion franchises in areas the ECHL had considered.

CENTRAL HOCKEY LEAGUE: HOCKEY RETURNS TO THE SOUTHWEST

The idea for the Central Hockey League, which began play in the fall of 1992, had taken shape a quarter of a century earlier, when Ray Miron and Bill Levins, executives of two teams in the Central Professional

Hockey League, were discussing the increasing costs of doing business in the league, which extended from Minneapolis to Houston. "There were very few bus trips; the teams flew just about everywhere, so you can imagine what the bills were like," Miron recalled in a 2005 phone interview. "Bill and I started to discuss ways that we could keep costs manageable and came up with the idea of having a league in which there were no individually owned teams—the league would own them all." A central office would avoid duplication of services; payrolls could be controlled and league geography made manageable.

Nothing came of their idea for many years. Miron went on to serve as the general manager of the NHL's Colorado Rockies and later became commissioner of the Atlantic Coast Hockey League and a consultant for the Vancouver Canucks. It was while representing the Canucks at IHL meetings in Salt Lake City in 1991 that he met Horn Chen, a successful Chicago businessman who owned the IHL's Indianapolis Ice and would later own teams and leagues in hockey, baseball and Canadian football. "I told him about the concept of a single ownership league," said Miron. Chen found the idea intriguing and offered his financial support. "He gave me the startup funds and left it to me to find league cities, facilities, front-office people, coaches and players." Miron hired his son Monte, and the two of them set up a league in the territories of the old CPHL, with teams in Wichita, Kansas; Tulsa and Oklahoma City, Oklahoma: Memphis, Tennessee: and Dallas and Fort Worth, Texas.

Creating the new league was both easy and difficult. "There were plenty of good players and coaches who wanted to be in pro hockey," Miron commented, "but the cities that owned the rinks were skeptical. Some of them didn't think the league would last until Christmas." However, a total of 983,613 paid to attend CHL games during the inaugural season, an average of 5,465 a game—well above the league's declared break-even point of 3,000 fans a game. The CHL posted a profit of over $1 million.

Why, after an absence of eight seasons, did professional hockey make so dramatic a return to the Southwest? Miron believed that the time was right. The 1988 trade of Wayne Gretzky from the Edmonton Oilers to the Los Angeles Kings brought the sport to the attention of hundreds of thousands of American sports fans. Miron also noted that the low price of tickets, under $10 a seat, along with the control on expenses exercised by the league, insured that revenues would exceed expenses. "We made sure that teams could reach other cities by bus, not air. And because we wrote the checks, we could enforce the $100,000 per team annual salary cap. We had a competitive balance on the ice. I've always said that no matter what the level of skill, if the two teams on the ice were evenly matched, you'd have an exciting game." Although the Oklahoma City Blazers earned the regular-season crown, the Tulsa Oilers, who had finished in second place, eight points back, won the playoff championship over the Blazers, four games to three, and took home the Bill Levins Memorial Cup, named in memory of the man who, with Miron, had envisioned the CHL so many years earlier, but who had died before the idea was realized.

One thing that Miron had worried about before the first season was the caliber of play. "Monte hired six coaches with NHL playing experience: Gary Unger in Tulsa, Ron Flockhart in Dallas, Peter Mahovlich in Forth Worth, Mike McEwen in Oklahoma City, Doug Shedden in Wichita and Steve Carlson in Memphis. They recruited their own players, and it turned out pretty well overall."

Miron remarked, years later, that "we wanted to give chances to players who hadn't been drafted—Tier II juniors and college students— and people who'd been let go by National Hockey League clubs after fall training camps." The Tulsa Oilers' roster during the team's successful playoff run provides a fairly typical example of a 1992–93 CHL team. Of the 17 players, only four were rookies and two were sophomores. On the other hand, one player had six years' experience, another seven, a third eight and a fourth nine. Seven had been chosen in the top 10 rounds of NHL drafts, and two had played in the NHL. Taylor Hall, a sixth-round pick in 1982, had appeared in 82 games for Vancouver and Boston, while Mike Berger, a fourth-round pick in 1985, had played 29 games for Minnesota. No Oiler would go on to play in the NHL after the 1992–93 season. Clearly, a large part of the roster was made up of players who had already reached their peak and were working at extending their hockey lives.

During the next three seasons, the CHL continued to be a financial success, with yearly profits in seven figures. The Tulsa Oilers improved their per-game average attendance by 1,000 fans to 6,500, and Wichita enjoyed two years with crowds averaging over 6,000 before dropping to 4,500 a game. Oklahoma City twice averaged over 10,000 fans a game before dropping back slightly, and the expansion San Antonio Iguanas, who joined the league in the fall of 1994, averaged 5,500 and 5,900 in their first two seasons. Three clubs experienced disappointing drops in attendance. The Memphis RiverKings' average dropped by over 800 people in each of the team's third and fourth years. However, the biggest declines occurred in the league's two largest markets. The Fort Worth Fire dropped by 1,400 fans a game over three years, while the Dallas Freeze, which had drawn a league low of just over 4,500 in the first season, had to contend after that with the presence of the NHL's Dallas Stars. After drawing fewer than 3,000 fans a game for the next two seasons, the club suspended operations.

Although the league had proved its stability, it was growing at a much slower pace than the other minor leagues around the country. Such cities as Albuquerque, New Mexico; El Paso and San Antonio, Texas; Lafayette, Louisiana; Jackson, Mississippi; and Davenport, Iowa were mentioned as possible locations for expansion teams, but San Antonio was the only new team in the league's first four years. The other cities became members of the Western Professional, Colonial and East Coast hockey leagues. The conservative fiscal policy underlying its central ownership may account for the league's slow expansion. Other leagues saw expansion fees as easy sources of revenue for their clubs, but because all of the CHL teams were owned by the league, it would not receive such revenues. It could move to new cities only if operations there could be profitable.

On the ice, the CHL product continued to improve slowly, but steadily. Several players were called up to the AHL and IHL to fill temporary roster vacancies, and in 1995–96, two players entered the NHL. Tulsa's Mike MacWilliam played 6 games for the New York Islanders, and Fort Worth's Alexei Yegorov played 11 games in two seasons for the San Jose Sharks. In the 1995–96 season, the CHL took steps to strengthen its profile as a developmental league. Only four three-year players (defined as those who were over 30 or who had played three full seasons in the CHL or 20 games in the NHL) would be permitted on each roster.

SUNSHINE AND SOUTHERN HOCKEY LEAGUES: CREATED ON THIN ICE

In the fall of 1992, another league began play in the South—but without the success of the CHL. The Sunshine Hockey League began as an outgrowth of the interest in the sport that increased with the NHL's announcement that it was expanding into Florida. Two groups sought to form leagues. Ed Broidy, a New York businessman, set about reviving the Southern Hockey League, which had ceased operations in the middle of the 1976–77 season, while Jordan Kobritz, a Lakeland, Florida, resident, set about forming Hockey South. A turf war quickly developed between the two because there were only five ice rinks in the state that had both the playing surfaces and seating capacity necessary for minor-league hockey.

This was when David McPherson, who was coaching a professional team in England, entered the picture. "A couple of European scouts who I knew lived in Florida," he explained to me in a 2005 interview, "and they told me about Broidy's and Kobritz's plans. So I phoned them and decided to put money into a franchise in Daytona Beach. By that time, the two weren't talking to each other." When both men announced that they were postponing opening their leagues for another year, McPherson decided to begin his own league, the Sunshine Hockey League. He signed rental agreements for arenas in Lakeland, Jacksonville, West Palm Beach and Daytona Beach (all in Florida) and found three more owners, one of whom, Bill Nyrop, was a graduate of Indiana's University of Notre Dame and had played in the NHL before pursuing a career in law. "I sought him out," McPherson explained, "because we knew that both his hockey and legal expertise would be invaluable to the league."

There were 3,600 fans at the West Palm Beach Blazers' opening game. Inaugural games of the Daytona Beach Sun Devils and Jacksonville Bullets attracted just under 2,000 each, while the Lakeland Ice Warriors drew 1,200. At the end of the season, West Palm Beach had an average of just under 3,000 fans, followed by Jacksonville with 1,500, and Daytona Beach and Lakeland with just over 1,000. "We fought football in the fall," league commissioner Nick Durbano commented in a 2005 phone interview. "Then in the winter it was basketball, and in March, major-league baseball spring training."

In addition to these four cities, which played in each of the league's three seasons, two other cities made brief appearances: the St. Petersburg (Florida) Renegades and the Fresno (California) Falcons. The St. Petersburg club, owned by Allan Harvie, who also owned the ECHL's Richmond Renegades, joined the league in January 1993, more than halfway through the first season. The team, which earned three points for each win, as opposed to two for other clubs, drew under 1,000 people a game, nearly 2,000 fewer than Harvie deemed necessary to break even. The Renegades' truncated season got off to a stumbling start. They missed a game in Daytona Beach because they thought the starting time was 7:00 p.m., not 1:00 p.m. The next day, their home opener had to be canceled because the ice was unsafe to play on. After waiting for over an hour, the 900 people who had shown up went home clutching "ice" checks for the rescheduled game. Just over 400 of them showed up the next night. The club folded after 20 games.

The Fresno Falcons, one of the top senior amateur teams in the United States, joined the league for the 1994–95 season in order to find strong-enough competition to get them ready for major senior tournaments. The California club, which played a home and home doubleheader against the four Florida teams, received 5.6 points for a win and 2.8 for an overtime loss. They finished third in the league.

Before the Sunshine Hockey League's first season began, commissioner Nick Durbano spoke of recruiting players from Junior A and college who hadn't been drafted. After a month of play, he rated the caliber of hockey as being just below the IHL. The athletes, he remarked, had "aspirations to play at a higher level."[5] McPherson had intended this when he held an open league-wide training camp in Daytona Beach for over 200 players. "I figured we'd get a good balance at the end of camp when the coaches held a draft to stock the four teams. But then I found that Bill Nyrop had signed a bunch of AHL veterans to play in West Palm Beach. They outshot us something like 85–20 in our home opener." The entire league was heavily weighted with old pros on the way down. The first season's rosters contained 21 former NHL draft picks. Three players (Doug Keans, Jim McGeough and Lou Franceschetti) had played in the NHL. One player, John Craighead, would appear in five games for the 1996–97 Toronto Maple Leafs. When the Fresno team joined the league, it had three members—Dwight Mathiasen, Jamie Huscroft and Steve Martinson—who had played in the NHL.

In 1995–96, the Sunshine Hockey League became the Southern Hockey League. Teams from Huntsville (Alabama) and Winston-Salem (North Carolina) joined West Palm Beach, Daytona Beach, Jacksonville and Lakeland. Poor attendance in five cities, high travel expenses and the presence of an ECHL team in Jacksonville doomed the league after a season. Huntsville, which had attracted over 3,000 fans a game, prepared to join the eastward-expanding CHL in 1997.

WEST COAST HOCKEY LEAGUE: OWNERS IN NEED OF A LEAGUE

The West Coast Hockey League began play in the fall of 1995. When the San Diego Gulls of the IHL moved north to Los Angeles after the 1994–95 season, Ron Hahn, who operated the San Diego Ice Arena, found himself without a team to play in his building. At the same time, Vancouver businessman Bruce Taylor, owner of the Fresno Falcons, was casting about for a nearby professional league in which his team could play.

In 2005, Taylor, now retired, recalled his time as a hockey team owner. "I'd owned several teams in the British Columbia Junior Hockey League.

A good workman takes care of his tools. Rookie Jarrett Konkle of the Elmira Jackals prepares his stick before a game against the Roanoke Valley Vipers.

One of my coaches, John Olver, and I looked into getting involved with hockey in the United States, and I bought the Fresno Falcons, who played in the senior amateur Pacific Southwest Hockey League." At the same time, he was interested in joining the IHL. "But when I found out it would cost me at least a million dollars, I called John Olver and said, 'Let's start our own league.'" He talked with Ron Hahn of San Diego, along with the owners of the Fairbanks and Anchorage senior teams the Falcons had played against, and visited civic officials in Reno (Nevada) and Bakersfield (California).

During the first season, six teams played: Hahn's new San Diego Gulls; Taylor's Fresno Falcons; two other teams Taylor owned, the Bakersfield Fog and the Reno Renegades; and the Alaska (Fairbanks) Gold Kings and Anchorage Aces. Plans to have a team from Albuquerque join the league fell through. Midway through the first season, the league announced plans to expand in the upcoming season to Tucson (Arizona), Boise (Idaho) and Colorado Springs (Colorado).

Organizers had announced their hope to create a balanced, competitive league. This did not happen during the first season. San Diego, icing six players with NHL experience and another seven who had spent time in the AHL and IHL, finished in first place with 100 points in 58 games, 33 more than second-place Fresno, and went on to win the playoffs.

During the WCHL's first season, three people involved with the league attracted attention that extended beyond the local sports pages. Keith Gretzky, Wayne's younger brother, was hired to coach the Bakersfield Fog. Heather McDaniel, a 24-year-old referee, the first woman referee in professional hockey, was kissed by a player when she went to break up a fight during a game between Reno and Fresno. Ron Duguay, a veteran of 864 NHL games, made a comeback with the San Diego Gulls. After three years of retirement, he played in 12 home games, scoring eight goals and assisting on nine others. He explained that not only did he want to help the injury-riddled Gulls, but he also wanted his children, who hadn't been old enough to see him during his NHL years, to watch him play.

"When I look back," Bruce Taylor recalled, "I realize how relatively inexpensive things were. We had deals with Alaska Airlines, and you could run things for just over a million a team. I laugh when I think that 10 years ago I ran three teams for the price it costs to run one now. We had players who hoped to be noticed and others who hadn't quite made it to the top and were looking for a place to finish their careers. Our league gave those people the opportunities they wanted."

COLONIAL HOCKEY LEAGUE: MOVING BEYOND THE MIDWEST
Between 1992 and 1996, the Colonial Hockey League moved its Fraser franchise to Detroit; the St. Thomas franchise to London, Ontario, and then Dayton, Ohio; and the Flint franchise to Utica, New York. Muskegon and Flint, Michigan; Chatham, Ontario (which moved after two years to Saginaw, Michigan); Madison, Wisconsin; and Quad Cities, Iowa/Illinois, were granted expansion franchises. In four seasons, 12 cities had hosted Colonial League teams and there had been five franchise shifts. The league's move to Utica was the first of many it would make to locations considerably distant from its midwestern center.

EXPLOSION

1996-2000

From 1988 to 1995, the various minor leagues had placed the majority of their new franchises in markets that had had experience with professional hockey. However, for four seasons beginning in the fall of 1996, a period in which the number of clubs increased from 85 to 111, and the number in the South from 34 to 56, teams played in such unlikely places as Lake Charles (Louisiana), Belton (Texas), Biloxi (Mississippi), Asheville (North Carolina), Augusta (Georgia) and Florence (South Carolina).

AMERICAN HOCKEY LEAGUE: SOUTHERN FORAYS

Although most of the American Hockey League teams were located in the northeastern United States and eastern Canada, four different southern cities hosted franchises between 1996 and 2000. The Carolina Monarchs played during the 1996–97 season, their second in the league, before relocating to New Haven, Connecticut. After that season the Baltimore Bandits relocated to Cincinnati, claiming one-year losses of over $1.5 million. The Kentucky Thoroughblades of Lexington began play in the fall of 1996. Three years later, in the fall of 1999, the Florida Panthers placed a team in Louisville.

The Kentucky Thoroughblades became a hit in the Bluegrass state even before they played their first game in the fall of 1996, as 5,000 people participated in a name-the-team contest; 300 people turned out to a press conference at which the club announced its affiliation with the San Jose Sharks; and 2,700 fans purchased season tickets. The enthusiasm was not simply spontaneous. The team's front-office staff worked hard to establish awareness of the new sport that would play in a building where college basketball was king, the Adolph Rupp Arena, home of the University of Kentucky Wildcats. One area television station regularly carried two-minute spots explaining and demonstrating the rules of hockey, and 50,000 copies of a "Hockey Handbook" were distributed around the state. A crowd of 17,503 people—a single-game AHL attendance record—was at the team's home opener, and for the first season the Thoroughblades drew an average of 7,600 fans per game—second only to the Philadelphia Phantoms' 9,200. The next year the average increased by 200. However, in succeeding seasons the average dropped by 1,500, 600 and 1,200 fans a game. Once the novelty wore off, hockey was not sufficiently popular to lure sports fans to the Adolph Rupp Arena when ice, rather than hardwood, was the playing surface.

INTERNATIONAL HOCKEY LEAGUE: MAJOR CONTRACTION

While the other minor leagues moved through four years of unprecedented expansion, the International Hockey League experienced four years of rapid contraction, with the number of clubs dropping by nearly one-third, from 19 to 13.

During the 1996–97 season there were 19 teams, the same number as in the previous season, but 5 of them were not returning to the same cities. San Francisco ceased operations; Peoria relocated to San Antonio; Atlanta moved to Quebec City, which had recently lost its NHL club; the Minnesota Moose became the Manitoba (Winnipeg) Moose; and Los Angeles went to Long Beach (California). Grand Rapids, Michigan, gained an expansion team. Five teams—Phoenix, Las Vegas, Houston, Orlando and San Antonio—played in the south. Twelve of the returning teams saw drops in attendance—five clubs averaged fewer than 6,000 fans a game. At the end of the season, the Phoenix Roadrunners, which had been competing for fans with the NHL's Phoenix Coyotes, withdrew from the league.

In spite of its continuing financial problems, in February 1997 the league announced plans to add more Canadian teams. Suburban Toronto and Montreal, along with Saskatoon (Saskatchewan), Halifax (Nova Scotia) and Victoria (British Columbia) were listed as possible cities. None of these locations materialized, and the 1997–98 season opened with 18 teams. Soon after the end of that season, Quebec City and San Antonio left the league. So, too, did Commissioner Bob Ufer. He had been criticized for setting unreasonable goals and had strained the league's tenuous relationship with the NHL, encouraging teams to move into established NHL markets and allowing clubs to sign NHL players who were holding out for higher salaries from their major-league teams. Ufer's successor was Doug Moss, a veteran hockey administrator who set about mending fences with the NHL.

The 1998–99 season, which began with 16 teams, would be the last for Fort Wayne and Indianapolis, which joined lower-level leagues (the UHL and CHL respectively), and Las Vegas, which ceased operations. Of the 14 teams that began the 1999–2000 season, two did not return the next year. Kalamazoo switched to the United Hockey League and Long Beach to the West Coast Hockey League. Only two southern teams—Houston and Orlando—remained. Unwise expansion, high player salaries, expensive arena fees and rising travel costs, made excessive because of the geographical expanse of the league, weakened teams that could no longer count on expansion fees to help defray their costs.

Neatness counts—but only before the players show up. Members of the equipment staff, generally the first people to arrive each morning, make sure that clean practice jerseys, sharpened skates and dry equipment are placed at each locker.

The life and death of the San Antonio Dragons provides an example of the fate of the IHL's attempts to establish itself in larger markets, frequently in the South. During the 1995–96 season, Bruce Saurs, owner of the Peoria (Illinois) Rivermen, which had experienced the financial pressures of being a small-market team in an increasingly big-market league, announced that he would move his team to San Antonio. The move appeared to be a good one. The Texas city was a fast-growing, lucrative market. However, there was a problem: Freeman Coliseum was in the middle of a five-year contract with the Iguanas of the Central Hockey League, and the two teams engaged in a battle for the ice during the Dragons' first season. The attendance of both teams suffered: the Iguanas dropped from near-ly 6,000 fans a game to just under 3,000, while the Dragons attracted 4,900 a game, the second-lowest number in the IHL. The Dragons won the turf war; the courts decided that, after the 1996–97 season, the club would not have to share the facility with the Iguanas, who then sus-pended operations for 1997–98. However, it was a Pyrrhic victory. In the Dragons' second and final season, attendance declined by 1,000 fans a game. Neither Bruce Saurs nor his partner, Don Levin, found the riches they had envisioned when they left Illinois two years earlier.

EAST COAST HOCKEY LEAGUE: SOLIDLY SOUTHERN

During the last half of the 1990s, the East Coast Hockey League contin-ued its steady course of expansion, adding seven teams over four years to bring the total number of clubs to 28 by 2000. The process involved the relocation of six teams and the granting of eight expansion franchises, along with the suspension of operations by three clubs. As the league moved into the new millennium, three-quarters of its teams were in the South. Fourteen of these were in cities with no prior professional hockey history; eight were located on the Interstate 10 highway corridor extend-ing from Jacksonville to Lafayette (Louisiana), and of these, seven were on the Gulf Coast.

For the 1996–97 season, Erie (Pennsylvania), one of the original five teams, became the Baton Rouge (Louisiana) Kingfish, and the Nashville Knights moved to Pensacola (Florida) to become the Ice Pilots. Expansion franchises were granted to Biloxi (the Mississippi Sea Wolves) and Peoria, where the Rivermen replaced the IHL team of the same name. The following year, the Knoxville Cherokees, another charter franchise, moved to Florence (South Carolina) to become the Pee Dee Pride. Expansion franchises were granted to a Maryland suburb of Wash-ington (the Chesapeake Icebreakers) and to New Orleans (the Brass).

During the 1998–99 season, Greenville (South Carolina) and the Fort Myers (Florida) area received expansion teams—the Grrrowl and Florida Everblades, respectively. Raleigh relocated to Augusta, Georgia, where, like many teams, it took an animal name—appropriately, for its new home, the Lynx. The Louisville RiverFrogs moved to Miami, playing one season as the Matadors before suspending operations. A year later, Little Rock (Arkansas) and Trenton (New Jersey) received expansion franchises, and the Arkansas RiverBlades and Trenton Titans entered the league. The Jackson (Mississippi) Bandits replaced the Chesapeake Ice-breakers, and when the NHL's Carolina Hurricanes moved to their new home in Raleigh (North Carolina), Greensboro returned to the ECHL after a four-season absence.

These franchise transactions didn't just occur because of the ECHL's desire to capitalize on the increased popularity of the sport. They involved a complex series of forces, including the wishes of higher-level leagues, especially the NHL; the desire of new arenas to acquire major tenants; the need for older facilities to fill in dates left vacant by departed tenants; and, quite simply, the failure of franchise operators to estimate the receptivity of a new market to hockey.

For example, the fates of the Greensboro and Raleigh clubs were determined by the relocation of the NHL's Hartford Whalers to Greensboro and then, two years later, Raleigh. The Louisville Panthers of the AHL were born because the NHL's Florida Panthers needed a farm team and the AHL wanted to add a franchise close to Lexington and Cincinnati. This forced the ECHL's Louisville RiverFrogs to relocate. They became the Miami Matadors, moving to downtown Miami and taking up residence in the arena the Florida Panthers vacated when they moved to the Miami suburb of Sunrise. Two of the ECHL's expansion franchises, the Greenville Grrrowl and the Florida Everblades, both of which have been among the most stable teams in the league, were born in part because cities with new facilities actively sought ECHL franchises.

Although the ECHL continued to grow, not all signs were positive. Of the 21 teams that began the 1996–97 season, 7 were not playing in 2001. And of the new cities, nine no longer had ECHL franchises after the 2004–05 season. Over the four seasons ending in 2000, clubs reported a decline in average per-game attendance from the previous season 52 times. Ten of these reports were for decreases of over 1,000 people a game. Eight of the franchises entering the league during this period experienced their highest per-game average attendance during their first seasons. Five saw consecutive decreases after that inaugural year.

On the ice, the product continued to improve and a steady stream of players advanced to the IHL and AHL. A few went on to the NHL.

By the end of the ECHL's 10th season, in 1998, 85 players, 13 of whom went on to substantial major-league careers, had advanced to the NHL.

CENTRAL HOCKEY LEAGUE: CHANGES IN PHILOSOPHY

The number of Central Hockey League teams increased from 6 in 1995–96 to 11 in 1999–2000. The league also underwent major changes in its operating philosophy. First, the Columbus (Georgia) Cottonmouths, Macon (Georgia) Whoopie, Huntsville (Alabama) Channel Cats and Nashville (Tennessee) Nighthawks, the expansion teams of 1996–97, were owned privately, rather than by the league. Second, the league moved from the Mississippi River, which had until that time marked its eastern boundary, to very near the Atlantic seaboard. A year later, when the Fayetteville (North Carolina) Force became a member, close to 1,300 miles separated the easternmost and westernmost clubs. Expansion continued in 1998–99 and 1999–2000, with the addition of the Topeka (Kansas) Scarecrows and the Indianapolis (Indiana) Ice, both privately owned teams.

Many vanity license plates in the south pay tribute to NASCAR, basketball or football. However, this plate, seen in the parking lot outside Bobcats Arena in Charlotte, North Carolina, refers to a long-standing hockey tradition.

Ray and Monte Miron, the league's commissioner and president respectively, had opposed the changes, believing that more travel and decentralized ownership would increase costs and weaken the league. "We approached Horn Chen for more capital to finance league-owned expansion, which had become necessary because the NHL was reportedly looking at Oklahoma City as a site for an expansion team," Ray Miron remarked when I talked with him in 2005. "Moreover, the IHL had moved into San Antonio." However, Chen believed that expansion was necessary in case Oklahoma City was lost, and he also saw franchise fees as a way to increase league revenues.

The CHL's options for expansion cities had narrowed, though. The ECHL had moved into Louisiana; the Colonial Hockey League into the western Midwest; the West Coast Hockey League into Arizona; and the

IHL into San Antonio. Most important, the Western Professional Hockey League (WPHL), which began its first season in the fall of 1996, placed franchises in four cities that might have been appropriate locations for the CHL: Austin, Amarillo and El Paso in Texas, and Albuquerque in New Mexico.

After the 1996–97 season, both Mirons retired, selling their shares in the league to Chen. Ray Compton and Thomas Berry Jr., two hockey executives from the Indianapolis Ice, took over as CHL president and commissioner respectively.

Between 1996 and 2000, Oklahoma City remained one of the strongest franchises in minor-league hockey, consistently averaging over 9,000 fans a game. Two other original CHL teams—Wichita and Tulsa—stayed near the 5,000 mark. However, on 20 different occasions, other teams posted per-game season attendance averages of under 4,000. The four eastern expansion teams drew considerably below the league average. Fort Worth and San Antonio were victims of turf wars in which clubs from two different leagues were playing in the same city. With increased competition for cities to play in, it is not surprising that, during the 1998–99 season, rumors of league mergers began to circulate. Many of them involved the WPHL and the CHL.

Tom Berry worked to develop affiliations between CHL and NHL clubs, thus strengthening his league's role as a place for developing younger talent. However, between 1996 and 2000, a relatively small number of players moved up from the CHL. A study of the scoring statistics for the league champions over these four seasons indicates that no players on these teams advanced to the NHL and that only 16 players—with a combined total of 417 games—played in the IHL or AHL.[1] None of the league's most valuable players—Trevor Jobe, Joe Burton, Derek Puppa, Chris MacKenzie or Yvan Corbin—moved to the higher leagues, and only 2 of 10 players to score 125 or more points in a season moved up.

WESTERN PROFESSIONAL HOCKEY LEAGUE: DEEP IN THE HEART OF TEXAS

The WPHL, the CHL's closest neighbor and fiercest rival for both players and desirable franchise locations, grew out of meetings between two owners of a major Canadian restaurant franchising business, the hockey-playing son of one of the owners, and one of the son's former coaches. Brad Treliving, nearing the end of a five-year minor-league career, ran into Rick Kozuback, who had become a coach for the Phoenix Roadrunners of the IHL, and the two began discussing Kozuback's idea of starting a professional league in one of the last relatively untapped regions in the minor-league explosion—the American Southwest.

"We brought the idea to my father and his partner," Brad recalled in a 2005 interview, referring to Jim Treliving and George Melville, whose Boston Pizza franchise business had expanded far beyond its Alberta and British Columbia base. "They said, 'Let's make it a franchise type of organization like Boston Pizza.'" The two businessmen gathered a group of investors, among them Kevin Lowe, then playing for the New York Rangers, and Darcy Rota, a former Chicago Blackhawk. The group provided $300,000 startup capital, $10,000 of which went to Brad Treliving and Kozuback to finance a trip from California to central Texas so they could visit cities that might have facilities suitable for hockey games.

Ralph Backstrom, who had been a member of the great Montreal Canadiens teams of the 1960s and later part-owner of the Chicago Cougars of the World Hockey Association, joined Treliving and Kozuback on their reconnaissance journey. "We looked at facilities in places like Sacramento, Long Beach and Oakland. But then we started thinking that Texas might have better potential markets," Backstrom, now the owner of the CHL's highly successful Colorado Eagles, told me in 2005. "They liked bull riding, which was a very physical, rough sport, and so hockey would probably work."

Kozuback also saw the parallels between hockey and football and felt that, as the Texas high school and college football seasons wound down, hockey would be there to provide fans with a winter sports fix. Most of the Texas buildings the trio inspected were, not surprisingly, rodeo and agricultural stadiums, and they had no ice-making equipment. "If it weren't for Rick," Backstrom remembered, "we might have moved on. I wondered, sometimes, what we were doing in these places. But he was very optimistic, and that's what got things started."

One of the biggest challenges the trio faced was selling civic officials and arena managers on the idea that professional hockey could work. "We talked to city and county officials and hockey operators about our ideas to see if they were interested. As Canadians, we had a real selling job to do," Brad Treliving explained. "We had to have the trust of the city and arena officials. Fortunately, we met many people who had vision and leadership, who realized what ice hockey could do for their cities and arenas."

The WPHL was officially incorporated early in 1995, but it was nearly a year later before the "original six" teams were announced: the El Paso Buzzards, Central Texas (Belton) Stampede, Waco Wizards, Austin Ice Bats, Amarillo Rattlers and New Mexico (Albuquerque) Scorpions. Only Amarillo and Albuquerque had ever hosted professional hockey before, and that was more than two decades earlier. The El Paso arena was the only one with an ice-making plant, so in addition to their $100,000 franchise fee, the owners of five of the new teams had to spend several hundred thousand dollars to renovate their buildings for ice hockey.

On October 15, 1996, the Central Texas Stampede defeated the Waco Wizards 5–4 in the first WPHL game. At the end of the second period, large numbers of fans, many of whom had apparently requested tickets on the 50-yard line, started to leave the building, nearly all of them quite pleased with what they thought had been the two halves of the hockey game. Three days later, the Austin Ice Bats played before a capacity crowd of 7,559 in an aging arena that their fans affectionately nicknamed "The Bat Cave." By the end of the season, a total of 864,020 fans, only a small number of whom were originally from Canada or the northern states, had watched this marvelous new sport—an average of well over 4,000 a game. Austin led the league in attendance, with a per-game average of 6,239.

League officials proclaimed the WPHL's opening season a great success and announced plans to expand by at least four teams for the second season. However, there were some problem areas. The New Mexico franchise had lost money and was reported to be close to bankruptcy, and in June the league took over operation of the Amarillo Rattlers, mired in a $750,000 debt.

San Angelo and Odessa, Texas, two of the six new teams that each paid a fee of $250,000 to join the league for the second season, were located in areas Kozuback had visited in his trip through western Texas two years earlier. Three others—Lake Charles, Monroe and Shreveport, Louisiana—opened for business in a state that had only recently been introduced to hockey by the ECHL. The sixth team—the Fort Worth Brahmas—would play head-to-head with the CHL's Fire. Although the league's per-game attendance average dropped by 500 during the second season, five new teams were added for the 1998–99 season: Little Rock,

Arkansas, where the ECHL would place a team a year later; Abilene and Corpus Christi, Texas; Alexandria, Louisiana; and Tupelo, Mississippi. Only Fort Worth showed an attendance increase in that third season.

Even though five teams were drawing fewer than the 3,500 people a game necessary to break even, the WPHL announced further expansion for the 1999–2000 season and predicted that the league would soon reach 24 teams. "Minor league hockey, in all its brutal glory, comes to Lubbock [Texas] in the fall," read an Associated Press headline for March 5, 1999. However, shortly into the 1999–2000 season, the WPHL contracted. In December, two teams folded: the Abilene Aviators, in their second season, and the Waco Wizards, one of the "original six." The Aviators, playing in a building where beer sales were prohibited, owed over $8,000 in rent; paychecks for players were late; and the league, which had taken over day-to-day operations of the club, announced that its "slush fund was running low." The Wizards, meanwhile, were in danger of being locked out of their building because of nonpayment of rent. On December 15, a league press release stated that both teams had ceased operations and added: "The WPHL believes that the move is clearly in the best interests of the Western Professional Hockey League and its 16 other member teams."[2]

At the conclusion of the season, the league announced that the Arkansas GlacierCats of Little Rock were going to cease operations after two seasons of play, one of them in competition against the ECHL's RiverBlades, who played in a brand-new crosstown arena. A few weeks later, the Alexandria Warthogs announced they would not be back for the 2001–02 season either. An unstable ownership group and front-office mismanagement were among the reasons given for the team's demise.

In marketing hockey to its nontraditional southern markets, the WPHL created a marketing slogan—"We Play Hockey Loud"—based on the initials of its name. The phrase placed the emphasis on body checks that sent players crashing against the boards or errant shots that noisily and harmlessly ricocheted against the glass. However, the league also saw itself as having a developmental role, preparing players for teams in higher-level leagues. Some of the coaches and athletes had more realistic views. In "Lone Star Skate," an article that appeared in *Sports Illustrated* in February 1998, Gary Unger, coach of the New Mexico Scorpions, remarked that "there are guys here with certain NHL skills, but not the complete packages ... But they're realistic, and their objective is the [IHL], or the [AHL], not the [NHL]."[3] During the inaugural season, many of the 200 players were veterans on their way down rather than prospects on their way up. Fourteen had had brief NHL careers, and only three had played more than a hundred major-league games: Herb Raglan, 343; Paul Lawless, 239; and Daniel Berthiaume, 231. Ryan Tobler and Darcy Verot, both of whom played for the Lake Charles Ice Pirates in 1997–98, were the first to make the NHL after playing in the WPHL. Tobler appeared in four games for the Tampa Bay Lightning during the 2001–02 season. Verlot played 37 games for Washington in the 2003–04 season. None of the league's MVPs for the first four seasons made it to the NHL, and only two advanced, seeing limited experience in the AHL and the IHL.

The experiences of Derek Shybunka, a goaltender who played two years of professional hockey, first with the Tulsa Oilers of the CHL and then with the New Mexico Scorpions and Waco Wizards of the WPHL, are not unlike those of many athletes who enjoyed brief careers in the early years of the WPHL. "I'd finished my university degree and wanted the chance to play professional hockey," he told me when we talked in 2005. "It was like a two-year paid vacation. The competition was good; we met some great people, traveled to new places, and after that we were ready to get on with regular lives." Neither the CHL nor the WPHL was really a developmental league in Shybunka's recollection, unless they were developing "the fighters. It seemed as if they were preparing some of them for jobs in the [AHL] or the [IHL]. But there were more guys on the way down than the way up. In fact, some of them seemed to be ready to play in the CHL or WPHL until they weren't wanted anymore."

He remembered that the WPHL fans weren't as knowledgeable as those in the CHL. "My wife told me that, one time, at the end of the third period, she got up to leave and said goodbye to the people sitting next to her. They were puzzled and told her that it was only the end of the third quarter. When she said that the game was over, they wouldn't believe her."

But a WPHL game was an event. "They marketed events. And the rinks had character, even if they were old. In Austin, we dressed in a trailer outside the stadium and walked to the ice on a long rubber mat. In El Paso, there was a hole in the roof and I remember it raining on me one time. Now I think these things made playing in the WPHL more fun than the CHL. I wasn't always so sure at the time.

"Waco was a tough place to play, right in the heart of Texas, football country. The owner wasn't a hockey person, and he was very thrifty. It was a revolving door—coaches and players were always coming and going. It showed on the ice. When I arrived, the team had won 4 and lost 24. Payday was an adventure. We'd all rush to the bank when we got our checks; we wanted to be there before the account emptied out. As I look back at it, it was funny. But at the time it was scary. There we were, a bunch of Canadians in the middle of Texas, living from paycheck to paycheck. Things were pretty uncertain at times. It was a great experience. I wouldn't trade it for anything."

UNITED HOCKEY LEAGUE: HEADED EAST AND SOUTH

The other two minor leagues, the Colonial Hockey League and the West Coast Hockey League, made tentative advances on the edges of territories occupied by the WPHL, CHL and ECHL, moving into the Southeast and Southwest respectively. However, their incursions into these areas were short-lived.

The Colonial League, which changed its name to the United Hockey League after the 1996–97 season, remained centered in the Midwest, but expanded eastward into upstate New York, to Utica and Binghamton, after AHL teams had departed. In the spring of 1997, the owners of the Utica Blizzard, claiming that they were unable to negotiate an acceptable lease at the Memorial Coliseum, relocated to Winston-Salem, North Carolina, a city that had lost two minor-league teams in the preceding five years. The team became the IceHawks. After two seasons, with attendance figures under 2,000 fans a game and losses of half a million dollars a season, owner Art Shaver expressed optimism for the future. However, a month later, when the Detroit Red Wings announced that they were removing their AHL affiliate from Glens Falls, New York, he relocated the IceHawks there.

The following season, the Brantford (Ontario) Smoke, one of the two remaining Canadian teams in the league, moved to Asheville, North Carolina, a city famous for its art deco architecture, but one that needed ice-making facilities in its stadium. The Smoke drew an average of 3,500 fans during the first season. Attendance decreased steadily after that.

A third team moved south for the 1999–2000 season: the Madison (Wisconsin) Monsters became the Knoxville Speed, giving the eastern

Tennessee city its first professional team since the ECHL's Cherokees had moved to South Carolina two years earlier. The presence of two southern clubs—Asheville and Knoxville—just over two hours apart, but so far away from the other UHL clubs, led commissioner Richard Brosal to express his interest in seeing the league form a southern division and to suggest Chattanooga and Bristol, Tennessee, neither of which had hockey rinks, as possible franchise locations. However, when Knoxville and Asheville withdrew from the league after the 2001–02 season, Brosal's idea was dropped.

During this four-year period, nine UHL players appeared in the NHL. For some of them, their UHL stops were brief, under 10 games. For one, Mel Angelstad, the road to the majors was a long one. He played five seasons in Thunder Bay before becoming an IHL and then AHL regular. In 2003–04, he appeared in two games for the Washington Capitals.

WEST COAST HOCKEY LEAGUE: EASTWARD EXPANSION
The WCHL, which added four new franchises, experienced a lower number of attendance declines between 1996 and 2000 than did other leagues. In fact, clubs reported per-game average increases from one season to the next 13 times. San Diego, which some jokingly referred to as the league's "Yankees," a reference to their on- and off-ice achievements, was the most successful club. They won three division, one regular season and two playoff championships. Over the four years, they averaged more than 6,300 fans a game.

Neither the Reno Renegades nor the Alaska Gold Kings was as fortunate. The former, in spite of such promotions as a pre-game exhibition by figure-skating bad girl Tonya Harding, never drew more than an average of 3,000 fans. The Fairbanks club never made it above 2,000. Renegades' owner Bruce Taylor folded the team after the 1997–98 season and took over ownership of the expansion Tacoma Sabrecats. The Gold Kings sat out a season before moving to Colorado Springs, still a plane trip away from their closest opponents.

When the league moved to Phoenix and Tucson in the fall of 1997, it claimed squatter's rights to territories that both the WPHL and CHL wanted. It also gave the WCHL two more cities within a fairly short distance of each other. Phoenix, which had iced teams in the "old" Western Hockey League, the World Hockey Association and the "old" CHL and the IHL, had been home to the NHL Coyotes since 1996. Tucson was relatively virgin territory—the CHL's Mavericks had played one season there in the mid-1970s.

Things got off to a bad start for the Tucson team. Before the Gila Monsters played their home opener in mid-October 1997, they had already gone through two owners and three general managers. Without a nickname, coach or players, the new owner and his new general manager had little time to market the team. The opening game attracted 4,101 people to the Convention Center, but by December the average attendance was under 2,000, with half the attendees reportedly receiving free tickets. By Christmas the team had suspended its radio broadcasts, filed for bankruptcy, accumulated debts of $140,000 and borrowed $400,000 from its shareholders. In the spring of 1998, a new owner, Stephen Mandell, expressed ill-founded optimism, but shortly after fewer than 400 people attended one game in late November, the team announced it was suspending operations.

The Phoenix Mustangs fared better, averaging just over 3,000 fans a game during their first three seasons. However, in the 13,700-seat Veterans' Memorial Coliseum, that number didn't generate enough money to meet expenses.

On the ice, the WCHL teams provided competitive, high-scoring action. In four years, players reached the 100-point plateau 27 times. However, only 19 of these scorers appeared in the higher majors, playing a combined total of 97 games.

MELTDOWN

2000-01

Between the early spring of 2000 and the early fall of 2001, the minor-league hockey landscape changed radically. When the 1999–2000 season ended in April 2000, 110 teams played in seven leagues. Eighteen months later, when the 2001–02 season began, 92 clubs played in five leagues. The rapid expansion of the 1990s had ended abruptly, and the process of contraction and consolidation began quickly.

RELOCATIONS AND DISAPPEARANCES

A small part of the change occurred at the end of the 1999–2000 season and was part of the routine franchise shuffle that occurred every summer. The Hampton Roads Admirals, occupying a territory long coveted by the American Hockey League, left the East Coast Hockey League to become the AHL's 20th franchise, the Norfolk Admirals. The International Hockey League lost its last small-market midwestern team as the Michigan (Kalamazoo) K Wings moved to the United Hockey League. One of its big-market franchises, the Long Beach Ice Dogs, after four years of seven-figure losses, joined the West Coast Hockey League. The UHL's Madison Monsters expired after one season, while New Haven was granted a UHL expansion franchise. Although the ECHL lost three clubs—Hampton Roads, Jacksonville and Huntington—the last of the three would reemerge as the Texas Wildcatters three years later. The Central Hockey League lost no teams and added the Border City Bandits from Texarkana, Texas. The Western Professional Hockey League folded the Arkansas GlacierCats and the Alexandria (Louisiana)

Warthogs and announced that an expansion team would begin play in Tucson in the fall.

At the end of September 2000, the various minor-league training camps began and league presidents and publicity directors released season-opening messages of optimism. Their statements may have been hollow public-relations utterances or the sounds of people whistling in the dark in spite of, or because they were blissfully ignorant of, the storm clouds massing just beyond the horizon of the season ahead. Certainly there had been signs and warnings. Articles had appeared criticizing the undue haste with which leagues had moved into untested, nontraditional markets and awarded franchises to inexperienced and sometimes underfinanced owners. It was noted that leagues overlapped each other's territories, engaging in mutually destructive turf wars, and that expansion had sometimes left league cities so distant from each other that travel budgets were becoming excessive. In the summer of 1999, Brad Lund, then the general manager (now CEO) of the CHL's Oklahoma City Blazers, commented: "In general, minor league hockey is a mess. Minor league hockey exploded too fast. There's never been any sort of governing body. It's been a free fall. The way the leagues formed has driven up costs and taken away natural rivalries. There's been no sense and structure to it. It's not fair to the people who have invested time and money into it."[1]

Entering the 2000–01 season, 46 of the returning teams—nearly half—had posted attendance declines for the previous season. For 16 of the teams, it marked the second consecutive season of decreases; for three, the third consecutive season; for seven the fourth; and for two the sixth. Twenty-two of the teams showing multiple-year declines were in the South, and for many of these the per-game decrease was considerable. Huntsville had lost 1,800 people a game in four years; Tallahassee, 3,700 in three; Orlando, 4,000 in four.

The first signs of the meltdown that would characterize the season occurred in Tucson in early October. The WPHL, which had long wanted to place a team in the southwestern Arizona city, quickly stepped in to claim the ice left vacant by the departure of the WCHL's Gila Monsters. The league awarded a franchise to Joe Milano, Jr., whose Waco Wizards had folded in the middle of the previous season. However, the Tucson Scorch's season was even shorter. On October 5, 2000, as players were preparing for their first road trip, a five-hour bus ride to El Paso, site of their opening game, WPHL officials announced that the Scorch franchise had been suspended. The club had fallen behind on lease payments to the arena and dues to the league. Moreover, it had sold fewer than 200 season tickets and thus lacked the upfront money needed to see it through the early weeks of the season. League communications director Steve Cherwonak stated: "You have to take chances with some markets ... It's a franchise business."[2]

The WPHL faced more problems as the season approached its mid-point. On January 6, 2001, the Central Texas Stampede, one of the "original six," played its last game. Dick Young, a spokesman for the ownership that had taken over the club eight months earlier, explained that low attendance (the team's per-game average had dropped by over 2,000 since the opening season), lack of sufficient sponsorship revenue, and rising costs led to the team's demise. He added that his group had lost $750,000 so far that season. Will Wright, sports editor of the *Temple Daily Telegram*, remarked cynically about "the popular belief that the league wanted too much, too soon by franchising too many teams. Demographics and marketing are taught in high school and college. And it seems that the league's powers-that-be, a bunch of rich guys from Canada, didn't know this part of the United States very well."[3] He suggested that "with four or five strapped teams ... the WPHL ... will live up to another acronym. Won't Play Hockey Long."[4]

Just 324 miles northeast of Belton, home of the Central Texas Stampede, another crisis was developing in Texarkana, home of the CHL's Border City Bandits. The expansion team's arrival a few months earlier had been met with skepticism when Jeff Minor, a reporter for the *Texarkana Gazette*, announced that the owner, Canadian developer John Barath, had abandoned an earlier team he'd owned, the WCHL's Tucson Gila Monsters, only a few weeks before it filed for bankruptcy. Barath had arrived in Texarkana, the CHL's smallest market, announcing that he expected many sellouts during the inaugural season.

By mid-November 2000, the team was in trouble on and off the ice. It was well on the way to a season record of 11 wins, 36 losses and 4 ties; was on its third general manager; and had seen crowds drop from nearly 4,000 a game to under 2,200. The first coach had been fired and then rehired after his replacement had been let go. The ticketing service canceled its contract with the team because the Bandits weren't paying their bills, and the office furniture was repossessed. Players cashed their paychecks as soon as possible, hoping they wouldn't bounce. On February 20, 2001, the CHL terminated the franchise, noting that it had fallen $80,000 behind in its dues payments to the league.

The UHL, meanwhile, was having its own problems with the Mohawk Valley (Utica) Prowlers. The upstate New York city had never been a strong hockey town; earlier teams in the UHL and the AHL had drawn between 2,000 and 2,400 a game. In the 2000–01 season, the Prowlers' attendance had dropped below the 2,000 mark, and corporate sponsorship had fallen considerably. On February 6, 2001, the team filed for bankruptcy protection. Expenses were reported to be exceeding income by more than 40 percent, and 117 creditors had not been paid. The Prowlers canceled one game after the team refused to take the ice, then played another with replacements, losing 18–4. On February 17, the UHL, fearing that the club would injure the league's credibility, closed the team down, stating that it had contravened league regulations.

Several years later, B.J. Stephens told me about his two months playing with the Prowlers. "It was my first year of pro hockey. I was brought in around Christmas. I think it was because I was cheap; the coach was letting the higher-priced veterans go. In January, our checks bounced, but the management asked us to wait for a week or so. Finally, we said, 'No pay, no play.' The management hadn't paid the rent on the players' apartments and guys were getting eviction notices. It seemed like right out of a movie—that outfit was as minor-league as it gets. I wondered why I'd chosen this profession."

During the season, several other clubs were reported to be in financial trouble: Topeka, Huntsville and Macon in the CHL; New Mexico, Lake Charles and Monroe in the WPHL; Phoenix in the WCHL; Port Huron in the UHL; Birmingham, Mobile, Roanoke and Tallahassee in the ECHL; Detroit and Cleveland in the IHL; and Kentucky and Louisville in the AHL. At the end of the seven minor leagues' regular seasons, 73 teams had seen attendance decrease; 18 of them had experienced drops of over 1,000 fans a game. For Greenville of the ECHL and Cincinnati of the IHL, the drop was over 2,000; for Cleveland and Detroit of the IHL it was over 4,000.

E-MERGING SOLUTIONS

In previous years, the leagues addressed their problems in a variety of ways, from relocating franchises to using expansion fees to provide temporary relief for cash-strapped teams. Sometimes owners sold to new owners who had neither the requisite experience nor the money. However, these were only stopgap solutions. During the 2000–01 season, another solution was frequently being discussed: league mergers, which would eliminate weak franchises and avoid overlapping territories. Until late May 2001, the AHL and the IHL continued to speak of business as usual in spite of season-long rumors about ongoing talks between the leagues. In contrast, the CHL and the WPHL did not hide the fact that they both believed it was necessary for them to merge.

In early March, *In the Crease*, a now-defunct hockey news website, reported that "after years of trying to kill each other, the WPHL and the CHL have agreed to put past differences aside and merge in the best interests of minor league hockey ... Rick Kozuback, President of the WPHL's parent company Global Entertainment, has confirmed a

meeting last week with CHL founder Horn Chen ... [Brad Treliving, WPHL president, said] both leagues can only benefit from working together."[5] Kozuback spoke of a quest "to combine the marketing skills of the WPHL with the tradition and mature hockey markets of the CHL."[6]

Like an army, a hockey team travels on its stomach. Here, unidentified members of the Lubbock Cotton Kings enjoy a post-game meal supplied by the Jack-Pack, the booster club of the Odessa Jackalopes.

After the season, two mergers took place, although, for legal reasons, the terms "joint operating agreement" and "expansion" were used. On May 31, 2001, the WPHL and CHL announced that they were entering a 10-year joint operating agreement. The league would be called the Central Hockey League, but it would be administered by WPHL, Inc., the legal name of the Western Professional Hockey League. The need to reduce travel expenses led to the demise of the CHL's southeastern teams—Columbus and Macon, Georgia; Huntsville, Alabama; and Fayetteville, North Carolina. Tupelo, Lake Charles and Monroe—the WPHL's most financially unstable clubs—did not return either.

Less than a week later, on June 4, 2001, the IHL commissioner announced that his league was disbanding. Six IHL teams—Salt Lake City, Houston, Manitoba (Winnipeg), Milwaukee, Chicago and Grand Rapids—would apply for expansion franchises in the AHL. The fee would be $1.5 million a team, with each surviving team contributing another $1 million to a fund to settle the IHL's remaining business. Consolidation, along with the elimination of weaker franchises, it was stated, would make the enlarged AHL stronger and more stable.

Although much of the media attention during the 2000–01 season focused on financial difficulties and the "merger" processes, a lot of very good hockey was played. Two players who toiled in the lower minors eventually moved up to the NHL. Jason Labarbera of the Charlotte Checkers (ECHL) later played for the Los Angeles Kings, while Raitis Ivanans of the New Haven Knights (UHL) went to the Montreal Canadiens. Nineteen players scored over a hundred points in the season—Yvan Corbin of the CHL's Indianapolis Ice (129 points) and Hugo Belanger of the UHL's Adirondack IceHawks (125 points) led the way—although none of them made it to the NHL.

A small number of players in the lower minors were advancing to higher leagues. In addition, a small number of players were being paid salaries that were too high. An essential aspect of maintaining competitive balance among teams in a league, and of keeping salary expenditures from creating too great a drain on a team's financial resources, is the imposition of salary caps, which limit the total amount a team can pay its players each week. In March 2001, the ECHL announced that, for the second time in two years, the Tallahassee Tiger Sharks had violated the league's regulations by offering some players under-the-table payments. In addition to a $50,000 fine, which the cash-strapped club could ill afford, the league deducted 15 of the team's points in the standings. As a result, the team failed to make the playoffs for the first time in five seasons.

The New Mexico Scorpions of the WPHL found themselves in similar trouble. For several months, rumors circulated that they had violated the salary cap; in March, the league found the Scorpions guilty. Their fine was also $50,000, a blow to owner Michael Plaman, who had fallen behind in payment of league dues. More significantly, the club had 34 points taken off its total, so instead of being on top of the Western Division, it found itself struggling—ultimately unsuccessfully—for a playoff spot. It marked the second time the Scorpions had been punished for illegal payments, and the second time Plaman had been punished. His Shreveport Mudbugs had been fined for a similar offense two years earlier. Plaman took the league to court over its decision against the Scorpions, but the case was dismissed. Shortly afterward, he sold the club to Corpus Christi businessman Doug Frank.

CONSOLIDATION

2001-05

The 2001–02 season marked the beginning of four years of relative stability in the minor leagues. With the American Hockey League taking in teams from the International Hockey League, and the Central and Western Professional hockey leagues entering into a joint operating agreement, the number of minor leagues dropped to five. During the 2003–04 season, the East Coast Hockey League accepted six members of the West Coast Hockey League as expansion franchises. A new league, the Atlantic Coast Hockey League, emerged in 2002–03, split into two smaller leagues for a season and then reunited in 2004–05 as the Southern Professional Hockey League. There were 94 teams operating during the 2001–02 season; in subsequent years the numbers were 93, 98 and 95. By the beginning of the 2005–06 season, 17 southern cities that had hosted minor-league clubs during the previous decade found themselves without teams. The southern ice age was slowing down.

AHL: FOCUS ON DEVELOPMENT

With the inclusion of Salt Lake City, Milwaukee, Chicago, Houston, Manitoba and Grand Rapids from the IHL; the transfer of the Kentucky franchise to Cleveland; and the addition of teams in Manchester (New Hampshire) and Bridgeport (Connecticut), the AHL began the 2001–02 season with 27 teams. It was close to realizing NHL commissioner Gary Bettman's goal of 30 teams, one developmental club for each NHL team. Over the next two years, three franchises—Louisville (2002), Quebec City (2003) and Saint John (2003)—had to suspend operations because they were unable to obtain affiliation agreements with NHL teams.

Although each AHL club's roster included a few older, more experienced players who could become short-term NHL replacements for
injured players and who could help younger players adjust to the intan-
gible elements of playing in the higher levels of the minors, the focus was
on development. The 2004–05 *American Hockey League Guide and
Record Book* made this point clear. The cover included a photograph
of Tampa Bay's Martin St. Louis, the NHL's Most Valuable Player in
2004, hoisting the Stanley Cup. President Dave Andrews's introductory
letter began by stating: "The AHL is proud to have produced over
100 members of the Hockey Hall of Fame and thousands of National
Hockey League players." A two-page spread announced that 80 percent
of NHL players for the preceding season were AHL grads and that 15
NHL head coaches had come from the AHL ranks, along with all of
the NHL's referees and 25 of the 38 linesmen.

For the 2001–02 season, the entry of the Houston Aeros from the
IHL gave the AHL two southern teams, the other being the Norfolk
Admirals. A year later, the dormant Louisville franchise moved to south-
west Texas to become the San Antonio Rampage. The arrival of the
AHL team in the Alamo city forced the CHL's San Antonio Iguanas
to suspend operations. It marked the second time a CHL team in San
Antonio had to cease operations because of the arrival of a club from a
higher league.

ECHL: PREMIER AA HOCKEY LEAGUE

The ECHL, which ended the 2000–01 season with 25 teams, added new
clubs in 17 cities during the next four years, but lost 18—15 of them in
the South, and 6 of these along the Interstate 10 corridor. Six of the new
teams had been members of the WCHL: nine had relocated from other
league cities. After announcing the acceptance of the WCHL clubs,
the ECHL had confidently revealed plans to expand to 40 teams in a
matter of three or four years. It reached 31 during the 2003–04 season,
but shrank to 28 a year later. By the start of the 2005–06 season it was
down to 25 teams.

When the ECHL relocated the troubled Huntsville, Alabama, franchise to Tallahassee, Florida, after the 1993–94 season, it was hailed as
a bold move into a nontraditional market. Soon the "I-10 Corridor," or
"Ice-10" as it was dubbed by sports writers, was being described as the

brave new frontier of minor-league hockey. However, beginning with the 1999–2000 season, the Ice-10 experienced a number of closures, and by the end of the 2004–05 season, only the Mississippi Sea Wolves remained. Jacksonville, playing in an aging and unsuitable facility, left after the 1999–2000 season. Tallahassee left after the next. The Mobile Mysticks, having seen attendance declines in five of their six seasons, followed suit after the 2001–02 season. The New Orleans Brass, which had enjoyed good crowds in its three seasons at the New Orleans Arena, found itself without a place to play when the Hornets, the National Basketball Association team that had moved from Charlotte, became the principal tenant beginning in the 2002–03 season.

The Baton Rouge Kingfish dropped out after the 2002–03 season. Owner Scott Bolduc, who had rescued the team from bankruptcy in October 2001, criticized local businesses for lack of support and threatened to sell the club to people who would move it elsewhere unless 4,000 season tickets were sold, an almost impossible goal considering that fewer than 2,000 people were presently attending each game. Locals, annoyed by his brash, outspoken attitude, did not buy.

By spring 2005, 12 other ECHL clubs ceased operations: Macon and Columbus, Georgia; Richmond and Roanoke, Virginia; Arkansas (Little Rock); Jackson, Mississippi; Lexington, Kentucky; Greensboro, North Carolina; Cincinnati, Ohio; Peoria, Illinois; Atlantic City, New Jersey; and Pee Dee (Florence), South Carolina.

With so many franchises going dark, it might seem the ECHL had become the "Incredible Shrinking League." However, it finished the 2004–05 season with 28 clubs, only three below its all-time high. Two factors accounted for its relative stability. First, many of the clubs relocated to new cities. For example, the Baton Rouge Kingfish resurfaced as the Victoria (British Columbia) Salmon Kings; the Mobile Mysticks transformed themselves into the highly successful Gwinnett (Georgia) Gladiators; and the Tallahassee Tiger Sharks became the Macon (Georgia) Whoopie for a year and then the Lexington (Kentucky) Men O'War. Unlike the WPHL, which allowed failing franchises to disappear permanently, victims of an attrition process that the league claimed made it stronger, the ECHL actively helped its troubled franchises in the search for new locations or for new owners who might relocate teams. When I asked him recently about the cost of an expansion franchise in the ECHL, Jack Carnefix, the league's director of communications, replied, "Two million." But he quickly added, "We'd encourage qualified buyers first to talk to owners of dormant franchises, which might be less expensive."

The WCHL also contributed to the ECHL's numerical stability. After the 2001–02 season, the West Coast Hockey League's Tacoma Sabrecats and Colorado (Colorado Springs) Gold Kings suspended operations, and one of the six surviving WCHL clubs, the Anchorage Aces, filed for bankruptcy. (Owner Michael Cusack put the club up for sale on eBay, but the listing was withdrawn when a $2.3 million bid turned out to be a college student's prank. Local ownership was later secured.)

A growing number of minor-league hockey teams play in brand-new, state-of-the art facilities. Since the fall of 2005, the Charlotte Checkers of the ECHL have called Bobcats Arena, built for the National Basketball Association team, their home.

With its high travel costs, $12,000-a-week salary cap and very high worker's compensation fees in California, the WCHL realized it could no longer continue in its current form. By June 2002, the possibility of a merger with the ECHL was openly discussed in newspapers, and on September 11, 2002, the ECHL announced that it would accept nine expansion franchises. Six teams from the WCHL would join in 2003. Three more—based in Las Vegas and Reno, Nevada, and Ontario, California—would begin play when their proposed arenas were completed. (By fall 2005, only Las Vegas had joined the league.) ECHL Commissioner Rick Adams stated that the expansion fee of $300,000 per team was a "group rate discount."

Over the next several months the ECHL worked to establish a uniform salary cap and a limit on the number of veterans allowed on each team, both of which ended up being considerably lower than the numbers previously set by the WCHL. The league then tackled the problem of what to call itself now that it bordered the Atlantic, Gulf and Pacific coasts. Two options were considered: the Premier League, which emphasized its role in developing young talent; and a corporate designation, in which the league would sell naming rights to a sponsor, who would pay as much as $1 million a year for a decade. Both possibilities were rejected, and the league decided to use the initials ECHL followed by the slogan "Premier AA Hockey League," a phrase that implied its superiority over the CHL and UHL.

During the summer of 2003, as it prepared to welcome its new western teams, the ECHL faced a major crisis. Its collective bargaining agreement with the Professional Hockey Players' Association (PHPA), which represented players in both the ECHL and the AHL, was due to expire. Each side advanced positions unacceptable to the other. The league wanted to restrict the size of its rosters to 19 and decrease the salary cap from $10,000 to $8,000 a week. The players wanted no limits on the number of veteran players (those who had appeared in more than 250 professional games), a salary cap of $8,500 and, most important, 12-month health insurance coverage for themselves and their families.

On August 18, 2003, the PHPA announced that its membership was on strike. Although this was a largely symbolic gesture, as the regular season was two months away, it could have had real consequences when training camps opened in early October. Canadian players would not have been granted work visas and thus would have been unable to attend the camps. However, the strike was settled, and the weekly salary cap was set at $10,000 in order to bring it closer to the salary caps of the former WCHL teams that were about to join the league. Each team was permitted to sign four veterans (who were now defined as players who had appeared in more than 288 professional games, half a season's difference from the earlier figure) and health benefits were increased. Signing this agreement further strengthened the ECHL's claim to be the premier AA hockey league. Neither the CHL nor the UHL had such a contract.

The ECHL continued its role as a developmental league. Its *2004–05 Official Guide and Record Book* contained a short article, "ECHL Today ... NHL Tomorrow," which summarized the achievements of ECHL graduates: "With a record of 40 former players taking the ice for the first time ever in the National Hockey League in 2003–04, the ECHL has firmly established its place as the Premier 'AA' Hockey League."[1] The article went on to mention that three players, the radio announcer and the equipment manager—all of whom had been in the ECHL—were members of the 2004 Stanley Cup champions, the Tampa Bay Lightning.

When the NHL locked out its players and canceled the 2004–05 season, the movement of players from the ECHL to the AHL and NHL was reversed. Many top prospects who might have spent some or all of the 2004–05 season with their NHL clubs were assigned to AHL teams, bumping AHL players to the ECHL. A few NHL regulars chose to stay in shape by playing in the minors. The most notable of these was New Jersey's Scott Gomez, who returned to his native state and played 61 games for the Alaska Aces, scoring 86 points and earning the league's Most Valuable Player award.

CHL: "NO NIGHTMARE TO BEHOLD"

Sixteen of the 24 teams that finished the 2000–01 season in the WPHL or the CHL entered the first season of the consolidated CHL. Over the next four seasons, only six teams left the league, while four joined. It was a small number of changes compared to the arrivals and departures of earlier years, and it reflected the CHL's attempt to avoid the financial problems that had been so frequent in the past. Now, financially stable owners ran clubs, many of which played in new multipurpose entertainment centers. By the end of the 2004–05 season, eight teams occupied arenas built since 2000.

In an interview with the Shreveport *Times*, CHL president Brad Treliving spoke positively of the first year of the merger: "It's a continual daily process. We continue to upgrade. From a business standpoint, we have to continue to solidify markets." He noted with pride the CHL's growing role as a developmental league, pointing out that four clubs had secondary affiliations with NHL teams. Writing about the process and results of the merger, Brian Vernellis, a reporter for the *Times*, humorously commented that "the powers that be had to play Dr. Frankenstein. They cut their loses, salvaged the remaining teams, and stitched together their strongest assets into a 16-team league. Whether it was the WPHL which bailed out the CHL or the CHL which bailed out the WPHL is a strong topic of conversation, but the resulting conglomeration of teams has become no nightmare to behold."[2]

Halfway through the 2002–03 season, the league faced a major problem. On January 7, the El Paso Buzzards—which had fallen $22,000 behind in rent payment, missed payrolls, fired front-office employees and lost their radio broadcasts—were locked out of their arena. A day later, each member of the team had to pay five dollars to enter the rink during a public skating session for a makeshift practice. Owner Bill Davidson, whose share of the Corpus Christi club had several months earlier been bought out by unhappy fellow owners, declared bankruptcy. The general manager, who hadn't been paid, resigned, and the league took over players' salaries. Attendance dropped to under 300 a game. Coach Craig Coxe, who at times was only able to dress 9 or 10 players, had not been paid in nearly a month and a half. On June 6, 2003, the CHL announced that it was shutting down the El Paso franchise. However, the team continued to make headlines in the sports pages during the summer. El Paso police issued a warrant for former owner Davidson. He was accused of stealing 14 pairs of skates from the team locker room in February. The skates had been returned the day after they disappeared, and charges against Davidson were later dropped.

During the first four years of the joint operating agreement, the reorganized CHL showed a modest but steady increase in per-game attendance, each season drawing approximately 200 more fans for each game. This was due largely to the development of new buildings in existing and expansion markets. In 2000, the founders of the WPHL had created Global Entertainment Corporation, which, in addition to WPHL, Inc., ran International Coliseums Company, GetTix and GEMS (Global Entertainment Marketing System), all of which were involved in the arena entertainment business. Two of the expansion clubs—the Rio Grande Valley (Hidalgo, Texas) Killer Bees and the Colorado (Fort Collins) Eagles—played in buildings developed by International Coliseums. Located in an area that was home to more than three-quarters of a million people, the Killer Bees developed a natural rivalry with Corpus Christi to the east and Laredo to the west and drew close to capacity crowds, including many people from Mexico, to its 5,000-seat arena. More than 1,200 miles to the north, the Colorado Eagles enjoyed similar success playing at the Budweiser Events Center, which was located in the middle of the best American hockey country outside Michigan, Minnesota and New England. Season-ticket sales were capped at just over 4,000, and the Eagles played to capacity crowds during their first two seasons.

In addition, Laredo, which had joined the league in the fall of 2002, consistently drew crowds of over 6,000 to games in its new building, while the always strong Oklahoma City Blazers averaged over 8,000 a game in the Ford Center, which had opened in 2002.

Family-priced, competitive hockey was the focus in these and other CHL arenas. However, teams were not above publicity stunts. In the fall of 2002, retired NBA player Manute Bol, who was 7 feet 7 inches tall, signed with the Indianapolis Ice. Even though he couldn't skate and never played a game, he gained international publicity for the team and raised money to aid children in his native Sudan. In the winter of 2005, Angela Ruggiero, a member of the American women's hockey team, briefly joined the Tulsa Oilers, playing defense in front of her goaltender brother, Bill.

UHL: ELITE PROFESSIONAL HOCKEY

Between the fall of 2001 and spring 2005, the UHL worked hard to become worthy of the motto it presently uses, "Elite Professional Hockey." It wished to establish its superiority over the CHL and to approach the level of excellence of the ECHL. However, in 2004, Peoria *Journal Star* reporter David Eminian provided another, less-flattering slogan, "The Unsound Hockey League," and remarked that it is "busy again this season trying to complete a schedule while some of its members die along the trail."[3] He was referring to the fact that the Columbus (Ohio) Stars folded in the middle of the season and two other teams—Missouri and Adirondack—were in serious danger of going under. During the four seasons, the UHL iced teams in 18 cities; however, membership went from 14 to 10 to 12 and back to 14.

Richard Brosal, the league commissioner, attempted to put a positive spin on losing teams. In October 2002, he told reporter Justin A. Cohn that "a strong league doesn't necessarily equate to how many teams you have … But one thing I've learned in this industry is that it turns on a dime. For us to speculate on what would happen would be foolish. It could all change on May 1."[4] At the end of the season he mentioned Canton, Ohio; Lehigh Valley and Williamsport, Pennsylvania; Cherry Hills, New Jersey; Mount Vernon, New York; Bloomington, Illinois; and Des Moines, Iowa, as possible franchise locations. None of the cities mentioned had teams in the league by the 2005–06 season, but Bloomington was to begin play in the fall of 2006.

The league did, however, grant four new franchises: Columbus

(Ohio) and Richmond (Virginia) in 2003, and Danbury (Connecticut) and Kansas City (Missouri) in 2004. Columbus didn't make it through its first season; Kansas City lasted one year. The move to Richmond, to the building vacated by an ECHL team, proved moderately successful. However, it also necessitated the admission of another southern city in order to decrease the traveling expenses of midwestern teams. In the spring of 2005, the league announced that Ken and Kristen Dixon would relocate their financially struggling Port Huron, Michigan, franchise to Roanoke, Virginia, in the fall of 2005.

During the four-year period, UHL teams reported average per-game attendance increases from the previous year only 22 times. Fort Wayne attracted more than 7,000 people a game for three seasons and more than 6,000 for another, but there were 23 instances where UHL clubs posted per-game attendance averages under 3,000.

ACHL, WHA2, SEHL, SPHL: NEW LEAGUES FOR OLD CITIES

By the spring of 2002, enough southeastern towns had lost their minor-league hockey teams to form a good-sized league. Businessmen from three of the cities—Knoxville (Tennessee), Fayetteville (North Carolina) and Columbus (Georgia)—approached Bill Coffey, one of the founders of the ECHL, to ask for his help in forming a new league. "From my experience in Greensboro and later Fayetteville, I knew that we needed at least four solid franchises, along with some others that could draw enough people to make expenses. And we needed owners who could run teams in a business-like way," Coffey remarked.

He developed a simple plan: ensure that expenses were within reason by reducing travel, shortening the length of the season and keeping salaries low. "You also needed to provide an entertaining product at an affordable price. Southerners don't understand the intricacies of hockey; this is NASCAR country," Coffey explained. "But if you provide competitive, balanced teams and an entertaining show and establish rivalries between relatively nearby cities, people will come out."

Finding players was not difficult. There were plenty of older players nearing the ends of their careers, along with undrafted junior and college athletes, who would be happy to skate in southern cities for teams whose weekly salary caps were less than $6,000 a week. Finding enough good owners to create a league that had a sufficient number of teams was not so easy. In March 2002, when he announced the creation of the Atlantic Coast Hockey League (ACHL), Coffey stated that he hoped there would be 10 to 12 teams. However, when the season opened in October, only Knoxville, Tennessee; Fayetteville, North Carolina; Jacksonville, St. Petersburg and Orlando in Florida; and Macon, Georgia, iced teams.

The league began to experience problems early in the first season. The St. Petersburg Parrots, run by Coffey himself, played at the aging Bayfront Center. Coffey was the team's third owner in four months, and he had purchased the franchise just before the season began so that the league would have an even six teams. On December 4, 2002, he announced that he was moving the club, which had drawn fewer than 800 fans a game, to Winston-Salem, North Carolina.

As the season progressed, it became apparent that there were other troubled operations. David Waronker, a Florida developer who had purchased the Orlando Seals early in the season, assumed controlling interest in the troubled Jacksonville and Macon teams. The Orlando Seals won the only ACHL championship, and Knoxville averaged 3,600 fans a game.

As soon as the season was over, Waronker withdrew his three teams from the ACHL and announced the formation of the World Hockey Association 2 (WHA2), which would begin play in the fall of 2003. His intention was that, during its second season, the league would provide farm clubs for the proposed World Hockey Association, which was scheduled to begin play in the fall of 2004 (it didn't get off the ground). The remaining ACHL owners announced that Fayetteville, Knoxville and Winston-Salem would become the core of the South East Hockey League (SEHL). The two leagues were frequently in competition for the same cities. Waronker predicted that WHA2 would be an 8- to 10-team league, while the SEHL owners expected to have six or eight teams.

By the end of the summer of 2003, the two new leagues had lined up their teams. The WHA2 established clubs in Pelham, a suburb of Birmingham, Alabama; Macon, Georgia; and Jacksonville, Lakeland, Orlando and Miami, Florida. The SEHL had clubs in Huntsville, Alabama; Knoxville, Tennessee; Fayetteville and Winston-Salem, North Carolina.

In early December 2003, the WHA2 began to experience difficulties. Crowds were less than expected; expenses were greater. Reports began to circulate of missed payrolls, bounced checks, players buying their own sticks and driving their own cars on road trips. The Miami Manatees, drawing just over 1,000 fans a game, became a road team in January 2004. As the season limped to a close, only Jacksonville was drawing an average of more than 3,000 fans a game. In Orlando, where the team staged a "guaranteed fight night" promotion, the 20,000-seat TD Waterhouse Centre rented for $12,000 a night. Proceeds from over half of the 3,000 tickets sold for each game were used to cover lease fees. The league held no playoffs; the Jacksonville Barracudas were declared champions.

Although the SEHL fared better—three of the four teams drew an average of just over 2,500 people a game—it, too, was not without problems. In the six weeks before the season began, it gained one team (Winston-Salem) and lost another (Tupelo, Mississippi). The Winston-Salem club was initially named the Moosehead after a Canadian beer, one of the major sponsors. However, just as the season was about to begin, the name was withdrawn and a name-the-team contest began. By November 26, when the new name, the Thunderbirds, was announced, the club was in the middle of a six-week road trip; another organization had booked the arena before the team had joined the league. The Thunderbirds attracted fewer than 800 fans a game. Huntsville won what would be the league's only championship, defeating Knoxville three games to one.

At the end of the season, officials from both leagues set to work creating a new league consisting of teams from the WHA2 and SEHL. Known first as the Eastern Hockey League, then the Southern Hockey League, it finally became the Southern Professional Hockey League (SPHL) and was made up of eight teams: Knoxville, Fayetteville, Jacksonville, Macon, Huntsville and Winston-Salem from the old leagues, and two new teams, Columbus (Georgia) and Asheville (North Carolina).

The league made no claims to be as good as the UHL, CHL or ECHL, each of which had previously located teams in these cities. The SPHL's aim was to provide competitive hockey with rosters that would fall within the salary cap of $5,600 a week, and it succeeded. In the final standings, the top six teams were separated by only 10 points. Fifth-place Columbus won the championship.

For 79 players, their time in the SPHL did provide a stepping stone to higher leagues. By the middle of the 2005–06 season, two SPHL veterans had appeared on AHL rosters, 21 on ECHL lists, 26 on UHL rosters and 30 on CHL rosters. Two of the eight teams, Knoxville and Fayetteville, averaged over 3,100 people a game. Buoyed by the strong showings of four of the teams, the SPHL began plans for a second season, something their predecessors had not accomplished, and started a search for expansion clubs.

CONSOLIDATION CONTINUES: THE 2005–06 SEASON OPENS

In the spring and summer of 2005, the various minor leagues began to line up teams for the new season. By October, the number of teams had shrunk to 88. Four teams had relocated, 8 cities had received expansion franchises and 15 cities found themselves without minor-league teams.

Both the Toronto Maple Leafs and the St. Louis Blues announced that they were moving their AHL franchises. The St. John's Maple Leafs became the Toronto Marlies and played in Ricoh Coliseum, a 15-minute drive from the parent team's Air Canada Centre. Citing insufficient corporate support, the St. Louis Blues transferred the Worcester IceCats to Peoria, Illinois, displacing the ECHL Rivermen.

With the AHL expanding to Omaha (Nebraska) and Des Moines (Iowa), and with teams already in Chicago, Illinois, and Milwaukee and Grand Rapids, Michigan, the league increased its Midwest presence. Because of high travel costs, the Utah Grizzlies dropped out of the AHL. Cincinnati requested a voluntary suspension because it had been unable to secure the required NHL affiliation. The Edmonton Roadrunners, after one season in the league, requested a one-year leave. The San Antonio Rampage, Houston Aeros and Norfolk Admirals remained the AHL's only southern teams. In October, the league began play with 27 teams, one less than in the previous season.

The ECHL made the greatest changes during the off-season and started the 2005–06 season with 25 clubs, three less than in 2004–05. The Atlantic City Boardwalk Bullies, who had never reached the 4,000-per-game attendance average in four seasons, relocated to Stockton, California. A new team, the Roadrunners, owned by the Phoenix Suns of the National Basketball Association, became the first minor-league hockey team to play in the Arizona city since 2001. The Louisiana Ice-Gators franchise, which had been run by the league since January and averaged fewer than 1,200 people a game, was terminated. Although the IceGators was one of only seven minor-league clubs to have posted a season average per-game attendance over 10,000 (which it did twice in the late 1990s), its audience had declined rapidly and drastically over seven seasons. A succession of inexperienced owners, poor marketing and the loss of ice hockey's novelty factor were blamed for the decline. The Pee Dee Pride, which played in one of the league's smallest markets and had seen attendance decline by nearly 3,000 a game over six seasons, withdrew from the league.

After June 15, the date the owners of the Utah Grizzlies announced that the Salt Lake City team would be joining the ECHL, the league's off-season reorganization seemed to be complete. However, in early September, the Mississippi Sea Wolves, whose seaside arena in Biloxi had been heavily damaged by Hurricane Katrina, applied for and received a year's leave of absence. Then Hurricane Rita hit the Texas Gulf Coast. Beaumont's Ford Arena was commandeered for use in long-term relief efforts, so the Texas Wildcatters also requested a voluntary suspension. With the Wildcatters' withdrawal, only Pensacola remained of the nine ECHL teams that had played in cities along the I-10 corridor.

In the CHL, the Topeka Tarantulas, owned by Horn Chen, one of the league founders, had drawn an average 2,300 fans a game, 800 fewer than the breakeven number of 3,100, and it ceased operations after one year. The San Angelo Saints of Texas, playing in the league's smallest market, also discontinued operations. Attendance had remained between 2,100 and 2,400 fans a game for the previous four seasons. In early May, the New Mexico Scorpions surprised Albuquerque hockey fans when the franchise announced that it would suspend operations for one year. Forced to share prime weekend dates with a new minor-league basketball team, owner Doug Frank opted not to play until the team's new arena in nearby Rio Rancho was complete.

The CHL added one franchise. The Youngstown (Ohio) Steelheads would play in a new arena built and managed by International Coliseums, a subsidiary of the league's parent company, Global Entertainment. Located 768 miles from Memphis, the nearest league city, the Ohio team would have to fly to many away games and would pay a travel subsidy to fly opponents to Youngstown. The CHL began the season with 15 teams, two less than in 2004–05.

In March 2005, the UHL granted Port Huron, Michigan, an expansion team, replacing the Beacons, which had moved to Roanoke. Late in the spring, the Kansas City Outlaws disbanded after playing only one season. This left the UHL with 14 teams, the same number as it had the previous year.

Shortly after the conclusion of its inaugural season, the SPHL lost three of its eight teams and announced the addition of two new clubs. The Macon Trax, which had been operating with a skeleton front-office staff since Christmas, folded after owner David Waronker failed to find local owners. The Winston-Salem Polar Twins, whose announced attendance of 1,265 a game was the lowest in all of the minor leagues, survived to the end of the season only because they received financial assistance from Keith Jeffers, owner of the Huntsville Havoc. He, too, searched in vain for local owners before closing the organization. Richard Hoodenpyle withdrew the Asheville Aces from the league because he was unable to renegotiate what he considered an unreasonably expensive lease with the Asheville Civic Center. He then announced that he would operate an expansion franchise in Florence, South Carolina, which had just lost its ECHL team. The Orlando Seals, which had not played in 2004–05, moved to Kissimmee and became the Florida Seals.

The 2005–06 minor-league season began with 88 teams, 36 of them in southern cities, playing in five leagues.

CONCLUSION

Thoughts on Dixie Hockey

In early March 2006, as I began a four-day drive from Albuquerque to Edmonton, I passed by Tingley Coliseum, where 15 months earlier my interest in minor-league hockey had been rekindled. Since I'd watched the New Mexico Scorpions play the Tulsa Oilers on December 19, 2004, many changes had taken place. Bill MacDonald had resigned as coach and become the new coach of the Austin Ice Bats. In early May 2005, owner Doug Frank announced that the team would not play during the upcoming season. Annoyed that the Coliseum administration had offered the majority of the attractive weekend dates to a newly formed minor-league basketball team, Frank decided to place the team on voluntary suspension until the fall of 2006, when a new facility in nearby Rio Rancho would be completed. In January 2006, he sold the team to a group that included former NHL player Dave Ellett. The group would be the franchise's fourth set of owners since it was formed in 1996.

I had been surprised when I first heard about the various events. However, as I turned onto Interstate 25 and drove north, I began to see that they reflected the one major constant of the minor-league hockey boom that began 18 seasons earlier: constant change. In fact, in the months before the 2005–06 season began, 26 cities had been affected as franchises relocated and dissolved, expansion franchises were granted and clubs shifted between leagues. Already this year, reports and rumors regarding various franchises were circulating widely.

In the American Hockey League, there was talk that Cincinnati might return to the league after a year's absence and that the Edmonton Oilers were going to place their dormant Roadrunner farm team in Quad Cities, Iowa/Illinois. The CHL's plans to place a team in Broomfield, Colorado, only 35 miles away from the Colorado Eagles' arena, angered the owners of that CHL club, and rumors circulated that the group was seeking a franchise in either the ECHL or AHL. It looked like the UHL was going to add two teams in Illinois, but the league's second excursion into the southern states seemed likely to end as both the Richmond and Roanoke franchises in Virginia were rumored to be ceasing operations after the current seasons. Those rumors went on to say that either or both of the Virginia cities might be candidates for expansion teams in the Southern Professional Hockey League. There were no rumors about the ECHL, but the Mississippi Sea Wolves, whose Biloxi arena had been damaged by Hurricane Katrina, were not going to ice a team for the 2006–07 season. The Texas Wildcatters, who, along with the Sea Wolves, had sat out the 2005–06 season, would be back.

Thinking about the articles I'd read and the interviews I had conducted over the previous 12 months, I tried to come up with answers to the questions I'd asked over a year earlier. Why had minor-league hockey expanded into southern markets—and why had the expansion occurred so quickly? Why did people want to form leagues and purchase teams? Why did cities actively seek franchises? Why did coaches, players and on-ice officials want to work in places where crowds had little knowledge of the game, where travel was usually grueling and where the pay was very low? What was it that drew fans—in very large numbers initially—to watch a game that was completely foreign to most of them? What caused leagues to merge or fail and teams to relocate or cease operations? Why had minor-league hockey lost a significant number of teams, particularly in the South, during the past five or six seasons? Finally, what was the future of minor-league hockey in the South?

The boom began in part because cities in the Southeast and Southwest that had had a long history of hockey were either without teams or without leagues for existing teams to play in. Hockey was no stranger to sports fans in Roanoke, Charlotte or Greensboro in the east or Oklahoma City, Tulsa or Dallas–Fort Worth in the west. Run by people experienced in the hockey business, most of these southern teams had been successful.

Finding players was not a problem. There were plenty of undrafted junior and university players, as well as older athletes who realized that their dreams of playing in the National Hockey League were over. They still had the passion for playing and enjoyed the camaraderie and the competition. Pay was sufficient, if not great, and the weather was much better than it was in Canada, the northern states or Europe. Many players enjoyed long careers in the lower minor leagues. Only one of the three leaders in total games played in each of the ECHL, CHL and UHL had ever appeared in an NHL game: Cam Brown, now with Gwinnett of the ECHL, played in one game for the Vancouver Canucks during the 1990–91 season. However, as the NHL expanded, the ECHL provided teams in which promising, but not the top, draft choices could develop, progressing to the AHL and, in over 200 instances, the NHL. The CHL and later the UHL and West Coast Hockey League provided players who could, on occasion, be called up as emergency replacements for AHL teams.

The early successes of the ECHL and, a few years later, the CHL attracted the attention of cities in nontraditional markets, places with acceptable facilities in need of primary or secondary tenants. It also attracted people with money—sometimes not enough!—who wanted to own a professional hockey team. As new teams joined leagues, the increasingly expensive expansion fees provided extra revenue to the leagues and, sometimes, much-needed cash for existing teams. Between 1993 and 2000, both the ECHL and CHL expanded into nontraditional markets in South Carolina, Georgia, Alabama, Mississippi, Louisiana and Arkansas.

Southern sports fans—whose awareness of hockey had been increased by Wayne Gretzky's trade from Edmonton to Los Angeles in 1988 and, later, by the NHL's placing franchises in Dallas, Phoenix and North Carolina—responded enthusiastically to the new sports teams in their midst. The game from the frozen north had the physicality of football, the speed and danger of NASCAR racing, the aggression of professional wrestling and the violence of bull riding. Fans also responded to the players themselves, welcoming them to their cities, treating them often like sons and grandsons. In many instances, players became permanent residents in the towns in which they played. Attendance figures for many first-year expansion teams were amazing: an average of over 9,000 a game in Baton Rouge (Louisiana) and North Charleston and Greenville (South Carolina); more than 7,000 in Pensacola and the greater Fort Myers area in Florida; over 6,000 in Biloxi, Mississippi; and over 5,000 in San Antonio (Texas) and Mobile (Alabama).

The initial successes of the ECHL and CHL in these southern markets did not go unnoticed. For three years the Sunshine and Southern Leagues operated in Florida and neighboring states. In 1997, in its second year of operation, the Western Professional Hockey League began an ambitious program of expansion in the Southwest. From 1997 to 2002, what was then the Colonial Hockey League placed franchises in North Carolina and eastern Tennessee.

The rapid expansion was not without its challenges. The early success of several teams did not last. In fact, 26 expansion teams in the ECHL, CHL and WPHL experienced their best per-game attendance average during the first season of operation. Once the novelty of the sport and, in some cases, of a new facility had worn off, many people found other entertainment diversions. Some clubs did not develop marketing strategies designed to retain fans or to develop a fan base sufficient to keep the teams in business.

The New Mexico Scorpions finished the 2004-05 season at Tingley Coliseum, the oldest facility in the Central Hockey League. They will open their 2006-07 season at Rio Rancho Events Center, one of three new CHL facilities that will begin operation in the fall of 2006.

Part of the problem arose from the fact that many new owners did not know how to run and market a sports entertainment business. Some of them lacked the necessary capital to sustain an organization for the first few seasons. Unfortunately, some of these owners, after failing in one location, moved their franchises elsewhere, with similar results. In some cases, owners departed in haste, leaving an organization in shambles and in debt, earning the ill will of local businesses and fans, which made it difficult if not impossible for a new team to succeed in the same market. Some of these owners resurfaced in other areas and were granted expansion franchises in different leagues. It often seemed that league officials, in their desire to expand as quickly as possible (sometimes to claim squatter's rights to certain territories), did not always thoroughly examine the finances and experience of new owners.

Expansion created further stumbling blocks. Often, teams in one league were located too far apart geographically. This was particularly the case for the CHL, which in the late 1990s extended from southwestern Texas to eastern North Carolina, and the UHL, which reached from the greater St. Louis area in Missouri to New Haven, Connecticut. Such distances created either enormous travel expenses or the necessity of a few geographically clustered teams playing the majority of their games against each other—a situation that often displeased fans, who demanded more variety. Leagues often overlapped. The WPHL and the CHL, the UHL and the ECHL, and the CHL and ECHL frequently occupied the same territories. Six times, teams from different leagues played in the same cities: San Antonio and Fort Worth, Texas; Little Rock, Arkansas; Jacksonville, Florida; Albany, New York; and Dayton, Ohio. One team usually lost the territorial battle, and in the cases of Jacksonville and Little Rock, both clubs disappeared.

Using expansion fees as an important source of operating revenue proved disastrous for the International Hockey League, which struggled, unsuccessfully, to survive after expansion had ceased. Other leagues learned that they had to generate revenues from ticket sales and sponsorships if they were to maintain financial stability. Finally, it should be noted that expansion and relocation were frequently unsuccessful: 52 expansion franchises or relocated teams either ceased operations or moved within five years or less.

In the late 1990s, leagues frequently attempted to solve problems by seeking new ownership groups, allowing franchises to relocate, taking over operations of teams or allowing clubs to cease operations, usually at the conclusion of a season, but in a few instances in midseason. However, during the past five seasons, leagues have merged, and the new combined leagues have established stricter ownership controls and vetted new franchise applications more carefully. In addition, leagues have encouraged local groups and individuals to assume ownership of clubs. A team's extensive, positive involvement with its host city is now recognized to be an essential component of success.

Although there have been difficulties and failures, the history of the minor-league boom in the South is not entirely a study of the distressing results of too much, too fast. Each of the four lower-level minor leagues has a core group of successful franchises that provide stability. These include Fayetteville, Knoxville, Huntsville and Columbus in the SPHL; four of the ECHL's southeastern teams, Florida, South Carolina, Charlotte and Gwinnett; and several CHL clubs: Oklahoma City, Wichita, Bossier-Shreveport, Laredo and Rio Grande Valley.

Some of the successful teams began with markets that had both a tradition of hockey and an existing core of knowledgeable fans. The other clubs capitalized on the novelty factor at first. However, all of them, as well as another two dozen or so teams in the lower minors, are now successful for two reasons: they have a knowledgeable front-office staff, and the members of that staff work hard for 12 months of the year. In addition, the increasing number of local owners inspires confidence about a team's longevity.

Front-office staffs have left the on-ice hockey activities to coaches, focusing instead on selling advertising and group and season tickets and developing the non-hockey events surrounding a game. Recognizing that a large number of attendees are not devotees of hockey, but people looking for an evening's entertainment, they have choreographed activities between periods and during stoppages of play that will keep spectators amused and engaged. They have also made sure that the team regularly interacts with the community, sending players to schools, churches, hospitals and service clubs.

Back in Edmonton, I followed the closing weeks of the regular seasons and the ECHL, CHL, UHL and SPHL playoffs. In the ECHL, the Alaska Aces won the Kelly Cup, defeating Gwinnett four games to one. The season's per-game average attendance increased by 366 to 4,370. Kalamazoo won the UHL's Colonial Cup four games to one over Danbury. The league's per-game attendance average dropped by 161 to 3,074. The Laredo Bucks won the CHL's Ray Miron President's Cup four games to one over Bossier-Shreveport. The per-game average of 4,663, an increase of 185, was second in the minor leagues to the AHL's 5,487. In the Southern Professional Hockey League, the Knoxville Ice Bears won the championship three games to one over the Florida Seals. The league per-game attendance average increased by 280 to 2,720.

When the playoffs ended, I spoke with the senior administrators of each of the four leagues. I asked each man how he would describe the current state of his league, what he thought were the major changes it had undergone since its inception, and what he believed the nature and status of the league might be in 2011.

Brian McKenna, who has been ECHL commissioner for the past four seasons, focused on two elements that he felt had changed during the years he'd been associated with the league. "On the ice it has become more and more a developmental league. This year we have 100 players under contract with NHL teams and another 100 with AHL teams. And this season, 43 ECHL graduates made their NHL debuts. We're not primarily a destination league anymore; a lot of our players have a good chance of moving up. Off the ice, we are focusing more on the concept that entertainment is key to our success. We want our teams to be competitive, but winning doesn't necessarily lead to business success. Seven teams that have won the playoff championships are no longer in the league. The successful clubs work hard at catering to fans. Each league city has between 1,000 and 2,000 hard-core fans, but that's not enough to pay the bills. You need to attract the casual fans, the groups, and then give them such a good entertainment experience that they become repeat fans."

McKenna admitted that the novelty of the sport—its action, speed and physicality—accounted for its initial success. However, in the rush to acquire franchises, many new owners—some of them absentee—did not take the time to make their teams part of the community or to understand what the initially large fan base wanted. "You need to connect with the community, to give to it, to show your commitment to it. I think this is particularly important in the South. That's why local ownership is important. It makes it easier for a new team to become part of a community."

"Total success," McKenna commented, "is a utopian concept. But the league is constantly working at helping everyone get better. Certain markets may ultimately fail, but that number is shrinking. Three or four years ago, seven or eight of our teams were struggling; this year we have only two or three in that situation."

In 2003, shortly after the ECHL announced that it was accepting seven clubs from the West Coast Hockey League as expansion franchises, officials raised the possibility of the league growing to 40 teams. It has not reached that number, and when McKenna was asked what he thought the league might be like in five years, he spoke of between 25 and 30 teams. "Some cities that have lost teams might be successful with new owners, and there are many good cities that don't have the facilities. On the ice, I think you'll see the ECHL continue to grow as a developmental league. Off the ice, I think we'll have more stable teams."

Brad Treliving, who had been one of the founders of the WPHL and, since 2001, president of the CHL, with which the WPHL merged, used the word "evolution" to describe how his league had changed. "First, the facilities: next year 11 of our 18 teams will be playing in new buildings. Second, the fan base: our fans have grown tremendously in the knowledge of the game. And third, the players: each year we have better players coming to us from colleges and Junior A leagues, and we're sending more players up to the AHL." He also used the terms "maturity" and "professionalism." "We've grown into a much better understanding of how this business works, and we've refined our formula. We know how to help a new team start up and set its priorities."

Like McKenna, Treliving stressed the importance of a team's making itself part of the community. "It takes time," he remarked. "In our cities, we've spent time introducing people to skating and playing hockey. Now we have youth leagues in all our cities, and our teams have helped amateur hockey. We're creating a new group of fans to come to our games." Noting that the CHL is in the entertainment business, he stressed that good customer service is essential. "We're competing for both the time and the money that people have for entertainment. If we provide a good product and treat our customers well, they'll come back. There have been places where we've had teams that failed, but I'd say that nearly all our problems were self-inflicted. Now that we're also in the coliseum building and management business, we have a better opportunity to avoid many problems."

Asked for his vision of the league five years in the future, Treliving replied, "Our goals and mission will remain the same: to continue building strong foundations for our business. We will continue to look for opportunities to grow the league under our model. How big will we become? We've never focused on the number. In fact, we've not taken some of the opportunities that have been offered. We don't want growth just for the sake of growth; all the pieces have to be in place. When we see the right market in an area that needs an events center, we investigate the possibilities of building and then placing a team there."

Richard Brosal, who during his nine-year presidency of the UHL saw the league extend from its Michigan center to upstate New York and Connecticut, the western Midwest, and twice into the upper Southeast, enthusiastically described the changes he'd overseen. "On the ice, the game has risen to unbelievable heights. The quality constantly improves, and our affiliations with the NHL and the AHL continue to grow. At first the Colonial League was a real gong show. But we cleaned it up: there's no more stupid stuff; no bench-clearing brawls; no stick-swinging melees. Off-ice, we're offering affordable family entertainment, and our product continues to improve. We're very active in our communities, and we're involved with charitable causes." He referred with pride to the "UHL Cross-Checks Colon Cancer" program, which involved Molly McMaster, an employee of the Adirondack Frostbite who had beaten colorectal cancer. During the month of March, McMaster, an amateur hockey player, appeared in one game for each of the league's 14 teams in a campaign to increase awareness of the disease.

Looking ahead, Brosal expressed his belief that the UHL would probably remain near its present size with "14 or 15 teams that are profitable and stable. We want to maintain the quality of play and the entertainment value. If we do add teams, we'll move into new, virgin markets. We don't need retreads like Utica, Winston-Salem or Greensboro. Owners shouldn't have to keep beating their heads against a wall; you can't expect them to keep spending money if people aren't receptive. How long can you keep pushing a rock up a hill?" He did not feel that the South would be part of the league's future, suggesting that hockey there was a fad. He spoke of strengthening the core areas, in each of which the teams are only a few hours' bus ride from one another.

Surprisingly, the SPHL, whose teams are located in cities that had been abandoned by the CHL, UHL and ECHL, is becoming stronger each season, partly because of its smaller expansion fees, controlled budgets and limited geographical area. Entry fees for the league are $100,000—those in the other three leagues range from $0.5 million to $2 million—and team budgets average $800,000 a year. Bill Coffey, the director of hockey operations, who was one of the founders of the ECHL in 1988, spoke of how important it was for the league to stay within what he termed its "geographical footprint," which currently includes five southeastern states. He added, "I thought it would succeed if everyone stayed within their budgets." The four most successful clubs—Knoxville, Fayetteville,

Huntsville and Columbus—all have local ownership, "which certainly helps establish connections with business and media people."

Coffey predicted moderate growth for the league, all of it within the "geographical footprint." He spoke of 10 to 12 teams in two divisions. However, he felt it would be to the league's disadvantage to expand for expansion's sake and believed that increasing the number of games would deprive too many teams of valuable Friday and Saturday home games. There were only a limited number of weeks that the season could be pushed back into the fall or advanced into the spring, and the alternative was scheduling more games on poorly attended weeknight dates.

By mid-June, the 2006–07 lineups for the five minor leagues with teams in the South had been "tentatively finalized." As in previous seasons, unanticipated changes could take place during the summer. However, the AHL planned to ice 27 teams, the same number as in the 2005–06 season. Cleveland relocated to Worcester, Massachusetts. The dormant Cincinnati and Edmonton franchises were not reactivated. Norfolk (Virginia) and Houston and San Antonio (Texas) remained the league's three southern teams.

The ECHL would begin the season with 26 teams, an increase of one, as the Texas Wildcatters and Cincinnati Cyclones announced their return. The Greenville (South Carolina) Grrrowl suspended operations.

In the CHL, the New Mexico Scorpions returned after a one-season absence, and expansion franchises were added in Prescott (Arizona) and Broomfield (Colorado). The Colorado Eagles did not jump leagues in response to the establishment of the Broomfield franchise. The Fort Worth Brahmas suspended operations. For the 2006–07 season, the number of CHL clubs would increase by two teams, to 17.

The UHL lost Roanoke and Richmond (Virginia), Motor City (Fraser, Michigan), Missouri (St. Charles), Adirondack (Glens Falls, New York) and Danbury (Connecticut), but added two teams in Illinois (Bloomington and Hoffman Estates, a Chicago suburb). The league was now scheduled to open the 2006–07 season with 10 teams, 4 fewer than in the previous season. However, there were questions as to whether the Elmira (New York) Jackals would return. Their nearest rival was now Port Huron, Michigan, 395 miles to the west. The UHL no longer had any teams in the South.

The SPHL added Richmond, Virginia, but not Roanoke, and would begin the season with eight teams, all of them in the South.

The number of teams slated to begin the 2006-07 season would be 88, up one from the previous season. Thirty-five teams would play in the South, the same number as in 2005–06. Of course, these figures represent a considerable decrease from the numbers in the 1998–99 season, when 110 teams, 56 in the South, played in seven leagues. However, those figures were the result of expansion at its most reckless and unplanned, when it seemed that, if there were a building in which a regulation hockey rink could be placed, someone was prepared to pay a league expansion fee or relocate an existing team. Twenty-six of the southern teams from that season no longer existed. By contrast, 18 of the southern teams returning for the 2006–07 season had played at least seven consecutive seasons as members of their leagues.

During the 2005–06 season, 4.5 million people watched minor-league hockey games in the American South. Six southern teams were among the top 20 teams in per-game average attendance. The Oklahoma City Blazers of the CHL, which averaged over 8,000 fans a game, were second only to Manchester of the AHL. Clearly the meltdown or rapid contraction that began at the turn of the century had ended. Most of the still-existing southern franchises appeared to have the fan base and the financial stability necessary to insure, for many seasons, the continuation of the phenomenon of Hockey Night in Dixie.

POSTSEASON POSTSCRIPT

In mid-summer, the San Diego Gulls of the ECHL ceased operations. The total number of teams to begin the 2006–2007 season was now 87; the ECHL would now ice 26 teams.

APPENDIX

Minor-League Hockey Teams in the United States and Canada, 1988–2006

ACHL	Atlantic Coast Hockey League 2002–03
AHL	American Hockey League 1988–
CHL	Central Hockey League 1992–
CoHL	Colonial Hockey League 1991–97
	(renamed United Hockey League in 1997)
ECHL	East Coast Hockey League 1988–
	(renamed ECHL in 2003)
IHL	International Hockey League 1988–2001
SEHL	South East Hockey League 1995–96
SHL	Southern Hockey League 1995–96
SPHL	Southern Professional Hockey League 2004–
SuHL	Sunshine Hockey League 1992–95
UHL	United Hockey League 1997–
WCHL	West Coast Hockey League 1995–2003
WHA2	World Hockey Association 2 2003–04
WPHL	Western Professional Hockey League 1996–2001

UNITED STATES

ALABAMA

Birmingham	Bulls ECHL (1992–2001)
Huntsville	Blast ECHL (1993–94)
	Channel Cats SHL (1995–96)
	Channel Cats, Tornado CHL (1996–97 to 2000–01)
	Channel Cats SEHL (2003–04)
	Havoc SPHL (2004–05 —)
Mobile	Mysticks ECHL (1995–96 to 2001–02)
Pelham *(suburb of Birmingham)*	
	Slammers WHA2 (2003–04)

ALASKA

Anchorage	Aces WCHL (1995–96 to 2002–03)

| | Alaska Aces ECHL (2003–04 —) |
| Fairbanks | Alaska Gold Kings WCHL (1995–96 to 1996–97) |

ARIZONA
Phoenix	Roadrunners IHL (1989–90 to 1996–97)
	Mustangs WCHL (1997–98 to 2000–01)
	Roadrunners ECHL (2005–06 —)
Tucson	Gila Monsters WCHL (1997–98 to 1998–99)[1]
	Scorch WPHL (2000–01)[2]

ARKANSAS
| Little Rock | GlacierCats WPHL (1998–99 to 1999–2000) |
| | RiverBlades ECHL (1999–2000 to 2002–03) |

CALIFORNIA
Bakersfield	Fog, Condors WCHL (1995–96 to 2002–03)
	Condors ECHL (2003–04 —)
Fresno	Falcons, Fighting Falcons WCHL (1995–96 to 2002–03)
	Falcons ECHL (2003–04 —)
Long Beach	Ice Dogs IHL (1996–97 to 1999–2000)
	Ice Dogs WCHL (2000–01 to 2002–03)
	Ice Dogs ECHL (2003–04 —)
Los Angeles	Ice Dogs IHL (1995–96)
San Diego	Gulls IHL (1990–91 to 1994–95)
	Gulls WCHL (1995–96 to 2002–03)
	Gulls ECHL (2003–04 to 2005–06)
San Francisco	Spiders IHL (1995–96)
Stockton	Thunder ECHL (2005–06 —)

COLORADO
Colorado Springs	Colorado Gold Kings WCHL (1998–99 to 2001–02)
Denver	Rangers, Grizzlies IHL (1988–89 and 1994–95)
Fort Collins	Colorado Eagles CHL (2003–04 —)

CONNECTICUT
Bridgeport	Sound Tigers AHL (2001–02 —)
Danbury	Trashers UHL (2004–05 to 2005–06)
Hartford	Wolf Pack AHL (1997–98 —)
New Haven	Nighthawks, Senators, Beast of New Haven AHL (1988–89; 1992–93; 1997–98 to 1998–99)
	Knights UHL (2000–01 to 2001–02)

FLORIDA
Daytona Beach	Sun Devils SuHL (1992–93 to 1994–95)
	Breakers SHL (1995–96)
Estero *(suburb of Fort Myers)*	
	Florida Everblades ECHL (1998–99 —)
Jacksonville	Bullets SuHL (1992–93 to 1994–95)
	Lizard Kings ECHL (1995–96 to 1999–2000)
	Bullets SHL (1995–96)

	Barracudas ACHL (2002–03)
	Barracudas WHA2 (2003–04)
	Barracudas SPHL (2004–05 —)
Kissimmee	Florida Seals SPHL (2005–06 —)
Lakeland	Ice Warriors SuHL (1992–93 to 1994–95)
	Prowlers SHL (1995–96)
	Loggerheads WHA2 (2003–04)
Miami	Matadors ECHL (1998–99)
	Manatees WHA2 (2003–04)[3]
Orlando	Solar Bears IHL (1995–96 to 2000–01)
	Seals ACHL (2002–03)
	Seals WHA2 (2003–04)
Pensacola	Ice Pilots ECHL (1996–97 —)
St. Petersburg	Renegades SuHL (1992–93)[4]
	Parrots ACHL (2002–03)[5]
Tallahassee	Tiger Sharks ECHL (1994–95 to 2000–01)
West Palm Beach	Blaze SuHL (1992–93 to 1994–95)
	Barracudas SHL (1995–96)

GEORGIA

Atlanta	Knights IHL (1992–93 to 1995–96)
Augusta	Lynx ECHL (1998–99 —)
Columbus	Cottonmouths CHL (1996–97 to 2000–01)
	Cottonmouths ECHL (2001–02 to 2003–04)
	Cottonmouths SPHL (2004–05 —)
Gwinnett	Gladiators ECHL (2003–04 —)
Macon	Whoopee CHL (1996–97 to 2000–01)
	Whoopee ECHL (2001–02)
	Trax ACHL (2002–03)
	Trax WHA2 (2003–04)
	Trax SPHL (2004–05)

IDAHO

Boise	Idaho Steelheads WCHL (1997–98 to 2002–03)
	Idaho Steelheads ECHL (2002–03 —)

ILLINOIS

Chicago	Wolves IHL (1994–95 to 2000–01)
	Wolves AHL (2001–02 —)
Moline	Quad City Mallards CoHL/UHL (1995–96 —)
Peoria	Rivermen IHL (1988–89 to 1995–96)
	Rivermen ECHL (1996–97 to 2004–05)
	Rivermen AHL (2005–06 —)
Rockford	IceHogs UHL (1999–2000 —)

INDIANA

Fort Wayne	Komets IHL (1988–89 —)
	Komets UHL (1999–2000 —)
Indianapolis	Ice IHL (1988–89 to 1998–99)
	Ice CHL (1999–2000 to 2003–04)

IOWA
Des Moines   Iowa Stars AHL (2005–06 —)

KANSAS
Topeka   Scarecrows, Tarantulas CHL
                 (1998–99 to 2000–01; 2004–05)
Wichita   Thunder CHL (1992–93 —)

KENTUCKY
Lexington   Kentucky Thoroughblades AHL
                 (1996–97 to 2000–01)
                 Men O'War ECHL (2002–03)
Louisville   Icehawks, RiverFrogs ECHL
                 (1990–91 to 1993–94; 1995–96 to 1997–98)
                 Panthers AHL (1999–2000 to 2000–01)

LOUISIANA
Alexandria   Warthogs WPHL (1998–99 to 1999–2000)
Baton Rouge   Kingfish ECHL (1996–97 to 2002–03)
Bossier-Shreveport *(see also Shreveport)*
                 Mudbugs WPHL (2000–01)
                 Mudbugs CHL (2001–02 —)
Lafayette   IceGators ECHL (1995–96 to 2004–05)
Lake Charles   Ice Pirates WPHL (1997–98 to 2000–01)
Monroe   Moccasins WPHL (1997–98 to 2000–01)
New Orleans   Brass ECHL (1997–98 to 2001–02)
Shreveport *(see also Bossier-Shreveport)*
                 Mudbugs WPHL (1997–98 to 1999–2000)

MAINE
Portland   Maine Mariners, Pirates AHL (1988–89 to 1991–92; 1993–94 —)

MARYLAND
Baltimore   Skipjacks, Bandits AHL
                 (1988–89; 1992–93; 1995–96 to 1996–97)
Upper Marlboro   Chesapeake Icebreakers ECHL (1997–98 to 1998–99)

MASSACHUSETTS
Lowell   Lock Monsters AHL (1998–99 —)
Springfield   Indians, Falcons AHL (1988–89 —)
Worcester   IceCats AHL (1994–95 to 2004–05)

MICHIGAN
Detroit   Vipers IHL (1994–95 to 2000–01)
Flint   Spirits IHL (1988–89 to 1989–2000)
                 Bulldogs, Generals CoHL/UHL (1991–92 —)
Fraser   Michigan Falcons, Detroit Falcons,
                 Motor City Mechanics CoHL/UHL
                 (1991–92 to 1995–96; 2004–05 to 2005–06)
Grand Rapids   Griffins IHL (1996–97 to 2000–01)

	Griffins AHL (2001–02 —)
Kalamazoo	Wings, Michigan K Wings IHL (1988–89 to 1999–2000)
	Wings UHL (2000–01 —)
Muskegon	Lumberjacks IHL (1988–89 to 1991–92)
	Fury UHL (1992–93 —)
Port Huron	Border Cats, Beacons, Flags CoHL/UHL (1996–97 —)
Saginaw	Hawks IHL (1988–89)
	Wheels, Lumber Kings, Gears CoHL/UHL (1994–95 to 1999–2000)[6]

MINNESOTA
St. Paul　　　　Minnesota Moose IHL (1994–95 to 1995–96)

MISSISSIPPI
Biloxi　　　　　Mississippi Sea Wolves ECHL (1996–97 to 2004–05)
Jackson　　　　Bandits ECHL (1999–2000 to 2002–03)
Tupelo　　　　　T-Rex WPHL (1998–99 to 2000–01)

MISSOURI
Kansas City　　Blades IHL (1990–91 to 2000–01)
　　　　　　　　Blades Outlaws (2004–05)
St. Charles　　Missouri River Otters UHL (1999–2000 to 2005–06)

NEBRASKA
Omaha　　　　　Ak-Sar-Ben Knights AHL (2005–06 —)

NEVADA
Las Vegas　　　Thunder IHL (1993–94 to 1998–99)
　　　　　　　　Wranglers ECHL (2003–04 —)
Reno　　　　　　Renegades WCHL (1995–96 to 1997–98)

NEW HAMPSHIRE
Manchester　　Monarchs AHL (2001–02 —)

NEW JERSEY
Atlantic City　Boardwalk Bullies ECHL (2001–02 to 2004–05)
Trenton　　　　Titans ECHL (1999–2000 —)

NEW MEXICO
Albuquerque　New Mexico Scorpions WPHL (1996–97 to 2000–01)
　　　　　　　　New Mexico Scorpions CHL (2001–02 to 2004–05)

NEW YORK
Albany　　　　Choppers IHL (1990–91)[7]
　　　　　　　　River Rats AHL (1992–93 —)
Binghamton　Whalers, Rangers, Senators AHL
　　　　　　　　(1988–89; 1996–97; 2002–03 —)
　　　　　　　　Broome County Icemen UHL (1997–98 to 2001–02)
Elmira　　　　Jackals UHL (2000–01 —)
Glens Falls　　Adirondack Red Wings AHL (1988–89 to 1998–99)

	Adirondack IceHawks, Frostbite UHL (1999–2000 to 2005–06)
Rochester	Americans AHL (1988–89 —)
Syracuse	Crunch AHL (1994–95 —)
Troy	Capital District Islanders AHL (1990–91 to 1992–93)
Utica	Devils AHL (1988–89 to 1992–93)
	Bulldogs, Blizzard, Mohawk Valley Prowlers CoHL/UHL (1993–94 to 1994–97; 1998–99 to 2000–01)[8]

NORTH CAROLINA

Asheville	Smoke UHL (1998–99 to 2001–02)
	Aces SPHL (2004–05)
Charlotte	Checkers ECHL (1993–94 —)
Fayetteville	Force CHL (1997–98 to 2000–01)
	Cape Fear FireAntz ACHL (2002–03)
	Cape Fear FireAntz SEHL (2003–04)
	FireAntz SPHL (2004–05 —)
Greensboro	Monarchs ECHL (1989–90 to 1994–95)
	Carolina Monarchs AHL (1995–96 to 1996–97)
	Generals ECHL (1999–2000 to 2003–04)
Raleigh	Icecaps ECHL (1991–92 to 1997–98)
Winston-Salem	Carolina Thunderbirds ECHL (1988–89)
	Thunderbirds ECHL (1989–90 to 1991–92)
	Mammoths SHL (1995–96)
	Icehawks UHL (1997–98 to 1998–99)
	Parrots ACHL (2002–03)[9]
	Thunder-Birds SEHL (2003–04)
	Polar Twins SPHL (2004–05)

OHIO

Canton	Ohio Gears UHL (1999–2000)[10]
Cincinnati	Cyclones ECHL (1990–91 to 1991–92; 2001–02 to 2003–04)
	Cyclones IHL (1992–93 to 2000–01)
	Mighty Ducks AHL (1997–98 to 2004–05)
Cleveland	Lumberjacks IHL (1992–93 to 2000–01)
	Barons AHL (2001–02 to 2005–06)
Columbus	Chill ECHL (1991–92 to 1998–99)
	Stars UHL (2003–04)[11]
Dayton	Bombers ECHL (1991–92 —)
	Ice Bandits CoHL (1996–97)
Toledo	Storm ECHL (1991–92 —)
Youngstown	Steelhounds CHL (2005–06 —)

OKLAHOMA

Oklahoma City	Blazers CHL (1992–93 —)
Tulsa	Oilers CHL (1992–93 —)

PENNSYLVANIA

Erie	Panthers ECHL (1988–89 to 1995–96)
Hershey	Bears AHL (1988–89 —)
Johnstown	Chiefs ECHL (1988–89 —)

Philadelphia   Phantoms AHL (1996–97 —)
Reading   Royals ECHL (2001–02 —)
Wilkes-Barre/Scranton
                    Penguins AHL (1999–2000 —)

RHODE ISLAND
Providence   Bruins AHL (1992–93 —)

SOUTH CAROLINA
Charleston   South Carolina Stingrays ECHL (1993–94 —)
Columbia   Inferno ECHL (2001–02 —)
Florence   Pee Dee Pride, Pride ECHL (1997–98 to 2004–05)
                    Pee Dee Cyclones SPHL (2005–06 —)
Greenville   Grrrowl ECHL (1998–99 to 2005–06)

TENNESSEE
Knoxville   Cherokees ECHL (1988–89 to 1996–97)
                    Speed UHL (1999–2000 to 2001–02)
                    Ice Bears ACHL (2002–03)
                    Ice Bears SEHL (2003–04)
                    Ice Bears SPHL (2004–05 —)
Memphis   RiverKings CHL (1992–93 —)
Nashville   Knights ECHL (1989–90 to 1995–96)
                    Nighthawks, Ice Flyers CHL (1996–97 to 1997–98)

TEXAS
Abilene   Aviators WPHL (1998–99 to 1999–2000)[12]
Amarillo   Rattlers WPHL (1996–97 to 2000–01)
                    Rattlers, Gorillas CHL (2001–02 —)
Austin   Ice Bats WPHL (1996–97 to 2000–01)
                    Ice Bats CHL (2001–02 —)
Beaumont   Texas Wildcatters ECHL (2003–04 to 2004–05)
Belton   Central Texas Stampede WPHL (1996–97 to 1999–2000)[13]
Corpus Christi   Ice Rays WPHL (1998–99 to 2000–01)
                    Ice Rays/Rayz CHL (2001–02 —)
Dallas   Freeze CHL (1992–93 to 1994–95)
El Paso   Buzzards WPHL (1996–97 to 2000–01)
                    Buzzards CHL (2001–02 to 2002–03)
Fort Worth   Fire CHL (1992–93 to 1997–98)
                    Bulls, Brahmas WPHL (1997–98 to 2000–01)
                    Brahmas CHL (2001–02 to 2005–06)
Hidalgo   Rio Grande Valley Killer Bees CHL (2003–04 —)
Houston   Aeros IHL (1994–95 to 2000–01)
                    Aeros AHL (2001–02 —)
Laredo   Bucks CHL (2002–03 —)
Lubbock   Cotton Kings WPHL (1999–2000 to 2000–01)
                    Cotton Kings CHL (2001–02 —)
Odessa   Jackalopes WPHL (1997–98 to 2000–01)
                    Jackalopes CHL (2001–02 —)
San Angelo   Outlaws WPHL (1997–98 to 2000–01)

Outlaws, Saints CHL (2001–02 to 2004–05)

San Antonio Iguanas CHL (1994–95 to 1996–97; 1998–99 to 2001–02)
Dragons IHL (1996–97 to 1997–98)
Rampage AHL (2002–03 —)
Texarkana Border City Bandits CHL (2000–01)[14]
Waco Wizards WPHL (1996–97 to 1999–2000)[15]

UTAH

Salt Lake City Golden Eagles, Utah Grizzlies IHL
(1988–89 to 1993–94; 1995–96 to 2000–01)
Utah Grizzlies AHL (2001–02 to 2004–05)
Utah Grizzlies ECHL (2005–06 —)

VIRGINIA

Norfolk Hampton Roads Admirals ECHL (1989–90 to 1999–2000)
Admirals AHL (2000–01 —)
Richmond Renegades ECHL (1990–91 to 2002–03)
RiverDogs UHL (2003–04 to 2005–06)
Roanoke Virginia Lancers ECHL (1988–89 to 1989–90)
Roanoke Valley Rebels, Roanoke Valley Rampage,
Express ECHL (1991–92 to 2003–04)
Roanoke Valley Vipers UHL (2005–06)
Vinton Virginia Lancers, Roanoke Valley Rebels ECHL
(1988–89 to 1990–91)

WASHINGTON

Tacoma Sabrecats WCHL (1997–98 to 2001–02)

WEST VIRGINIA

Huntington Blizzard ECHL (1993–94 to 1999–2000)
Wheeling Thunderbirds, Nailers ECHL (1992–93 —)

WISCONSIN

Madison Monsters, Kodiaks CoHL/UHL (1995–96 to 1999–2000)
Milwaukee Admirals IHL (1988–89 to 2000–01)
Admirals AHL (2001–02 —)

CANADA

ALBERTA

Edmonton Roadrunners AHL (2004–05)

BRITISH COLUMBIA

Victoria Salmon Kings ECHL (2004–05 —)

MANITOBA

Winnipeg Manitoba Moose IHL (1996–97 to 2000–01)
Manitoba Moose AHL (2001–02 —)

NEW BRUNSWICK

Fredericton	Canadiens AHL (1990–91 to 1998–99)
Moncton	Hawks AHL (1988–89 to 1993–94)
Saint John	Flames AHL (1993–94 to 2002–03)

NEWFOUNDLAND

St. John's	Maple Leafs AHL (1991–92 to 2004–05)

NOVA SCOTIA

Halifax	Citadels AHL (1988–89 to 1992–93)
Sydney	Cape Breton Oilers AHL (1988–89 to 1995–96)

ONTARIO

Brantford	Smoke CoHL/UHL (1991–92 to 1997–98)
Chatham	Wheels CoHL (1993–94)
Cornwall	Aces AHL (1993–94 to 1995–96)
Hamilton	Canucks, Bulldogs AHL (1992–93 to 1993–94; 1996–97 —)
London	Wildcats CoHL (1994–95)
Newmarket	Saints AHL (1988–89 to 1990–91)
St. Thomas	Wildcats CoHL (1991–92 to 1993–94)
Thunder Bay	Thunder Hawks, Senators, Thunder Cats CoHL/UHL (1991–92 to 1998–99)
Toronto	Roadrunners AHL (2003–04)
	Marlies AHL (2005-06)

PRINCE EDWARD ISLAND

Charlottetown	Prince Edward Island Senators AHL (1993–94 to 1995–96)

QUEBEC

Quebec City	Rafales IHL (1996–97 to 1997–98)
	Citadelles AHL (1999–2000 to 2001–02)
Sherbrooke	Canadiens AHL (1988–89 to 1989–90)

Notes

5 BEGINNINGS: 1988-92

1. Mike Mastovich, "Celebrating Ten Years," *ECHL Media Guide 1997–98* (Princeton, NJ: East Coast Hockey League, 1998), 8.

6 EXPANSION: 1992-96

1. Amy Rosewater, "IHL has no plans to slow down," Cleveland *Plain Dealer*, January 29, 1995.
2. Michael Farber, "Putting on a Show," *Sports Illustrated*, October 17, 1994, 16.
3. Trent Angers, ed., *The Louisiana IceGators' Phenomenon: The Story of the Successful Introduction of Professional Ice Hockey to Louisiana* (Lafayette, LA: Acadian House, 1996).
4. Jan Spaulding, *East Coast Hockey League Official Guide and Record Book* (Princeton, NJ: East Coast Hockey League, 1994), 6.
5. Paul Hunter, "Leafs Getting More Respect from Las Vegas Oddsmakers," *Toronto Star*, January 24, 1993.

7 EXPLOSION: 1996-2000

1. From 1997 to 2000 the champions were Fort Worth Fire, Columbus Cottonmouths, Huntsville Channel Cats and Indianapolis Ice.
2. Glen Rosales, "2 WPHL teams collapse," *Albuquerque Journal*, December 16, 1999.
3. Mike Shrepshire, "Lone Star Skate," *Sports Illustrated*, February 16, 1998, 88, 73.

8 MELTDOWN: 2000-01

1. Quoted in Marc Foster, "A Proposal for the Realignment of AA Hockey Leagues," June 1999 (www.hockeyresearch.com/mfoster/realignment/proposal.html)
2. James Cohen, "WPHL Searches for Stability," *Austin American-Statesman*, November 24, 2000.
3. Will Wright, "What Might Have Been for the Stampede? Now, We'll Never Know," *Temple (Texas) Daily Telegram*, January 7, 2001 (http://www.temple-telegram.com/story/2001/1/7/20495).
4. Quote from now-defunct website www.icestormspond.com/CTXfate.
5. "Merger Needed If Minor League Hockey Is to Survive," *In the Crease*, March 6, 2001 (www.inthecrease.com/warrior/warrior_030601.html).
6. W. Scott Bailey, "Hockey Leagues Close Ranks," *San Antonio (Texas) Business Journal*, May 18, 2001 (www.bizjournals.com/sanantonio/stories/2001/05/21/story2.html).

9 CONSOLIDATION: 2001-05

1. "ECHL Today ... NHL Tomorrow," *ECHL 2004–05 Official Guide and Record Book* (Princeton, NJ: ECHL, 2004), 18.
2. Brian Vernellis, "CHL Brass Likes Progress," Shreveport *Times*, January 25, 2002.
3. David Eminian, "ECHL Teams Circle as UHL Club Folds," Peoria *Journal Star*, January 13, 2004.
4. Justin A. Cohn, "Less Is More: UHL Scales Down to 10 Teams," Fort Wayne (Indiana) *Journal Gazette*, October 11, 2002.

APPENDIX

1. Team ceased operations during the 1998–99 season.
2. WPHL revoked Tucson franchise the day before the opening of the 2000–01 season.
3. Team ceased operations during the 2003–04 season.
4. Team joined SuHL during 1992–93 season and withdrew before end of season
5. Team relocated to Winston-Salem during the season.
6. Team relocated to Canton, Ohio during the 1999–2000 season.
7. Team ceased operations during the 1990–91 season.
8. Team ceased operations during the 2000–01 season.
9. Team relocated from St. Petersburg during the 2002–03 season.
10. Team relocated from Saginaw during the 1999–2001 season.
11. Team ceased operations during the 2003–2004 season.
12. Team ceased operations during the 1999–2000 season.
13. Team ceased operations during the 1999–2000 season.
14. Team ceased operations during the 2000–01 season.
15. Team ceased operations during the 1999–2000 season.

Index

This index includes the names of people associated with minor league hockey from 1988 to 2006 (players, coaches, and team officials; referees and league officials; fans, writers, and family members, etc), of cities that hosted teams, and minor leagues active during this period. In cases where teams had names different from the cities in which they were located, both the full team names and cities are listed and cross-referenced.